THE USE AND ABUSE OF THE BIBLE

A study of the Bible in an age of
rapid cultural change

Dennis Nineham

BOOKS
10 East 53d St., New York 10022
(a division of Harper & Row Publishers, Inc.)

First published 1976 by
THE MACMILLAN PRESS LTD
London and Basingstoke

Published in the U.S.A. 1976 by
HARPER & ROW PUBLISHERS, INC.
BARNES AND NOBLE IMPORT DIVISION

ISBN 0-06-495178-2
LCN 76-15690

Printed in Great Britain

Christianity is always adapting itself into something
which can be believed.

T.S. Eliot

For
RUTH

sine qua non

Contents

Preface

The rather chequered history of the writing of this book has affected the contents sufficiently for the reader to be entitled to some explanation. In 1967 I was honoured with an invitation to deliver the Edward Cadbury Lectures at Birmingham University in 1969, and I gladly accepted; but a little later the pressure of unexpected administrative duties at Cambridge, where I was teaching at the time, compelled me to withdraw my acceptance. An invitation then came for 1971 and again I gladly accepted, but between the acceptance of the invitation and the delivery of the lectures I was involved, again quite unexpectedly, in a move from Cambridge back to Oxford and in all the extra-academic activities attendant on a change of post and on participation in my new college's centenary celebrations in 1970. The result was that when the lectures were delivered early in 1971 they were not as fully prepared as I could have wished, and I therefore decided — against the advice of Professor J.G. Davies, the wisdom of which I now appreciate! — to do considerably more work on the text before it was published.

Further work in connexion with something already written is always hazardous because one ends up wanting not to alter the text but to write a new one; and had I followed my inclination in this case I should have written something quite new. That, however, would hardly have been consistent with a Cadbury lecturer's obligation to 'publish the lectures', and I therefore finally decided on a compromise, namely to publish the lectures in something like their original form together with a good deal of new material. In what follows Chapters 2–5 and 8–10 reproduce seven of the eight original lectures in more or less the form in which they were delivered.

Chapters 6–7 contain a very extended version of a single lecture which, as originally delivered, consisted largely of commentary on blackboard diagrams. The long chapters at the beginning and the end are entirely new, the former designed to explain the general background-considerations on which many of the detailed arguments in the lectures ultimately rest, the latter to explain why I believe the sort of position with regard to the Bible which emerges from the lectures is compatible with a lively religious, and indeed specifically Christian, faith. Readers are asked to forgive such slight elements of repetition as all this has made inevitable.

There is one question I am fully conscious that I have not confronted directly, namely why I am a Christian and look to the Christian scriptures for guidance and enlightenment with such confident expectation. That is clearly too large a matter to be entered on in the preface to a book on a different topic. All I can do is to draw attention to various hints scattered through the last chapter and answer baldly: the reason is because within the community which has preserved the scriptures, and had its life and beliefs to a considerable extent moulded by them, my experience has been such that, unless I deny what I am deeply convinced on many grounds is real, I am bound to affirm the existence and initiative of God and the possibility and reality of personal encounter with him. How far that affirmation can, or should, be spelled out in traditional terms and how the truth of it should be defended are subjects for another book.

In this, as in previous writings, I recognise that my debts to other people and books are so many that it would be impossible to remember, let alone acknowledge, them all. The quotations and references in the text should make clear the writers to whom I am most directly indebted, and I should like in addition to thank the various friends who have helped me in various ways and encouraged me when the task of getting my multitudinous material into shape seemed almost beyond my powers. Professor Gordon Davies of Birmingham issued the original invitations to deliver the Cadbury Lectures and has been endlessly patient with delays and set-backs; and he and his colleague, Professor John Hick, have helped and encouraged me in connexion with their publication, as indeed have the long-suffering publishers. My secretary, Miss Ruth Lawrence, worked wonders to get the original text of the lectures typed in time from an illegible manuscript and Mrs P. Broadbent worked equally quickly from final copy almost equally illegible. Two former pupils, the Reverend M.F. Perham and Mr A.R. Roake, undertook respectively the arduous tasks of reading the proofs and preparing the indexes. I have also received much help from Professor Maurice Wiles and from my son-in-law, Canon John Drury, while my old friend, Leslie Houlden, Principal of Ripon College, Cuddesdon, has read, re-read and criticized drafts until he must almost be regarded as co-author of the book. However, I have not always taken his advice and must accept sole responsibility for the final inadequacy of the work. It is indeed inadequate; the only excuse for publishing it must be the hope that it may help to spark off a vigorous debate on issues which I sincerely believe the contemporary church, at any rate in England, is seriously ignoring to its peril.

Finally, in this, as in all other things, my deepest debt for help and encouragement is to my wife.

Keble College,   DENNIS NINEHAM
Oxford

January, 1976

1 Introduction: Cultural change and cultural relativism

One of the main convictions underlying the lectures which follow may be expressed like this: people of different periods and cultures differ very widely; in some cases so widely that accounts of the nature and relations of God, men and the world put forward in one culture may be unacceptable, as they stand, in a different culture, even though they may have expressed profound truth in their time and expressed it in a form entirely appropriate to the original situation. Since it will be a central contention of the lectures that a situation of this sort has arisen in connexion with some of the teaching of the Bible, the truth or falsity of the initial conviction is obviously a matter of crucial importance.

Reasons for it are naturally given in the course of the lectures themselves, but discussion with the audience after the delivery of the final lecture suggested, what subsequent discussion with others has confirmed, that the point is one which needs further exposition and defence if the argument of the book is to be fully intelligible or convincing.

An objection which has been raised more than once in one form or another runs something like this: It is perfectly true that men of different cultures often differ widely. They may differ, for example, in their estimate of the size and age of the universe; they may differ in their expectations of the future or their picture of various events in the past. They may differ in their scientific or psychological outlook or in their beliefs about the existence and activities of demons or witches. Examples could no doubt be multiplied *ad infinitum*, but in the end they would all be found to refer to things relatively superficial. When all is said and done, whatever the differences between their cultures, human beings are all fellow-members of the human race and, as such, subject to the same basic drives, urges and needs — the survival instinct, the sexual urge, the drive to satisfy hunger and thirst, and so on. What is more, they all know the meaning of pride, jealousy and greed; they all have experience of joy, terror, grief, temptation, sin and guilt and the need for forgiveness. At bottom human nature does not change; and since it is with the problems of this basic human nature and its relation to God that religion is concerned, religious beliefs are not affected by the problems of cultural change to anything like the extent the lectures imply.

This objection is such a compound of truths, half-truths and untruths that some attempt must be made to sort them out, though it is not to be expected that any universally acceptable conclusions will emerge. The reason for that is not only limitation of space or the present writer's relative unfamiliarity with the subject-matter; many of the issues involved are so complex and have been under discussion for so short a time that the scholars most expert in the field are the first to insist that the time for definite conclusions is still a long way off. Two leading American sociologists, for example, have written recently: 'contemporary Western men, by and large, live in a world vastly different from any preceding one. Yet just what this means in terms of the reality, objective and subjective, in which these men conduct their everyday lives and in which their crises occur is very far from clear. Empirical research into these problems, as distinct from more or less intelligent speculation, has barely begun.'[1]

The stress which Berger and Luckmann lay on the novelty of the situation deserves to be noted very carefully. Since we are dealing with an essentially new situation, there can be no possibility of settling the issues it raises by direct recourse to any orthodoxy or tradition formulated before the issues in question had come to light. Which means in effect that we cannot look for direct enlightenment to any period much earlier than the beginning of the last century. For it was only in the eighteenth and nineteenth centuries when, as a result of better communications and improved methods of research, a veritable mass of historical material relating to societies and civilisations in all parts of the world began to be accumulated, particularly in Germany, that the problem which is central to our concern was first clearly recognised. The sheer bulk of the new material and the vivid way it brought home the reality of the past, made it an essentially novel phenomenon. As it all began to be digested it became clear that human civilisation comprised cultures which differed from one another far more radically than anything in the thought of the Enlightenment or earlier periods had prepared people to expect. The recognition by the early Romantics that other societies and periods were dominated by outlooks and sets of values very different from their own, was not only vindicated; it was shown to have done, if anything, less than full justice to the truth. It was not just that various societies differed in the amount and extent of their knowledge and technological development, or in the opinions and theories they held about particular matters; they differed in their basic understanding of, and approach to, reality as a whole.

Clearly this raises vast issues, but luckily it is only necessary for our purposes to deal with certain aspects of them. According to Freud's teaching, for example, the human condition is indeed unchanging, fixed for all eternity by the unconscious drives; but since — quite apart from the question whether Freud's teaching can be accepted in its entirety — it is not in this sense that the objectors we have in mind are contending for an unchanging human nature, this aspect of the matter can be left on one side in the present context.

Perhaps the best way of opening up the aspects of the matter which are of concern to us will be by making baldly five statements which will then be clarified and justified in the course of the subsequent discussion. The statements are these:

(*i*) Although man, like other animals, is subject to a variety of urges and drives, in his case they are relatively unspecialised and can be developed in a variety of ways. Man is only imperfectly programmed by his bodily organism.

(*ii*) A great deal turns, from our point of view, on the way men understand their urges, drives and needs.

(*iii*) The first two statements are closely connected in a two-way relationship. Not only does the way men understand their urges and needs affect the way they deal with them; the way the drives are handled and developed affects the way they are understood. If they are developed differently, they will be understood differently. Marx was surely right in insisting that men's *praxis*, the way they develop and use their powers to cope with their environment, strongly affects their understanding of it, even if he stated the point in too simple and one-sided a form.

(*iv*) At any rate until recently, individual human beings have had virtually no freedom of choice about the way they understood their humanity and its environment and relationships. Their understanding has been almost entirely controlled by the understandings of the matter, and the categories of interpretation, available in the various communities to which they belonged. Although the position has gradually changed, freedom in this matter is severely restricted even in modern western societies. It follows that:

(*v*) To the extent that an individual has no more control over his understanding of a phenomenon than he has over the phenomenon itself, he will not normally be conscious of the two as distinct. Both will seem equally part of given reality, and a thing will be actually *experienced* as what it is understood to be.

The last two points may be clarified by means of an example. Suppose a man lives in a society in which all illness is understood as due to demon-possession. The only questions he will be able to ask about his health — or, *mutatis mutandis*, about other people's health — will be: Am I possessed by a demon; and if so, what sort of a demon is it and how can it be expelled? Because no alternative understanding is available in his community, the symptoms, real or imaginary, which lead him to ask the question will actually be *experienced* as demonic activity. The pains will *feel like* a demon biting at his vitals, the rash will be *seen as* a demon's claw-marks, and so on.

If we imagine a slightly more sophisticated situation, the man may belong to a community that permits the existence of an alternative religion which ascribes all illness to witchcraft. Even then the understandings of illness available to the man will be limited to these two. He will still not be able, for example, to interpret his symptoms as the end result of a chain of natural causes and effects after the manner of a modern doctor. Even his choice between the two available understandings will not be a fully free one. If he belongs to the one religion, he will still feel his pains as the action of a demon and he will dismiss the beliefs of the other religion as delusions only to be expected of a heresy. If in the course of time he should become converted to the other religion, he will simply reverse this position. In either case his physical condition will be *experienced as* the activities of a demon or the machinations of a witch, as the case may be.

The next point to be made is that when in this context we speak of 'understanding' something, the word means, as it does in most other contexts, relating the thing in question by a chain of cause and effect (which may often be far from scientific) to some fact regarded as ultimate and as needing no further explanation. For example, if a child asks me why a coin which is pushed out of a window always moves downward and never upward, I refer him to the law of gravity and do my best to describe the mutual attraction bodies exert on one another. If my account is clear enough, the child is satisfied. We have taken the matter as far as we can in our society. We have understood it. (And it makes no essential difference if, as often happens, the process takes place below the level of consciousness.)

This definition of understanding is important because it is becoming generally recognised that one of the main things which separates the outlook of one culture from that of another is precisely the different things each takes for granted and regards as self-evident — neither requiring nor permitting any further explanation. Writers on the subject put the point in different ways, but the variety of their terminology serves only to emphasise the underlying measure of agreement between them. By way of illustration we may cite the views of three English thinkers. T.E. Hulme, for example, expresses it as follows:

> There are certain doctrines which for a particular period seem not doctrines, but inevitable categories of the human mind. Men do not look at them merely as correct opinion, for they have become so much a part of the mind, and lie so far back, that they are never really conscious of them at all. They do not see them, but other things *through* them. It is these abstract ideas at the centre, the things which they take for granted, that characterise a period. There are in each period certain doctrines, a denial of which is looked on by the men of that period just as we might look on the assertion that two and two make five. It is these abstract things at the centre, these *doctrines* felt as *facts*, which are the source of all the other more material characteristics of a period.[2]

To cite another example, R.G. Collingwood speaks of every civilisation being dominated by some 'constellation of absolute presuppositions', which determine the types of questions, both practical and theoretical, all its members ask, and the types of answers they give, and find satisfying, without any of them being aware what their absolute presuppositions are.[3]

A further aspect of the matter is well brought out by Professor Basil Willey[4] who points out that different periods are dominated by different interests, and that these interests control not only the sort of questions people ask and the subjects about which they ask them but, even more significantly, the sort of answers that content them and the sort of explanations by which they are satisfied. If there is a change of interest, people begin to ask different questions — both questions about subjects previously neglected as uninteresting and also questions of a different sort about every subject, questions that is, which require a different sort of answer to satisfy the questioner.

A familiar example may help. The Middle Ages were a period dominated by religious interests. People tended, therefore, to be satisfied with answers to their questions which clarified in some way the relation of the subject under discussion to the divine. Thus, if questions were raised about the motions of things, even the most acute thinkers were satisfied with answers which spoke, for example, of things in a state of potentiality seeking to actualise themselves, that is, to exercise fully a divinely implanted potency; or they spoke of things seeking the place or direction proper to them — 'proper', that is, according to God's intention for them. Such explanations satisfied because they were consistent with the contemporary outlook with its strongly religious orientation. Copernicus and Galileo typified the growing changes of interest characteristic of their period when they ignored such explanations in their study of movement, because, however true, they shed no light on the manner in which bodies move in space and time, how, that is to say, one natural state precedes, and leads up to, another; and that was precisely what interested Copernicus and Galileo. In order to answer their questions and satisfy their type of interest it was necessary to devise experimental techniques and this in turn led to a further set of interests and enquiries. All this in its turn could easily lead to the discovery of many more 'secondary' causes, some of which might account completely at the natural level for phenomena previously thought to require special divine activity for their explanation.

If we now put together what has been said so far and draw out some of the implications, a more concrete picture may perhaps emerge. We will begin with the first of our five statements (see p. 3 above).

It is one of the basic differences between men and the other animals that the latter have a fixed relationship with the world into which they are born, more or less from the moment of birth. Despite some degree of individual learning and accumulation, every animal has a relationship to its environment which appears to be biologically determined and so is shared with all other members of the species concerned. For example,

> kittens do not consciously decide, or have to be taught, to catch mice; there is apparently something in their con-genital equipment which makes them do so. Presumably, when a cat sees a mouse, there is something in the cat that

keeps insisting, Eat! Eat! Eat! The cat does not exactly *choose* to obey this inner voice. It simply follows the law of its innermost being and takes off after the hapless mouse (which, we suppose, has an inner voice that keeps repeating: Run! Run! Run!)[5]

In this sense, all non-human animals live in closed worlds whose structures are predetermined by the biological equipment of the species to which each belongs. The world of every non-human animal is what von Uexkull calls a 'species-specific environment'.

With man the case is quite different; to a large extent his world is a world of his own devising, though of course the range of possibilities is limited by a number of physical and biological factors. For instance, as we have already seen, man has drives just like the other animals, but they are highly unspecialized and undirected, so that the human organism is capable of applying its constitutionally given equipment to a very wide and varying range of activities. Men can *decide* to do this and not that; to be meat-eaters, for example, and not vegetarians; nomads and not agriculturalists. And decide is precisely what human societies do. In the light of various factors — local conditions, geographical location, numerous individual decisions (stories such as those of Abraham or Moses are not intrinsically implausible) and no doubt a good deal of in-fighting, and also, as a rule, a sense of supernatural guidance which need not be regarded as illusory — different groups come to cope with their environment and the problems of survival in it in various ways. Some become nomadic communities, others settled agriculturalists, yet others seafaring and fishing communities and so on; and each one develops institutions and ways of doing things appropriate to its manner of life.

In the course of time each of these institutions will attract to itself an account of its origin which serves to specify its meaning, that is, the way it should be understood and carried on. These 'historical' accounts often seem to us to have something of the character of 'just-so stories', and the question how they came to be attached to the institutions they 'explain' is a fascinating one, though it is highly

complicated and controversial and too far from our immediate concern to be taken up here.[6] What is important
from our point of view is that the purpose, or at any rate the
effect, of these explanations is largely practical. By describing
the solemn or remarkable circumstances surrounding the
foundation of the institutions they encourage later
generations to take them and their continuation seriously. By
specifying the purposes for which each institution was
founded they ensure that succeeding generations will know
how to carry it on, or how to modify or extend it, if that
should become necessary. By rooting the various practices in
the will of the gods or the wisdom and experience of earlier
generations they provide assurance that the practices in
question are in accordance with the nature of things and can
be relied on to contribute to the well-being of the community
and keep at bay the chaos and ultimate disorder which
human beings of all periods so desperately fear — whereas it
is characteristic of a period of rapid technological change
such as ours that in many spheres it can no longer rely to any
great extent on the practice or opinions of the past for
guidance on how things are best done in the present.[7]

All this means that every child since the dawn of history
has found itself born into a human society of some specific
type with institutions of an appropriate kind. And unless it
has been born in comparatively recent times, the child will
have found the institutions and practices current in its
society accepted as an unquestioned, and almost unquestionable, part of the local way of life, and the aetiological stories
connected with them believed almost equally implicitly.
Indeed the corporate 'memory' enshrined in such stories is a
large part of what constitutes a society, particularly a
primitive society; and to have made the corporate memory
one's own is a large part of what is involved in becoming a
full member of an established community.[8] Halbwachs goes
so far as to say that society in its essence *is* a memory.[9] That
is to say, because the corporate 'memories' so largely control
the beliefs, institutions and practices of a society, it is
impossible to understand or participate in the life and faith
of a society apart from its memories and myths.

An illustration may help to make this clear. If a modern

anthropologist could have been present at a celebration of the Passover in post-exilic Israel he would have been unable to appreciate the full meaning of what was going on until the youngest male present had asked the ritual question: 'What mean you by these things?' and the father of the family had explained how the ceremony originated in, and brought to mind, the events of Israel's exodus from Egypt (Exodus 12:26, etc.). Apart from the anthropologist, no one present would have doubted that this was the true, indeed the only possible, explanation; and even the anthropologist, although he would not himself be able to accept the explanation, would have to take it very seriously if he wanted to understand what it meant to be a member of the ancient Jewish people.

If now we revert to the case of a child born into a relatively primitive society, two aspects of his experience deserve special attention. First, he will be subject as he grows up to the process known to sociologists as 'socialisation'. That is to say, in a thousand subtle ways he will be encouraged, or more accurately compelled, not merely to learn and understand the institutions and meanings of his community so far as they concern him, but to interiorise them and make them his own. The processes by which he is persuaded to do this will be partly on a conscious, and partly on an unconscious level. At the conscious level there will be education and training, both formal and informal. At the unconscious level one of the most potent influences will be learning to speak his native language. To an extent that is not always recognised, a particular language is both the expression and the vehicle of a particular community's self-understanding. It reflects, and impresses on those who speak it, the understanding of, and response to, reality of the society whose language it is. 'The very structure of our language, its grammar and syntax, as the new school of linguists has clearly shown, is itself dependent on unconscious presuppositions regarding the way in which experience should be divided into categories and those categories related to one another.'[10] Whatever language we care to consider, we shall find that there are certain things it cannot be made to express or communicate because of the character of its structure and the poverty of its vocabulary; and that is only one example of the way language conditions the outlook of those who use it. Thus, in primitive societies especially, the language young human beings are brought up to speak will play a considerable part in determining their view of things and in ensuring that their outlook conforms to that of the community whose language it is.

Training in infancy and learning a language thus go a long way towards ensuring that a human individual interiorises the culture of his society; the process goes all the deeper for being so largely unconscious, and it is backed up by a whole number of other socialising agencies; and if at any stage the individual should show signs of serious deviation, every society has an effective system of social controls, of varying subtlety complexity and openness, by which it can bring all but the most obstinate deviants back into general conformity with its outlook.

The influence of this socialising process can hardly be exaggerated. For when we speak of people 'interiorising' the society into which they are born, the word carries very profound connotations. It is not just that they take note of the institutions which make up their society, or even that they take them for granted and gradually discover how they work. They define their own identity and significance in terms of their relation to these institutions. For example, if a boy is born as the eldest son of the king in an early monarchical society, he not only learns the meaning of kingship in a general way, and how to do the things that kings in that society do; he accepts the position of heir-apparent as simply part of the reality of things, like the movements of the stars or the periodical flooding of the local river. He regards his possession of royal status in more or less the same way as he regards possession of a male human body; both contribute to define what he is and to constitute his being. In other words, 'the individual not only learns the objectivated meanings, but identifies with and is shaped by them. He draws them into himself and makes them *his* meanings. He becomes not only one who possesses these meanings, but one who represents and expresses them.'[11]

Even the example just quoted is a relatively superficial

one. It needs to be recognised that at the deepest levels of his being, in his capacity as parent, mourner, tempter, sinner, saviour and so on, the individual's understanding of, and response to, his humanity and his relationships will be largely conditioned by the institutions and meanings of his culture. There is nothing else in relation to which they can stand.

And what goes for his understanding of himself applies equally to his understanding of the divine. Let us assume for the purposes of argument — and it is of course an enormous assumption, but a book on the Bible is not the place for undertaking a defence of the reality of the supernatural — not only that a supernatural world exists, but that it reveals itself, that it transmits what Berger calls signals of transcendence: these signals can only be received if they are in a form that men can understand, which means that they must be related to the institutions and understandings of the human beings for whom they are intended. To give a grossly oversimplified example: if God is to reveal something of his character as Lord to a society which consists of only two classes, barons and serfs, it will have to be in the form that he is some sort of arch-baron and men are in a totally servile relationship to him. No doubt it will be recognised that as between God and men the relationship has certain peculiar features. God is a baron-with-a-difference and men in their relationship to him are serfs-with-a-difference. It may even be that the realisation of these differences will contain the seeds of revolutionary change which will eventually alter the whole character of the society. It will still remain that, in the short term at any rate, the baron-serf relationship will have to serve as the underlying model of the relationship between God and men. As should be clear by now, no doctrine of revelation or inspiration, however high, can affect that conclusion in the slightest. For if there is to be divine communication to men who dwell in history, it will inevitably be historically conditioned. As we have seen, if it is to be intelligible to those to whom it is made, it will have to be in terms of their institutions, assumptions and myths, which means that it will have to be in culturally conditioned terms. There can be no possibility of a revelation which transcends culturally conditioned terms altogether and is given in terms which are not peculiar to any one culture but apply equally to all cultures.

The same general point is reinforced by another important consideration. If taken by itself, the account so far given of the socialising process would convey a very one-sided impression. For it might suggest, what is emphatically not the case, that human beings are simply passive material for social moulding. The fact is that every normal human being is a *participant* in the process of his social formation. He does not absorb the social world like a sponge, but plays an active part in appropriating it. What is more, once he has begun to be formed as a person, he plays his part, however insignificant, in the continuation, and sometimes the modification, of it. He becomes in a small way a co-producer of his social world and of himself in it.

This book is in no way intended to call in question or belittle that truth. Yet the words 'in a small way' must be given their full force. It must be recognised that even the most outstanding human being can conceive and communicate only relatively modest changes of outlook. So limited are the measures of man's mind that no individual, or even group of individuals, can in their lifetime envisage more than a limited revision of the position they inherited; and if *per impossibile* they could envisage more, their contemporaries would not be able to comprehend it. The thunderings of a great prophet may demand changes which appear radical, and in comparative terms *are* radical. Yet when viewed from a historical perspective, what was demanded — however great its eventual implications — will be found to have left the greater part of the *status quo* unchallenged and unchanged.

We can see all this if we consider the achievements of men who are generally regarded as having been responsible for major changes of outlook, men like Mohammed, Martin Luther or Karl Marx. It implies no underestimate of their real achievements to insist that what they left unchallenged in the presuppositions of their times was far, far more than anything they challenged or changed. From our perspective the chief impression made by Luther, for example, is that of a late medieval theologian, while Karl Marx strikes us as in many ways a typical middle-class nineteenth-century German intellectual who took over unquestioned a great deal of Hegel's philosophy and a lot more of the generally accepted ideas of his period and class. Even the most revolutionary thinker must speak — and think — in the language of his day, and we have seen something of the significance of that.

The second aspect of our imaginary child's experience is much harder to discuss briefly. Even to broach it is to enter upon one of the most controversial areas of modern thought.

It is simply a psychological fact that as the child grows up, the various institutions and meanings of its society will seem to it to hang together in some sort of unity. Particularly if it has no knowledge of any other culture which can provide a standard of comparison, the state of affairs in its own community will appear to it simply as 'the way things are'. What is more, long before the child appears on the scene, specialists of various kinds will have been at work in its community seeking to provide a theoretical basis for such feelings of unity and to show that the various 'meanings' of the society do in fact cohere rationally. According to the character and historical situation of the community, they will attempt their task in religious, theological, philosophical or scientific terms or in some combination of these. The results of their labours will constitute what sociologists call the 'meaning-system' of the community in question; and to the members of that community its validity, at any rate in general terms, will seem self-evident. So far as they give the matter any thought, they will be convinced that each element in their society's outlook presupposes, necessitates and ties in with the others.

To observers from other cultures a good deal of the logic of any meaning-system will seem highly questionable, or even incomprehensible, and the whole process will smack strongly of rationalisation. Recognition of that, however, should not blind us to the fact that there is in sober truth a large measure of homogeneity and inter-relatedness — or perhaps we should say '*inner*-relatedness' — about the outlook of any well defined cultural period or group. One of the key difficulties about our subject is that this quasi-monolithic character of every culture is a reality, and a very important reality, and yet it is exceedingly difficult either to define, or explain. Professor Stuart Hughes writes of 'the old but still relevant matter of the "spirit of the times" ', and he goes on: 'Most of us think that such a spirit exists . . . But who is bold enough to say exactly what this spirit is? Who is confident that he knows how to locate it or define it? The paradoxical truth is that the discovery of the spirit of the times is at once a technical near-impossibility and the intellectual historian's highest achievement.'[12]

The phenomenon under discussion is what Ernst Troeltsch and other German thinkers have had in mind when they refer to a cultural group or epoch as a *Totalität*, a word which might be translated in this context as a 'unified and interrelated complex'. The general validity of this concept is attested by the practice of working historians who work, typically, not on isolated incidents comparable to the separate elements on which the natural scientist concentrates, but on slabs, or blocks, of the past singled out precisely because of their relative cultural coherence. These may be phenomena of very different sorts, for example, a nation, a period, a class or a trade union; but whatever they are, they will normally have this in common that each one falls under a single meaning-system. It is precisely the mark of a good historian that the subject he selects has sufficient cultural coherence to be capable of illuminating treatment; and if the historian turns biographer, and the figure he writes about belongs to a culture of the past, he will usually find it necessary to sketch out his subject's cultural background — the meaning-system within which he lived — in order to render his motives and behaviour intelligible to readers who belong to a different culture. The implication is clear and so is its importance for our topic: the original meaning of the words and actions of a person or group is only fully intelligible in the context of the cultural situation in which they were spoken or performed.

As we have seen, it was in Germany in the nineteenth century that the problems we are considering first began to be fully recognised, and the earliest discussions of them were by German historians and philosophers brought up in the tradition of German idealism and deeply influenced by the romantic movement. To such men the 'spirit' of a social or historical institution was what was of central importance, and they tended to see each cultural totality as the expression of a particular, unique *Geist*. (The word means 'spirit'; cp. *Zeitgeist*, the spirit of a period and *Volksgeist*, the spirit of a people.) All the manifestations of a civilisation — its philosophy, its science, its architecture, its painting, its religion and so on — were seen as necessarily constituting a unity because they were taken as being so many expressions of the single spirit to which the group or epoch owed its being and character.[13] These *Geister* (spirits) were held to be the deepest stuff of which history and society were made and, as such, to be beyond the power of men to penetrate or explain. They remained what Goethe had called them, 'ineffable' realities.[14] The more extreme among these German thinkers, most notably Oswald Spengler in the early part of the present century, went so far as to maintain that the spirit of one civilisation was necessarily incomprehensible to members of another;[15] even those who did not go to such lengths often suggested that the understanding of one culture and its members by the members of another must depend on the possession and exercise of some special intuitive insight usually designated by the word *Verstehen* (the ordinary German word for 'understanding' but used in this context as a technical term).

The difficulties in all this will be obvious enough. Not only is such language, if taken at its face value, unacceptably mythological; those who have used it have been far from consistent. Spengler, for example, by attempting to do at length in his *Decline of the West* what he himself had declared to be impossible, showed an implicit awareness that his position was untenably extreme. Moreover it is not a very far cry from the contention that each society is the expression of a unique and inexpressible *Geist* to the contention that the spirits of some societies are inherently superior to those of others and so to a doctrine of a *Herrenvolk*.

For that and other reasons this whole way of thinking has become deeply and increasingly suspect, especially in England. The trouble is, however, that in their quite natural reaction against this type of explanation thinkers have tended to discount the facts along with the bogus explanations of them, and the result has been a serious lack and one-sidedness in a great deal of modern thinking, particularly in this country. To repeat the quotation from Stuart Hughes, 'the matter of the "spirit of the times" may be "old" but "it is still" relevant.'[16] The deep differences between cultures and the close inner-relatedness within cultures to which nineteenth century German thinkers pointed, were both real enough; and it has been an undoubted weakness of a good deal of twentieth century philosophy and theology that it has not reckoned sufficiently seriously with that fact. (The present writer, for example, can remember being expected when he was an undergraduate studying philosophy at Oxford to discuss and evaluate the ideas of such thinkers as Descartes and Hobbes with only the most tenuous guidance as to their relation to the thought and conditions of their time. The syllabus included no thinker between Aristotle and Descartes, students presumably being expected to be able to understand the latter and his successors out of all relation to political, social and philosophical history between 300 B.C. and A.D. 1600!) Cultures *do* differ widely and it *is* very difficult for a member of one culture to understand the thought of another, let alone know how it should affect his own thought when he has understood it.

Perhaps we may succeed in emphasizing the facts without getting involved in speculative explanations, which are not in any case germane to our purpose, if we confine ourselves to an illustrative analogy. The analogy, that of the paradigm, is one which has been used a good deal in this sort of connexion recently but we shall be using it in our own way and purely for purposes of illustration.[17]

Every reader who looks at the figure on p. 18 will see either an elaborate cup or chalice of some sort, or else two faces in profile. Two points should be noted. First, both those who see a cup and those who see two faces will be looking at the same drawing. It is identically the same reality with which they will be dealing. Secondly, the difference between them is not due to a deliberate choice. It is not that either group begins by looking in a neutral way at a set of uninterpreted lines and then consciously decides to interpret them as a cup or a pair of faces. Each group simply *sees* a cup or two profiles.

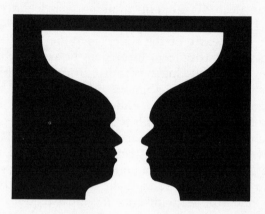

In a somewhat similar way (and let it be remembered that we are offering no more than an analogy) different human groups see the one environment, natural and supernatural, by which we are all surrounded, in different ways. Each society has what is sometimes called its own 'set' towards this environment. In this case of course the choice is not confined to two alternatives; there is an almost infinite range of possibilities. Nevertheless the analogy holds in certain important respects. We have deliberately put on one side the question why particular cultures adopt the 'sets' they do; but once a 'set' has come to be adopted by a society, the individual members of that society have, at any rate until recently, had virtually no choice in the matter. They have been brought up, in the way described just now, to accept the 'set' current in their society, with at most minor modifications.

Our figure illustrates a further truth, namely that the way the whole is seen governs the way individual items are seen. Those who see the figure as two faces will see A and B as eyes and C and D as pairs of lips. Those who see the whole as a cup will see C and D as parts of a decorative adornment on the stem and A and B as marks on the wall behind the cup.

This in turn illustrates a further point. Suppose someone

who at first unhesitatingly sees the figure as a cup begins for some reason to feel that A and B look like eyes. He and others with whom he discusses the matter may in the end become convinced that they *are* eyes. For a time they may content themselves with the supposition that the background against which the cup is set is part of a picture of a face to which the eyes belong; but this will not seem quite right, and they will begin to feel uneasy with their view of the figure as a whole. If this leads them to a close examination of other features of it, they will no doubt come to see C and D as

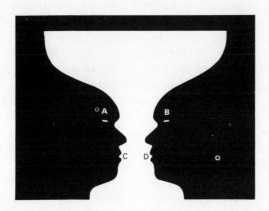

pairs of lips and so eventually the whole figure as a pair of profiles. This helps to make clear how, as we saw in the case of Copernicus and Galileo, the questioning of certain individual presuppositions, and the reinterpretation of certain specific phenomena, can lead to a radical change of 'set', and provoke — sometimes in the end relatively quickly — a major cultural revolution and a new way of seeing the whole.

The relation of individual items to the interpretation of reality as a whole may also be illustrated by a concrete instance. It is only in a society sufficiently advanced technologically to have produced large machines that it will be possible to interpret reality as a whole, after the manner of Bertrand Russell and others, as a vast impersonal, interlocking system of physical forces. The existence of large machines does not of course *compel* anyone to accept such a view. The point is that it is only in a society with machines big enough to provide the necessary analogue that such a general interpretation would be *possible*.

At this point it will be well to insert an extended illustration, if only to bring out how completely the adoption of a particular 'set' is likely to control people's way of seeing everything, including their own humanity. For the sake of example let us imagine a fairly primitive community — no actual historical society is intended. (As the example develops it will be obvious that the biblical community is not far from mind; but in order that a number of different points might be illustrated, it seemed best not to confine ourselves to any one historical society. See further p. 24 below.)

Having no means of discovering accurately the real size, shape and age of the universe, the members of this community envisage it as consisting of a flat disc some four hundred miles square (the earth) floating on a finite quantity of water, with the sky as a sort of inverted colander over the disc serving to keep out, or rather limit the entrance of, further 'waters that be above the firmament'.

The universe so conceived is envisaged as a plastic reality continually subject to the moulding hand of God, rather as the soft clay is shaped by the potter on the wheel. The community believes that it was only relatively recently that God formed the material into anything like the present universe; and he was able to do so only by dint of overcoming various supernatural powers opposed to him, some of whom have survived their defeat and now attempt to thwart his purposes from inside the universe. As he continues his moulding of the universe God is able to contain and counteract these activities of his opponents and he can be relied on in the end to give the universe the shape and character he originally intended it to have.

It does not require much imagination to recognise that such a way of seeing the universe will affect the way men see almost everything. For example, if the members of this community inherit a tradition which represents the past as having been very different from the present, that will not give rise to any doubts on the score that 'such things do not happen nowadays'; no one expects the later stages in the making of a pot to be the same as the earlier stages. Again, if life in the present seems to conform to a fairly regular rhythm, that will be because God has now reached a stage at which a relatively regular handling of the material is the appropriate procedure. At any time, however, it may become appropriate for him to interrupt this regularity of treatment; so if reports of some remarkable happening come in, there will be no particular incredulity: God is in any case bound to subject the universe to new modes of treatment before he has perfected it. The future will be bound to be radically different from the past and the present, though not, in the main, as a result of men's doing. The most that men can hope to do is to keep things going as well as their forefathers did.

'Miracle' in the modern sense of a decisive breach in an otherwise totally regular pattern of events will be inconceivable in such a society, and the language of the society will need no terms with which to express it. All its language will need words to express is that certain events are 'wonderful', highly unusual manifestations of God's power, sure signs that he is at work, as for example when he counteracts the activities of his supernatural opponents by stilling a storm, or refrains from sending the sun the whole way across the sky as he normally does once in each twenty-four hours. (Thus, what we think of as the miracles of Jesus are described in the New Testament as *dynameis*, 'acts of power', *sēmeia*, 'signs' or, less commonly, *terata* or *thaumasta*, 'wonders'.)

Likewise the members of this community will have no difficulty in believing that a famine or pestilence has been inflicted on a particular limited area in order to punish its inhabitants, without there being consequences of any sort for immediately neighbouring territories.

So far as the members of this community can discern regularities in the Great Potter's way of working — for example in the way he brings the crop from the seed each year — these regularities, being directly attributable to his personal activity, will provide them with a clue to his nature and his ways of working in other spheres; it will not provide a basis for scientific investigation as we understand it because the regularities in question will not be genuinely predictable. They, no less than the remarkable events, will be the direct workings of God and any attempt to investigate or predict his workings will be both arrogant and fruitless. 'The ways of the Lord are past finding out.'

When things go wrong, for example in cases of bodily or mental illness, the obvious response will be, not to investigate the working of impersonal secondary causes, which will not be recognised to exist, but to discover what evil supernatural power is at work and to bring countervailing divine power into play against it by sacrifice or magic or intercession or whatever is the accepted practice in such cases. It follows that so far as men are conscious of themselves as individuals, they will see their own *psyches* as the objects and playthings of external forces, both divine and demonic, and always liable to be so contaminated by the latter as to be good for nothing but destruction.

These are only a few of the beliefs and practices of this society which could be cited by way of example; but it is important to be clear what it is they exemplify. Perhaps we may say that they exemplify the outworkings of the original 'set', so long as it is understood that they are by no means *logically entailed* by that set. These beliefs and practices are by no means the only ones which could be combined with the original set, nor do they follow necessarily from it. The point is that they can be combined perfectly naturally and plausibly with it in a way that many other beliefs and practices could not; and on the other hand that they could not be plausibly combined with other 'sets' with which different beliefs and practices are fully compatible.

One further example deserves to be cited because it is so important for our subject, namely the attitude of a primitive community to the past. Such a society will have neither the records nor the sophisticated methods of handling them necessary for the production of any historical account in the modern sense of the term. What then will be the origin and status of the vivid accounts of the past which primitive communities preserve and treasure? In some cases oral tradition will lie at the basis of them, but in this connexion it needs to be remembered that the purpose of such accounts is mainly practical; it is not the satisfaction of intellectual curiosity. As we have seen, the 'memories' of a primitive community were part of its meaning-system and, as with the rest of the meaning-systems, their main purpose was to explain, legitimate, and ensure the continuance of, certain features of the present, or of what was at one time the present. (Thus laws which could be attributed to Lycurgus at Sparta or Solon at Athens or Moses acting as the mouthpiece of God in Israel enjoyed enhanced prestige and authority.) The real meaning of these memories is thus that the past 'must have been' of a certain character for certain features of the present to be as they are or ought to be. There is nearly always an element of projecting some present into the past.

The members of the community will have no means of knowing how far the picture of the past they inherit rests on sound oral tradition or how far such tradition, if it ever existed, has been modified or supplemented for ideological reasons. In fact such questions will hardly enter their minds; it will not occur to them that any alternative account of the past might be possible. Their attitude will be the same as it is toward the rest of their meaning-system. They will accept the traditional picture of the past as being just as much part of objective reality as the community and practices it legitimates.

When, as will often happen, the traditional account of the past gets expanded or modified, that will not normally be because new documents or archaeological evidence have come to light. It will be because new events have occurred, or new interpretations have emerged, which make it appear that God or man 'must have' done things in the past which had not previously been recognised. If the new accounts of the past which result are incompatible by modern historical standards with the accounts which were current before, that will worry no one in a primitive society. Their accounts of the past are not intended or understood as history in that sense. In mythological history logical or chronological incompatibilities can always be accommodated somehow. If members of primitive societies are aware of them at all, they can always find ways of explaining them. Indeed they must; for these accounts rest not on the authority of learned research but on the authority of a sacred tradition. Therefore, whatever the *prima facie* difficulties, things *must* have happened as the tradition represents.

A further point is involved. Because their beliefs about the past are all equally based on the authority of an un-questioned tradition, people in primitive societies make no distinction between statements which *we* should distinguish sharply according to whether or not they could in principle be verified empirically. Such people are not conscious that statements about the words and deeds of historical charac-ters, which could at the time have been verified or falsified by the use of the five senses, have what modern philosophers call a different 'logical status' from statements about the words and deeds of invisible divine figures which could never have been verified in the same way.

Perhaps that fairly extended illustration will have been detailed enough to make a little clearer the sort of internal coherence cultural groups exhibit. Furthermore, although the group described was imaginary, every one of the features ascribed to it could be documented from the history of some actual society (See above, p.20), so perhaps the gulf between its cultural situation and our own may make clear just how widely cultures can differ and how large an element of plausibility there is even in an extreme position such as that of Spengler. So far as Spengler's point was that members of one culture may be too remote from members of another to be able to identify imaginatively with them, far more sober writers could be cited in his support. Louis MacNeice, for example, although he was a professional classical scholar at the time, wrote about the ancient Greeks:

> These dead are dead
> . . . . .
> And how one can imagine oneself among them
> I do not know;
> It was all so unimaginably different
> And all so long ago.[18]

If it should be replied that in an avowedly polemical poem MacNeice had his tongue in his cheek, we may quote some words written recently about Jesus by a theologian, Professor A.D. Galloway: 'We cannot share his thoughts by re-thinking them after [him]. We could only do that validly by becoming ourselves first century Palestinian Jews . . . . we cannot put ourselves in his sandals.'[19]

From the point of view of a literary critic, Dame Helen Gardner quotes MacNeice's words with approval; and her own accompanying comment is well worth reproducing here: 'It is difficult enough', she writes,

> to enter imaginatively into anyone else's religious experience. When two thousand years and more of history separate us from authors and audience it seems rash indeed to attempt to imagine oneself viewing a Greek tragedy in the brilliant spring sunshine all those centuries ago. Responses that seem natural and obvious to-day might not have occurred to me then and elements I now overlook or regard as conventional might then have aroused in me deep religious response because they echoed my own religious experience. We necessarily project into the past our own concerns and our own way of seeing the world. Our concepts of the past are historically conditioned.[20]

That quotation is packed with relevance for our subject and we shall recur to it more than once later. Meanwhile let us note that all these writers are referring to *imaginative identification* with others, and that that is by no means the same thing as understanding what others say. However hard the distinction may sometimes be to draw in practice, it is often possible to understand what another says when it would be quite impossible to imagine what it would be like to be standing in his shoes as he speaks.

Secondly, Professor Gardner's words help to explain why it is sometimes difficult even to understand other people's meaning, especially if they lived in the distant past and our only access to their minds is through their writings. The difficulty, as she makes clear, is to know what experiences or assumptions their words leave unstated because they were taken for granted. As we saw earlier, it is precisely the things 'taken as read', the 'doctrines felt as facts' which it is essential to know for the full understanding of a people's outlook. The written word is not particularly well adapted to help in this connexion. For authors normally have no need to mention the things they and their intended readers agree in taking for granted. It is about things at the conscious level, concerning which there is interest or disagreement, that men tend to put pen to paper.*

The full interpretation of an ancient document is thus very often a laborious business requiring great skill and sensitivity. What we have to do in many cases is to read between the lines in the hope of bringing into the open what is at most implicit in the text itself, and that is no easy matter, as Faust recognises at the beginning of Goethe's play.[21] The procedure must be to begin by interpreting the words on the basis of the best guesses we can make as to the original assumptions and presuppositions. In the light of the interpretation which that yields we may hope to refine our understanding of the presuppositions and then re-read the text on the basis of our new understanding of its assumptions. The process may have to be repeated many times and it may seem circular — it is in fact often referred to as the 'hermeneutic circle'. If nevertheless it works reasonably well in practice, that is because good interpreters bring into play that intuitive insight nineteenth-century thinkers called *Verstehen*, both at the stage of initial guesswork and at subsequent stages of the interpretative process.

As a result, if we know *something* of the context, ancient documents usually yield their meaning at any rate in general terms, and certainly no one doubts that it is possible to discover with reasonable accuracy what most of the biblical writers intended to say, though that, as we have seen, is a very different thing from being able to imagine ourselves inside the skins of, let us say, Amos or Hosea or, still more impossibly, the historical Moses or Elijah.

Many biblical passages — more perhaps than is generally recognised — still remain to be cleared up or explored a great

---

* *Cp.* H. Butterfield, *The Discontinuities between the Generations in History* (CUP, 1972) p.6: 'behind the avowed differences . . . there exist more subtle and delicate differences, some of them in the realm perhaps of presuppositions — things not always avowed, indeed things which men do not always know to quarrel about, such ideas and assumptions being so much part of the air that one breathes. They are the things that the men of 1600 shall we say — but the men of 1900 similarly — do not have to explain to one another, and the result is that *they do not always get into the historian's evidence. Therefore they are apt to be a serious problem to the historian*' (italics mine).

deal further, and it is still all too common to hear the original meaning of the text being expounded on the basis of the interpreter's presuppositions rather than the writer's. Yet the Bible gives rise to less difficulty in this connexion than many other ancient documents. This is partly because of the relatively universal character of much of its subject-matter, partly because the great bulk and variety of its contents and the wealth of illustrative material from other sources make it easier for the interpreter to check his guesses about pre-suppositions; but above all it is because the Church has kept alive, at any rate until lately, many of the absolute presuppositions on which the majority of the biblical material was based. That is why simple Christians, who have never heard of the hermeneutic circle or the problems associated with it, have so often been able to interpret at least certain parts of the Bible with deep insight.

What then is the problem? How does what we have been saying so far bear on the use and interpretation of the Bible? The answer is sometimes put in the crude form of a distinction between what a document *meant* and what it *means*. By the sort of methods just described it is usually possible to get inside the mind of an ancient author sufficiently to understand a large part of his meaning. For example, if I am reading or watching Sophocles' play *Antigone*, I may learn to understand enough of the heroine's beliefs about the demands of the gods and the essential importance of funeral rites to understand her actions and appreciate her tragedy. I do all this, however, by dint of what Coleridge called the 'willing suspension of disbelief'.[22] I do not need to be *converted* to Antigone's beliefs on these matters, and when I stop attending to the play I no longer entertain them; or if her belief does linger in my mind it is as what Collingwood calls an 'incapsulated thought', that is to say, 'a thought which, though perfectly alive, forms no part of the question-answer complex which constitutes what people call the "real" life, the superficial or obvious present, of the mind in question'.[23] That is not to say that having understood and entertained Antigone's beliefs may not affect my own beliefs and behaviour in the present; what it does mean is that I cannot hold them, or be directly affected by them, in the precise form in which Antigone, or those on whom she was modelled, held and were affected by them.

By now most Christians have come to recognise that something of the sort obtains in connexion with many of the beliefs and attitudes in the Bible. For example, if I am to understand fully the accounts of creation in the first four chapters of Genesis, I shall have to enter into a way of picturing the universe not unlike that ascribed just now to our imaginary community. That is something I find little difficulty in doing if I give my mind to it; but it in no way commits me to being a 'flat-earther' in my ordinary everyday life.

What Christians have not so often recognised — or so our argument will run — is that because of the internal coherence of cultural totalities, what holds of such relatively indifferent things as the size and age of the universe, is very likely to hold of other, doctrinally more significant, things as well.

In the light of what has been said, it will be clear that, whatever else the Bible may be, it is the expression, or at any rate an outcrop, of the meaning-system of a relatively primitive cultural group. That being the case, the Bible is bound to pose a general problem in a sharp form.

As we have seen, members of one culture can often discover what the meaning-system of another culture meant in its original context; can they then derive enlightenment from it for their own time, and if so, how? Something of the gravity of this question may be indicated by pointing out that some of the acutest minds who have devoted themselves to it have returned a totally negative answer. The facts seem to them to point to complete relativism. Sir Isaiah Berlin, for example, feels that cultural totalities are entities so discrete that the attitudes and values of each are relative to it alone and can afford no guidance to members of other totalities.

About one thing we must certainly all be clear. Words and practices cannot be taken over in isolation from one culture into another without a profound change of meaning. If, for example, I take words of St Paul from the meaning-system which was their original context and quote them in the context of a quite different cultural situation, what they will say, if it is intelligible, will be something very different from what Paul said. (An instructive example is provided by 1 Cor. 15. Those who hear it read in a modern context, e.g. at a funeral, naturally suppose that the apostle's problem was what change the *dead* would need to undergo before they were ready for life in the kingdom of God. In fact Paul believed that he and most other Christians would still be alive when the kingdom arrived and his question was about how the *living* could suddenly be transformed into a heavenly state when the trumpet blew. 15:51a is meant literally.)

That in itself is not something we need take too tragically. Literary critics constantly tilt against what they call the 'intentionalist fallacy', that is, the assumption that the only meaning which may legitimately be attributed to a writing is that which the original author consciously intended. Some critics go further and deny that the author's understanding of what he writes has any greater authority than anyone else's. Paul Valéry, for example, wrote that 'Quand l'ouvrage a paru, son interprétation par l'auteur n'a plus de valeur que tout autre par qui que ce soit.'[24] Without going as far as that, we shall ourselves be claiming that the modern reader can find in the Bible meaning in abundance, much of which the original authors could not possibly have envisaged in the quite different cultural circumstances of their times.

The problem here, however, is that the Bible has usually been supposed to be something more than a work of artistic creation such as literary critics normally study. It has been believed to advance truth-claims and to provide information about the supernatural in a direct way which distinguishes it sharply from 'mere' works of art. No artist would accept such a way of putting the matter for a moment, but so far as there is any truth in it, the Bible poses a unique problem: on the one hand it claims to convey information; on the other hand it is involved in all the problems of cultural relativity familiar to historians and literary critics, which we have been discussing.

Not of course that the problem has gone unrecognised; in one form or another it has been intensively discussed for well over a hundred years. We shall argue, however, that the terms in which it has usually been formulated have been inadequately analysed and defined. The problem has been supposed to arise from the fact that the modern culture or meaning-system is incompatible with that of the Bible; but that way of putting it is altogether over-simplified and is misleading for a number of reasons.

To begin with, there *is* nothing which can be called 'the modern culture' or meaning-system. Dame Helen Gardner puts it like this:

> We live to-day . . . in a world where the immense extensions of knowledge in every sphere have made a synthesis of our knowledge into anything that could be called a 'world view' impossible. However much the 'world view' or 'world pictures' that have been constructed for earlier ages simplify what men actually thought and felt, it is difficult to believe that any future scholars will ever attempt to construct such a systematic picture of common beliefs and assumptions for the twentieth century. If they attempt to characterize our age at all, no doubt it will be under the metaphor of a 'climate' rather than a 'picture'.[25]

The truth of this is beyond dispute. The very vastness and complexity of the modern cultural enterprise mean that there is no person and no group competent to construct a single overarching world-view on the basis of it; and it may be doubted if there will ever again be a single universally, or even generally, accepted meaning-system. One of the most notable features of the modern cultural situation is its open texture and lack of homogeneity; thoughtful and well-informed people in it hold very widely differing interpretations of the nature of reality. Indeed some sociologists suggest that what prevents many people in the West to-day from subscribing to the Christian faith or to any other clearly defined position is not that they can see decisive objections to it but that they are bewildered by the variety of outlooks available to them and feel incompetent to make a definite choice between them.

Of course, some beliefs and convictions are more widespread than others and what everyone, including the theologian, is tempted to do is to accept as authoritative the opinion of the majority in the group or area in which he lives. Any such temptation should be sternly resisted. That a thing is true because most people believe it is a form of the *ipse dixit* argument no sounder than any other. From the standpoint of the sociology of knowledge Professor Berger has recently subjected it to penetrating criticism.[26] The extent to which a particular view prevails, especially among those who might be expected to be competent judges, is certainly something to be taken into account, but there is no reason at all why Schleiermacher's 'cultured despisers of religion' should be allowed to become the arbiters of our creed, if our own considered and sincerely held beliefs run counter to theirs. As Archbishop William Temple used to put it, we are under no obligation to restrict our faith simply to 'what Jones will swallow'.

That statement could be the vehicle of a dangerous half-truth, however, if it were taken to imply that we are at liberty to form and hold religious beliefs without any reference to the modern cultural situation. Such a suggestion might seem absurd were it not sometimes actually made, often in the form of pious questions. 'Has it not always been part of what Christian discipleship involves', it is asked, 'to be committed to the outlook of the Bible and of the classic Christian formularies derived from it? Is it not the duty of a Christian in every age to let the Bible stand in judgement on his own culture?' And the inability of our constantly changing cultural situation to supply any firm standing-ground is used to reinforce those questions. 'He who marries the spirit of the age', mocked Dean Inge, 'will soon find himself a widower.'

The answers to these questions will depend of course on the way the terms are defined, but one thing is certain: it can never be a Christian's duty to deny what he knows to be true or affirm what he knows to be false; and there are some things which no modern human being can affirm or deny with integrity.

The difficulty is to know what those things are. Some of them might seem obvious enough. It might be thought, for example, that no one could doubt the approximately spherical shape of the world or the heliocentric character of the solar system. Yet it was only just over twenty years ago that a geography student at London University obtained a first-class honours degree without at any point in her papers being false to her conviction, held on religious grounds, that the earth is flat. Which at least shows how difficult it is to *prove* that any given statement is incompatible with what a citizen of the modern world is bound to hold.

A rather less extreme example may be more illuminating. As a consequence of the progressive questioning of absolute presuppositions over the centuries, no one in the West to-day doubts that most illness is due not to demon-possession or witchcraft but to bacteria or viruses or other 'natural' agents.• To most people the evidence seems to have rendered impossible continued belief in any direct personal causation of illness; but it is obviously not self-contradictory to believe, as a minority continues to do, either that *some* cases of illness are due to direct demonic activity or that demonic activity lies behind the immediate operation of bacteria, viruses and similar agencies. In the latter case demonic activity is of course being understood in a different way and on a different scale from what it was in the ancient world; but the example nevertheless emphasizes how difficult it is to show that even a rare minority-view logically contradicts facts universally taken as established.

In order to provide an example where opinion may be much more evenly divided, at any rate among religious people, let us return to the case of miracle which we have already discussed briefly.

As a result of various shifts of interest and consequent changes in the type of question asked, many events at one time thought of as miraculous are now generally agreed to have been the result of regularities in nature previously unrecognised or imperfectly understood; or in some cases to have been due to an exceptional concomitance of physical factors in themselves now quite fully understood. The same cultural shifts have also meant that the very concept of a miracle has changed significantly. So long as the universe was thought of as being directly and continually under the personal control of God, the line dividing the miraculous from the normal was relatively thin. To use a different model from the one we used before, it was only to be expected that while God would often move the universe in a regular way, as a man moves his body rhythmically when walking across country at a regular pace, he would want occasionally — for reasons which approved themselves to him, even if men could not understand them — to move the world in an exceptional way, just as the man may suddenly take a flying run in order to leap over a stream, incomprehensibly to a distant onlooker who cannot see the stream.

As defined in terms of modern presuppositions, however, the word miracle takes on a greatly heightened meaning. That is not only because miracles, if they occur at all, are of much rarer occurrence than used to be supposed; but because in the light of our modern understanding of the physical universe as an impersonal interlocking system, a miracle would entail an exercise of divine power on a far vaster scale than previous periods envisaged. The halting of the sun for Joshua, for example, appeared simply as a signal expression of God's power to the ancient Jews who in any case thought of him as sending it across the sky each day; we who appreciate just what exercise of power would be necessary to neutralise the repercussions of a cessation of the earth's movement on the rest of the solar system, may feel, in the light of what we know of God, that the exertion of power on so literally astronomical a scale would be out of all proportion to the supposed purpose of it. At the very least we have here a further example of the truth that a single element cannot be transposed from one cultural context to another without a drastic change of meaning. To believe now in the halting of the sun, or for that matter in the raising of Lazarus, is to hold a quite different belief from that which was held by the biblical writers.

All this, however, is inconclusive and will make a different impact on different people. Some will insist that nothing in what has been said makes a miracle in the strictest sense logically impossible or comes anywhere near proving that 'miracles cannot happen'. Others will be so impressed by the number of events previously regarded as miracles which have now been explained naturally; and by the fact that they have never witnessed a miracle themselves or known anyone directly who has, that they will doubt if miracles in our sense, even if they can happen, ever do or ever have.

We have here a case of the sort alluded to just now where equally well-informed and intelligent people interpret the same evidence in quite different ways, and there is no question of 'the modern man's' being constrained by 'the modern world view'. Ours is a cultural situation in which some people have no difficulty in believing things about which integrity obliges others to say: 'that I cannot believe'.

Such a position frequently arises over quite general questions. The question of miracles, for example, is a part of a wider question. Thinkers such as Ernst Troeltsch regarded as axiomatic what they called the principle of analogy, that is, the principle that the way things happen in the present is a safe guide to the way they have always happened in the past. They assumed that the universe possesses sufficient uniformity to exclude the possibility of any pronounced deviation; and that is certainly a principle on which working historians normally proceed. In fact it is difficult to see how they could do their work if they did not. An artificially simplified example quoted from an earlier work may illustrate the point. Consider an historian attempting to decide whether in a particular campaign a certain general marched an army of a certain size across a certain tract of desert, as he is alleged to have done. The historian concludes that he did not do so in view of the number and size of the oases in the desert concerned, which could not possibly have provided sufficient water for even a tenth of the number of troops supposed to have been involved. The conclusion seems sound enough, but of course it presupposes that the oases in question were producing at the particular time roughly the same amount of water they are known to produce at all other times. If the historian could not assume that, he would have no criterion, no basis for accepting or rejecting the statements of his source; he could not in fact pronounce any scientific verdict on the historicity or otherwise of the alleged march.

To many people the universal validity of the principle of analogy will seem virtually self-evident. They will feel that no event can properly be claimed as 'historical' in the generally accepted sense of the term unless the evidence for it has been subjected to rigorous tests based on this principle. Others, however, will see it quite differently. They would concede that the principle in question is a useful working principle for ordinary historical research; and they would admit that the occurrence of any radical discontinuities in the historical process would put the historian in a difficult position, and even perhaps make it impossible for him to certify the events in question as historical in the ordinary sense of the word. But, they would insist, *ex hypothesi* the biblical events were not ordinary events, and no working principle gives anyone the right to lay down that even events of the most radically extraordinary character cannot, or do not, occur. Obviously if they did occur, their occurrence would place strains on the historian's normal working procedures because those procedures have been devised to deal with normal events; but that is a truism and gives the historian no ground for claiming that his inability to issue an event with a certificate of historicity in his special sense means that the event in question did not occur. No one can dictate that events of a certain sort shall not have occurred. The assumption of many modern historians that radically exceptional events have never occurred is quite arbitrary and simply denies the credibility of many of the biblical narratives by what amounts to a straight *petitio principii.*

To this the supporter of the principle of analogy in his turn may reply that since the whole of history is a seamless web of interconnected events, an event within history which could be described as 'wholly other' would be a meaningless concept. He may also attempt to cut the ground from under his opponent's feet by pointing out that he is claiming far more for the biblical narratives than they claim for themselves. In the cultural circumstances of their own day all the biblical writers were doing was to claim traditional testimony for the occurrence of certain relatively unusual 'signs' or 'wonders' (See p. 21 and p. 33 above); what their modern interpreters are doing is to try to turn this into solid historical evidence for the occurrence of miracles in the strict modern sense.

Obviously this difference of opinion will make a great deal of difference to the way the Bible is understood, and further examples of a similar sort could easily be produced. A book about the Bible is not the place in which to attempt to settle the philosophical issues involved, so the method adopted in these lectures will be to analyse some of the main ways in which Christians of various periods have handled the Bible and based their faith on it, and then ask to what basic presuppositions each of those ways commits anyone who adopts it. The hope is that each reader will thus be in a position to decide for himself whether those presuppositions are ones which he can adopt with integrity.

If the question is raised whether such an approach does not play down unduly that *sacrificium intellectus* which Christianity has always been supposed to demand, answers are attempted at various points in the lectures. Suffice it to say here that if God is God, his nature and his relations with the world must exceed the measures of man's mind. Some paradox is inevitable, and any system which claimed to give a complete account of the matter would justly incur the complaint Kierkegaard made *à propos* the Hegelian system, that 'the Absolute is gone out of things'. Nevertheless, despite the *credo quia impossibile* of Tertullian and his irrationalist successors, no one has ever seriously suggested that being a Christian entails what the little girl described as 'believing what you know can't possibly be true'.

Before we pass to the lectures there is a further very serious inadequacy in the way the biblical problem is usually formulated, which needs to be pointed out. As we have seen (Cp. p. 30 above), the problem has generally been supposed to arise from the fact that modern culture is incompatible with that of the Bible. Apart from the points we have already considered, there is a further very important point which has received curiously little attention.* It is this.

In practice the absolute presuppositions Christian readers

---

* An honourable exception to this is Professor R.P.C. Hanson in his book *The Attractiveness of God* (SPCK, 1973) e.g. pp. 30–1. Unfortunately, Dr Hanson has not seen, or at any rate has not drawn out, the real implications of his own observations. Existentialist interpreters of the school of Bultmann, with their strong Lutheran emphasis on the *sola scriptura*, have been strangely insensitive to the positive significance and value of interpretations of the Bible in cultures between the biblical and our own.

have normally felt obliged to accept in interpreting the Bible have been the presuppositions not so much of the biblical writers themselves as of those who have *interpreted* the Bible in whatever periods — patristic, medieval or reformation — the readers in question have regarded as classical and authoritative. In reading the Bible Christians have usually taken for granted the truth of the classical creeds and of the formularies of the denomination to which they belonged, and, with varying degrees of self-awareness, allowed them to influence and dictate their interpretation of the text.

The details of that will be spelled out later, but if in the meantime it may be taken as established, its significance deserves to be drawn out and emphasized. Every creed or formulary is the product of a particular cultural situation, and so far as it is derived from the Bible, it is derived from it in accordance with the mode of biblical interpretation current in that situation. It is therefore essential to recognise that the situations in which the various creeds and formularies of Christendom grew up were on the one hand different from the situations in which any of the biblical books was written, but on the other hand differed even more radically from our own situation. For as the lectures will show, at about the end of the eighteenth century a cultural revolution of such vast proportions broke out that it separates our age sharply from all the ages that went before.

From all this two things follow. First, since the categories in which the fathers, the schoolmen or the reformers interpreted the Bible were the categories of their own times and not those of the Bible, no interpretation based on their categories will be strictly, or exclusively, biblical.

Secondly, since the categories with which these various interpreters worked were only a little less foreign to our culture than the categories of the Bible itself, the same problems of cultural difference which arise between us and the biblical writers arise equally, or almost equally, between us and these pre-nineteenth century interpreters. And since it is on the work of one or more of these interpreters that the orthodoxy of every denomination rests, it could well be argued that the problems arising out of our cultural differences from them form a large part of the biblical problem.

Anyone who values the survival of the Bible will be bound to regard the activities of these earlier exegetes in a rather ambivalent way. On the one hand they deserve our gratitude and respect, not only for the intrinsic value of much of what they said, but because it was only through their interpretation of the Bible in their various periods, in ways which made it speak to their contemporaries, that it retained from age to age its reputation as a book of lively oracles, and so its capacity to survive. On the other hand, so far as the methods of biblical interpretation employed by these interpreters, and the sort of results obtained by them, have come to be regarded as timelessly valid and as binding on Christians to-day, they have become, through no fault or intention of their authors, a very serious stumbling-block.

All this will be exemplified at length in the lectures, but one brief example may be given at once. It is not always recognised that it is largely the thought of those who devised the classic formularies which has determined the type of unity Christians have traditionally ascribed to the Bible. Although it may be true that in developing their ideas on the subject these theologians were taking up hints in the Bible itself, the fact remains that their ideas go far beyond anything actually found in the Bible; and the type of unity they ascribe to the Bible belongs to the question-answer complex of their cultural situation rather than to that of the biblical writers themselves, for most of whom the question of the unity of the Bible did not arise at all, or was not a particularly pressing one.[27] In any event modern critical scholarship has its own ways of explaining such unity as the Bible possesses, and it should be left an entirely open question how far these need to be supplemented by such categories as type-antitype or promise and fulfilment. (So far as these categories were in the minds of the biblical writers or their pre-critical interpreters, they must of course be taken with the utmost seriousness for the purpose of understanding what both classes of writers wrote. The question is how far they need or should figure in *our* understanding of the relationship between God and men.)

Whether anything that has been said disproves the widely held belief that 'human nature doesn't change' is a comparatively uninteresting question because the answer is in any case largely a matter of definition. At least we may have gone some way towards explaining why one of the leading English students of the question dismisses as 'fallacious' any 'belief in a fixed, ultimate unchanging human nature'[28]; more significantly, what has been said may have helped to show that, whether or not human nature changes, the understanding and expression of it change so radically as to raise a major problem for the current understanding of the Bible and of earlier interpretations of it. This introductory chapter will have served its purpose if it has made intelligible and convincing the following words of the American critic Lionel Trilling: "To suppose that we can think like men of another time is as much of an illusion as to suppose that we can think in a wholly different way. ... It ought to be for us a real question whether, and in what way, human nature is always the same. I do not mean that we ought to settle this question before we get to work, but only that we insist to ourselves that the question is a real one. What we certainly know has changed is the *expression* of human nature, and we must keep before our minds the problem of the relation which expression bears to feeling ... ' [We may add 'and belief'; it must be remembered that Professor Trilling is thinking primarily in this passage of works of art.] 'The problem ... is a very difficult one, and I scarcely even state its complexities, let alone pretend to solve them. But the problem with its difficulties should be admitted, and simplicity of solution should always be regarded as a sign of failure.'[29]

The last two sentences in particular should be underlined; for the rest, it must be a case of *solvitur ambulando*.

2 The nature of the biblical problem

It may be best to begin with some remarks about the title of these lectures. First a limitation must be stated. The lectures will be concerned only with the use — or possible *mis*-use — of the Bible by Christian readers, or at any rate people who read in the hope of receiving religious enlightenment; they will not, for example, be concerned with the Bible considered simply as literature or simply as source-material for the historian or the anthropologist.

Secondly, the title might seem arrogant if it were taken to imply a claim to know how the Bible should, or should not, be used. Let me at once disclaim any pretensions to such knowledge. At most, you can expect only hints and inklings; and even these, I hope I can say sincerely, are simply offered for the completely frank comments and criticisms of my fellow Christians.

My title might also be faulted on the grounds that it seems to deny to the Bible the spontaneity it often in fact exhibits. 'There are times', it might be said, 'when, if such language is to be used at all, it would seem more appropriate to talk of the Bible's using us than of our using the Bible. The Bible is a book which can, on occasion, stand in judgement over us, call in question all our self-understanding and self-conceit, and drive us to new attitudes, whether we like it or not.'

With that I am in complete agreement. The Bible can indeed be a 'bomb of a book', particularly perhaps when it impinges on people and cultures hitherto unfamiliar with it. The Bible can hit a man in such a way as to destroy and remake his whole outlook; it — or parts of it — can 'find' us as Coleridge put it.[1]

An obvious example is what happened to Karl Barth

during the first world war, when the Epistle to the Romans in particular 'found' him in this way, and the result was his commentary on the Epistle, itself a 'bomb of a book', in which new insights fairly poured forth in a red hot stream, calling in question many of the basic assumptions and presuppositions of Barth himself and most of his fellow Christians.

All that is incontrovertible; nevertheless it is possible to admit, indeed to assert, the reality of the impact on Barth and yet to have reservations about his response to that impact and his interpretation of it. As you know, his response was to take the Bible more seriously than his predecessors had done in the sense of taking it more literally. He attributed to what he took to be the biblical doctrine of God and his great acts in history, and to certain other key concepts of the Bible, a more or less absolute status, treating them as a given framework within which all genuinely Christian thinking must be done.

Barth's influence has been very profound and it has extended far beyond the circle of those who would call themselves Barthians. So it is probably true to say that at any rate in Protestant circles, variants of his view, or views very similar to them, dominate the scene. It will be necessary later to say quite a lot about such views; meanwhile we must note that there are current in the Church other responses to the impact of the Bible and some of these too we shall have to discuss later.

For the moment all I need do is to point out that all, or almost all, these responses have at least one thing in common with Barth's: they involve an attempt to derive more or less directly from the Bible an understanding and definition of what Christianity is — to extract from it the norms of Christian belief and behaviour.

To many this will seem entirely natural. Christians in the past have always sought to discover the content and norms of the Christian faith from the Bible in this way; by what warrant should we behave differently? It is not surprising if many Christians regard the use of the Bible in this way as at least *an* essential element in the definition of what it means to be a Christian. 'Christian teaching', writes Canon Ronald

Preston, 'must of course derive from the Bible'. From the Reformed side Professor J.K.S. Reid tells us that 'in the Scriptures ... nothing ... is lacking for the nourishment and rule of Christian life and faith', and the writer of a recent article on spiritual reading begins by saying that the obligation to know the Bible will be taken for granted by all serious Christians 'because all we are and do comes under the judgement of the norms there established'.[2]

Such an attitude is readily understandable and no doubt in varying measure we all share it. In all of us there is a strong drive towards continuing in the familiar ways of our fathers. Yet we cannot help noticing that in most realms of activity nowadays we do not succeed in doing so. To practise medicine or psychology or literary criticism, to do physics or chemistry, to study history or ethics in the ways our forefathers did even two hundred years ago would be absurd; and the same applies to practically every other type of activity. The question therefore at least deserves to be raised why the practice of the Christian religion, and the use of the Bible in particular, should be thought to be in any different case.

It will no doubt be replied that we do *not* try to practise our religion, or use the Bible, exactly as our fathers did. Christian believers are well aware of the cultural revolution that has taken place in recent times; indeed Christian theologians in the past two hundred years have done little else than try to cope with it.

There is obvious truth in that, but the question may still be asked whether the ways in which they have tried to cope have been along the right lines. An analogy which suggests itself is that of an individual suffering from the sort of emotional disturbance which results from a conflict, real or supposed, between some influence or relationship in his distant past and something arising out of the circumstances of the present or the recent past.

In such cases people's immediate impulse is often to minimise the seriousness of the conflict and to dismiss it from consciousness as far as possible; and then to try to live with the situation by confining their activities in the present to whatever can be done and borne while still remaining

under the dominance of the childhood influence or relationship. This, however, invariably leads to loss of effectiveness,
and if a psychoanalyst is consulted he will normally advocate
the opposite course — facing the conflict in its full scope and
trying to understand its nature and causes. He will then very
often encourage the patient to see the influence from the
past as one which, however healthy it may once have been, is
now baleful, and can be, and should be, outgrown.

So far as the analogy is valid, we may ask: what part have
modern theologians played, that of the minimiser or that of
the psychoanalyst? The influence from the distant past which
I have in mind in this case is not so much the existence of the
biblical writings as the way they have traditionally been used,
that is to say the way they were used during the sixteen
hundred years or so of what might be called classic
Christianity, the period when the orthodoxies of the patristic, medieval and Reformation eras were constructed on
the basis of the Bible. I hope to show that the use of the
Bible in that period was in certain important respects more or
less uniform, and that the understanding of the relation
between the Christian faith and the Bible was almost equally
uniform. If so, it is not surprising if that way of using the
Bible and that understanding of the relation between the
Bible and the faith have sunk so deep into the Christian
consciousness that they have come to seem to many
irreformable without the disappearance of Christianity
altogether.

We have already seen something of the importance for our
situation of the way the Bible has been handled in the past
(see above, pp. 36—8), but if anyone remains to be convinced,
let him indulge for a few moments in the fancy that immediately after the completion of the last New Testament book,
the sole text of the Bible was hidden and lost until its discovery in a cave near the Dead Sea some ten years ago. Whether
or not any church would have survived in those circumstances,
and whether or not any church which survived would have
been better than the existing church, our whole attitude to
the Bible would obviously have been completely different.
Just imagine for example what we should have made of the
purple passages which would have appeared in translation in

the Sunday papers; or just consider what the position would have been with regard to those essentially patristic constructions on the basis of the Bible, the doctrines of the Trinity and the Incarnation!

To revert briefly to our psychological analogy, the element in the present which seems to me to have given rise to conflict can be defined for the moment rather vaguely as the situation resulting from what I described just now as a cultural revolution of the last two centuries or so. I shall particularise later; for the moment I will simply register the impression that theologians, and biblical interpreters in particular, have seriously underestimated the scope and significance of this revolution. I say that in no spirit of blame; if the situation has changed radically, it has done so gradually; and at no stage, including the present, has the picture been clear. But if the reasons are understandable, the fact remains that the voice of the theologian has often been the voice of the minimiser which may well be, in this context, the voice of the Tempter.

In order to test this suspicion I should like, greatly daring, to assume the role of psychoanalyst for a while; let us try to see how serious the biblical problem will look if we analyse its essential character, and how radical the treatment it will need. May I remind you, in case you are looking for anything original, that the things psychoanalysts tell us are always things we know already? And you will not need to be reminded that the interpretations offered by psychoanalysts are notoriously — and quite avowedly — subjective. I shall be quite satisfied if I succeed in analysing the nature of this problem at all usefully and bringing the seriousness of it to the attention of others better qualified than I am to suggest a diagnosis and remedies.

Let us then look at the traditional use of the Bible, reminding ourselves that it is a psychoanalyst's, and not a historian's, look that we shall be taking. A historian would have to deal with many matters we cannot consider in the course of one or two lectures; and he would have to record and document the fact that there were numerous and important variations in this matter between different theologians and schools of theology, even if we define the word 'traditional' in such a way as to exclude the whole period since the rise of historical-critical study some two hundred years ago.[3] The psychoanalyst, on the other hand, is justified in considering the overall impact made by a period of the past in a more general way; and he is free to be more selective, treating only those features in a period which seem to him significant for the problem with which he is concerned. So from his point of view, even if it is not justifiable to speak of *the* traditional attitude to the Bible, it may be permissible to speak of a single interpretative tradition dominant in more or less all parts of the Church at least until about the eighteenth century. Whoever we are in the Christian west, we have, broadly speaking, a common past so far as the Bible is concerned. Certainly, even between Roman Catholics and Protestants, agreements about the Bible in this period can be seen from our perspective to have been far more significant than such differences of approach as there may have been. Even at the Reformation, although in one sense the biblical question was central, the issue was not so much the infallibility of the Bible, or the ways in which faith and morals could be elicited from it, as the relation between the authority of the Bible and other alleged authorities.

For this was the age of the authority. C.S. Lewis says of the Middle Ages that they were 'the ages of authority', and he goes on, 'if their culture is regarded as a response to environment, then the elements in that environment to which it responded most vigorously were manuscripts. Every writer if he possibly can, bases himself on an earlier writer, follows an *auctour*: preferably a Latin one. This is one of the things that differentiates that period . . . from our modern civilisation.'[4] And he remarks later of medieval people: 'they find it hard to believe that anything an old *auctour* has said is simply untrue'.[5], (To put the point in the language of our Introduction, we might say that a culture very much aware of its inferiority to previous cultures did not think of questioning the categories with which those earlier cultures had worked, or the answers to questions they had given in terms of those categories. The virtual infallibility of these earlier cultures was a 'doctrine felt as a fact'.) If that was true of the medieval attitude toward *any* ancient author, how much truer will it have been of the Bible which was regarded throughout this period as a sacred book with all the infallible authority, mysterious quality and virtual sanctity which attach to the sacred book in any religious tradition? To this day the formal title of the scriptures is the *Holy* Bible.

One consequence of its possessing this status as a sacred book was that the Bible was expected to reveal its message in mysterious and riddling ways and it was therefore no cause for surprise if allegorical and other non-literal methods of interpretation needed to be used in order to make it yield its secret; but that is to anticipate. Let us draw out the relevant features of the situation in order.

First there was the universal conviction that the Bible was, in some fairly strict sense, produced by God himself. It is true that the precise mode of God's working was not formally defined and the matter may have been one of universal assumption rather than explicit belief. Canon Charles Smyth goes so far as to say that 'nobody really believed in the verbal inspiration of the Holy Scriptures until the geologists began to question it' in the nineteenth century.[6] That is perhaps putting it rather strongly, for there were some, like Theophilus of Antioch, who thought of the biblical writers as completely passive instruments in the hands of God, and used such models as that of a flute and a flautist. Also there was widespread acceptance of the formula that the Bible had God for its *auctor* and was written at the dictation of the Holy Spirit (*dictante spiritu sancto*) — surely telling phrases, especially in the light of the passages quoted just now from C. S. Lewis, even though they did not then convey quite all they suggest to us, with our modern conventions about copyright and our experience of stenographers.

At any rate there can be no doubt about the correctness of Canon Smyth's subsequent words: 'broadly speaking, people believed everything they read in the Bible, in the same way that some people believe everything that they read in the newspapers'.[7] That was the attitude; every word was true because every word in some real, if undefined, sense had God as its author. Such an attitude was bound to have a very strong influence on the use to which the Bible was put and the way it was interpreted.

Apart from the obvious and important negative corollary that the Bible could contain no error, there was the positive implication that every passage must have some meaning, some truth to convey; otherwise God would not have arranged for its inclusion. Likewise in many circles the particular turns of phrase in the Bible took on deep significance; for God would not have arranged that any particular passage should be expressed as it was unless he had intended the particular turn of expression to be significant. Some even attributed the pointing and punctuation of the original text directly to God and so invested them with the character of vehicles of divine communication. Here again opinion and emphasis varied to some extent, but no one doubted that since the Bible was God's product, everything in it was there for a purpose and had some truth to reveal.

A further corollary, though it was not strictly a logical inference, was that little attention need be paid to the human author's historical situation in determining the meaning of a passage, or even to the context of the passage in the Bible; and the habit of seeing a specific meaning in individual passages taken in isolation, was reinforced by the practice of preachers who took a single short passage as the basis of each sermon and *appeared* at least to find in it a more or less self-contained meaning, without reference to its context.

The practice of taking small isolated passages as a unit of exposition has now become so habitual that its oddity often passes unnoticed. It may, therefore, be worth repeating some words from the *Times* first leader for 23 January 1971 about the communiqué of the Singapore Commonwealth Conference: 'It may be a bit early to start quoting isolated texts from the declaration as if they came from holy writ.' You note the implication; it is holy writ — and holy writ alone — which is normally treated in this extraordinary way. In the ordinary way the meaning of a passage in any document may be expected to be very largely defined by its context; but in the case of the Bible this expectation was frequently offset by another belief. Although every passage was believed to have a meaning, it was not felt that the meaning need

necessarily be the obvious and literal sense conveyed by the
words. From the beginning, the Christians, like the Jews — and
the Greeks with reference to such a text as Homer — became
convinced that many a passage in the scriptures could yield
no truth 'worthy of the dignity of God' unless it were
interpreted in an allegorical, or some other figurative,
manner. Without such figurative interpretations many Old
Testament passages could not have been interpreted in any
sense compatible with Christianity, and so, as everyone
knows, allegory 'saved the Scriptures for the Church'.[8] Given
a dead-level approach, according to which every passage was
equally attributable to direct divine initiative, such modes of
interpretation were inevitable, and as we have seen, they
seemed entirely natural in the case of a sacred book.
Accordingly, figurative modes of interpretation of many
types were applied, especially to Old Testament passages.

The results may often have been bizarre, but there was one
negative corollary which was to be of significance later. The
habit of figurative interpretation meant that Christians of the
pre-critical period did not always feel bound by the literal
statements of the Bible, at any rate on matters of history,
geography or natural science. To quote only two examples,
Cardinal Baronius is said by Galileo to have coined the
aphorism: 'The Holy Spirit wishes to teach us not how the
heavens go, but how to go to heaven'[9]; and long before that
Augustine had commented 'We do not read in the Gospel of
the Lord's having said: I send you a Comforter to teach you
about the course of the sun and moon. What he sought to
produce was Christians, not astronomers'.[10]

In general, however, the tendency was to accept the
statements of the Bible, literally interpreted, as giving
authoritative guidance on scientific and historical, as well as
religious, matters. Dr Leonard Hodgson, who in his youth
had first-hand experience of a basically pre-critical attitude to
scripture, points to the evidence that, as he puts it, the
Church was 'accustomed to take for granted the authorship
of the Pentateuch by Moses and of the other books of the
Bible by those to whom they were ascribed in their titles, *and
to think of their contents — in matters of science and history
as well as of faith and morals — as truths guaranteed by*

divine inspiration'.[11]

A further point which is to be noted here is more difficult to put briefly. Perhaps I can express it by saying that every statement in the Bible was taken to have a literal meaning. As we have already seen, this does not mean that every statement was taken literally. It was of course recognised that many biblical statements are, and were meant to be, figurative or metaphorical. John Donne, for example, writes in one of his sermons: 'the literall sense is not alwayes that, which the very Letter and Grammar of the place presents, as where it is literally said *That Christ is a Vine*, and literally *That his flesh is bread*, . . . in many places of Scripture, a figurative sense is the literall sense'.[12] What is more, traditional theology was insistent on the philosophical point that no statement which refers directly to God and the supernatural world can be literally true, whether it occurs in the Bible or elsewhere; all such statements must be understood in a symbolical, or to use the language of the schoolmen, analogical, sense (*per analogiam*). Nevertheless, it will be noticed, Donne assumes that all passages, even figurative passages, have a literal sense. The two passages Donne refers to are both unmistakably figurative, but the same principle was taken to hold for passages which were figuratively interpreted without express warrant in the text.

Whatever problems such a view involved, it had this important consequence: it provided the basis for the belief that every biblical passage has what may be called a factual reference and meaning, and that if these references are all correctly read off and put together, they will form a coherent account of things, which may fairly be described as *the* meaning of the Bible. Orthodox dogma was in fact an attempt to formulate such an account; and being a Christian meant accepting that account and endeavouring to live in the light of it.

Perhaps the point may be made clearer by means of examples. If Christ was said to have expelled demons, then it could be assumed that beings called demons must exist, whatever their true essence and character, or place in the hierarchy of being. Or, to take a more significant example, if the New Testament says that the Messiah has come, that was traditionally taken 'literally' in the sense that it was assumed to imply:

(i)   that there must exist an identifiable being, a super-natural entity (*hypostasis*), properly called the Messiah, and

(ii) that this being once effected a transition from another world to this world such as can properly be represented *per analogiam*, as 'coming into' this world.

Such an understanding of individual passages naturally encouraged attempts to extract the literal sense of each one and then combine the literal meanings of them all into a single coherent corpus of information.

This aspect of the matter links closely with another. It would be difficult to exaggerate the importance for biblical interpretation of the fact that Christianity, having begun as a near-oriental religion, moved west at an early date, and from then until quite recent times has been practised and interpreted almost exclusively in the context of western culture. This meant, among other things, that the educated men to whom the interpretation and exposition of the scriptures fell, tended to be men of a philosophical and systematizing bent of mind (even if, as in Tertullian's case, it was *malgré eux*). Moreover, these men were heirs to a particular philosophical tradition.

It is quite right — and as a corrective, very important — to insist, as Professor James Barr does, that phrases such as 'Greek thought' or 'Graeco-Roman culture' are so ill-defined as to be virtually meaningless. But that does not alter the fact — or the importance of the fact — that when, in its early days, Christianity was very much 'a religion seeking a metaphysic',[13] it found available to it a metaphysical outlook sufficiently congenial for an alliance to be possible.

We must not exaggerate the homogeneity of this philosophical outlook, composed as it was of Platonic, Aristotelian, Stoic and other elements. Different theologians found different elements in it congenial; but since almost every element adopted by Christians proved to require modification in the light of Christian belief, the Christian critique and control of the tradition gradually produced greater homogeneity.

The religion and the philosophical tradition exerted mutual influence, and the upshot, so far as the handling of the Bible was concerned, was a series of fairly similar variations on a basic philosophical theme, any one of which provided the biblical student with a metaphysical context in which he could happily work, and in particular, from our point of view, in which he could interpret biblical passages 'literally' in the sense defined above. The upshot was that readers and students of the Bible found themselves working in a situation where a certain set of philosophical pre-suppositions very widely prevailed.

This traditional Christian philosophy proved very long-lived and the earliest Protestants took it over largely unchanged from the Church of the Middle Ages. It was:

(*i*) essentially a 'substance' philosophy which saw reality as a dual structure. That is to say, the sum of things was taken to consist of two elements, rather as an iceberg does. There was 'this world', as it were the visible and less significant element in the iceberg; and there was 'the other world', which is hidden from view because it is not involved in space and time. Yet it was sufficiently like this world for language strictly applicable to this world to be used of it symbolically, provided proper safeguards were employed. The two worlds were thought to inter-act; this world depended for its very existence on the other, but by the same token things done in this world could by an essentially mysterious mode of operation have effects in and upon the other world.

(*ii*) Reality was also regarded as a hierarchy of being in which every existent, from God the Father, through angels and men, to the lowest animal, and even the stones, had its appointed niche.

The importance of all this for the literal interpretation of the Bible will be readily seen. For example, biblical references to various lesser supernatural beings, both good and bad, and all their goings and comings between heaven and earth, could easily be seen as descriptions, more or less figurative, of beings and activities which had a literal existence at their appropriate point on the great chain of being. And, to cite a more central matter, New Testament interpretations of the death of Christ were understood in the same frame of reference. The primary significance of Christ's death was assumed to lie not in any natural effects it may have had on his followers in this world, either at the time or since, but in the 'supernatural' effects it produced, quite independently, in the other world. As we shall see, a good deal of traditional theology consisted of attempts to understand the working, or 'mechanics', of these interactions between the natural and the supernatural.

Two interesting results, among others, flowed from all this. The philosophical tradition Christianity found available in the west was, as we have seen, essentially systematic in trend and therefore was such as to reinforce the tendency we have already noticed towards attempts to work statements of the Bible together into a coherent system; indeed, given the character and assumptions of this tradition, the obvious thing to do with the Bible was to read off the 'literal' meaning of all the passages and then attempt to put them together in such a way as to form a coherent account of things. As we have seen, such an account could be thought to enshrine *the* meaning of the Bible, and orthodox dogmatics was in fact an attempt to formulate such an account.

The only question at issue concerned the scope of the systematizing activity. Purists held, at least in theory, that the process should be confined entirely to biblical data, on the ground that the Bible contains all we need to know for our souls' health. Attempts to probe into extra-biblical matters were simply the products of the sort of curiosity which kills cats. 'Where is there any likeness between the Christian and the philosopher? between the disciple of Greece and the disciple of heaven?' asked Tertullian. 'What has Athens to do with Jerusalem? What has the Academy to do with the Church?'[14]

In practice, however, the basic presuppositions of the generally accepted philosophical stance seemed to everyone so obvious that this view differed little from that which ultimately prevailed and which took the knowledge and insights of non-biblical authorities with full seriousness, seeking to mould them and the biblical data together into comprehensive systems of universal knowledge. It seemed self-evident to everyone, needless to say, that in cases of conflict, absolute preference should be given to the divinely guaranteed deliverances of the Bible. 'The Philosopher' might have great authority; 'the Apostle' had *absolute* authority.

A further consequence of the position I have described is that it entailed a quite definite understanding of the nature and task of biblical exegesis. Given these presuppositions, the 'meaning' of a biblical passage *could* only be some statement or statements which fitted into the overall system derived from Christian and non-Christian sources. Thus exegesis was understood essentially as the translation of biblical statements into the categories of that form of the dominant philosophical tradition which appealed most to the exegete doing the work.

From our vantage point it is possible to see that this definition of exegesis was a very special one, and it led to what we can only regard as a great deal of distortion; but to a period which knew no alternative possibility it seemed the self-evident definition; and so both with regard to the Bible as a whole and to the interpretation of individual passages, the philosophical tradition went a long way towards defining the nature of traditional biblical interpretation.

Not only did it define its general character; in time it went a long way towards defining its detailed conclusions. For in the early days exegetes working along the lines described, performed their task so skilfully that by the end of the fifth century there emerged a widely accepted and authoritative formulation of Christian truth couched in current philosophical categories.

It is important to notice that this and later formulations had, in their turn, a profound effect on subsequent exegesis in all the orthodox branches of Christendom. For since the orthodox doctrines of the Trinity, the Incarnation and the rest, which arose out of early exegesis and were formulated in the course of the Councils and controversies of the first five centuries, were believed to enshrine *the* meaning of the Bible, they inevitably provided both a framework of reference and also an ultimate criterion for all subsequent exegesis. Anyone, for example, interpreting a New Testament passage which referred to 'the Son', now started from the conviction that the reference was to the Second Person of the Trinity as defined at Nicaea and Chalcedon; and he was also convinced that no interpretation of the passage could be correct which implied anything incompatible with the characteristics of the Second Person as laid down at those councils. Thus John 14:28b ['the Father is greater than I'] now became a *crux interpretum,* because it seemed *prima facie* to conflict with the Nicene and Chalcedonian doctrine; but on the presuppositions of traditional exegesis there could not be any real conflict, and therefore the orthodox doctrine of the Trinity indicated the area in which the correct interpretation must lie, whatever it eventually turned out to be. It would be easy to cite other examples — passages about 'the brethren of the Lord', for instance, against the background of the doctrine of the perpetual virginity of Mary — since there are almost innumerable examples to choose from. And when it is remembered that what applies to the definitions of Nicaea and Chalcedon applies equally to numerous other doctrinal definitions, it will be seen how very largely the scope and direction of traditional exegetical activity were determined and delimited by the philosophical and doctrinal context in which it was carried on.

As *we* see it, the alliance of Christianity with that particular complex of philosophical traditions is a contingent fact, even if we regard it as providential. But at the time, since Christianity soon became in practice an almost exclusively western phenomenon, no alternative was conceived or conceivable. Consequently what was in fact a *particular* way of handling the Bible, and a way which from our point of view had many defects and led to many distortions, would have seemed, had the question so much as been raised, to be *the* way, the only conceivable or meaningful way.

The philosophical tradition contributed to the same result by an almost opposite route. It is generally recognised that the *philosophia perennis* was much stronger on the deductive, analytic and systematic sides than it was on the experimental. What C.S. Lewis has to say about the medieval thinker can be applied more generally to thinkers in this tradition: 'At his most characteristic, he was not a dreamer nor a wanderer. He was an organiser, a codifier, a builder of systems .... Distinction, definition, tabulation were his delight'[15]. Consequently this tradition was slow to give rise to experimentation and natural science as we know them; and under its guidance European culture remained comparatively static for centuries. No doubt, as Mr Heath-Stubbs, for example, would point out,[16] any such generalisation requires a thousand qualifications; but the fact remains that the societies and cultures in which traditional exegesis was carried on were in many respects not basically different from the societies and cultures of New Testament, and even Old Testament, times. At any rate these societies were non-industrial, non-mechanized societies, with methods of agriculture, means of communication and an outlook on natural science not radically different from those of their predecessors; and their horizons, so far as concerned matters of astronomy and cosmology, chronology, psychology, demonology, medicine and the rest, were not all that wider than those of the biblical writers.* We may recall the remark of Dr Charles Galton Darwin that culturally 'London in 1750 was far more like Rome in A.D. 100 than like either London or Rome in 1950'.[17]

The effect of this on the understanding of the Bible was twofold. On the one hand it helped to prolong the assumption (as distinct from the self-conscious conviction) that certain methods of interpretation were timelessly valid. On the other hand it made plausible an assumption that statements could be timelessly true. Consequently everything in the Bible could be assumed to be timelessly true in some sense, if only the sense could be discovered. And as far as the

---

* Cp. now the remarkably similar statement in Dr Beryl Smalley's book *Historians in the Middle Ages* (Thames and Hudson, 1974) pp. 64—5. She points out that 'the medieval view of past ages as all alike was rational, in that essentials had not changed'. And to go beyond the Middle Ages, 'Napoleon va à la même lenteur que César' (Valéry). Although, as Valéry says, prosperity depends so much on speed of communications, even Napoleon could not do much about it. Paris—Toulouse had required about 200 hours in Roman times, and the stage coach still took 158 hours in 1782. See Ivan D. Illich, *Energy and Equity* (Calder and Boyars, 1974) pp. 43 etc.

ethical comments contained or implied in the Bible — or at any rate the New Testament — were concerned, they likewise were taken *au pied de la lettre* as literally binding in all circumstances and all ages, once their bearing had been grasped. (It would be interesting from this point of view to examine medieval and Reformation exegesis of biblical passages prohibiting usury, to see whether they constitute an exception. If so, it would be an exception which proved the rule in so far as the exegesis in question would have been influenced by a very definite social change.)

Before concluding this section of the lecture I should like to add two points loosely related to what I have said earlier. The first, which would require a good deal of qualification were it to be pursued in detail, is this. So far as the real authorship of the Bible was ascribed to God in the traditional approach, exegetes had no occasion to concern themselves with the individuality or relativity of the human authors. No questions needed to be asked about the grounds on which the human writers made their statements, or the possibility that the meaning and validity of what they said was essentially bound up with their individual experience and the cultural *milieu* in which they enjoyed it.

The second point I find hard to put concisely or in a way that is not misleading. From the way I have described matters so far, it might appear as if the Christians of the pre-critical period were simply precursors of that strand in modern theology which sees the Bible as essentially a vehicle of revelation; as if, that is to say, their emphasis was not on the literal (the word is used here in its normal modern sense) and factual accuracy of what the Bible reported or taught, but solely on the timeless truths that could be elicited from its statements by means of allegorical interpretation. In fact, however, that could be said only with considerable qualification.

It is true that they regarded the Bible as revelatory in all its parts; and, as we have seen, they were quite happy about interpreting passages to mean something of a very different sort from what they appeared to say. One thinks for example of their discussions of the ages of the patriarchs or of the Chapter headings to the Song of Songs in the Authorised

Version and the attempt they represent to show that the poem is 'really' about the relations of Christ and his Church. On the whole, however, they took the text, and especially the narrative and descriptive parts of it, to mean what it said. On the basis of the birth narratives in the Gospels, for example, they took it as a straight physiological fact that Jesus was conceived without the introduction of male sperm. In general they gladly took the whole rich variety of biblical material — historical, legal, moral, proverbial, scientific, religious and the rest — at its face value. They saw the whole as a great panorama of events that had happened in the past, including direct divine interventions and appearances in this world; and the theological question they asked was: What can we learn about the nature of God and the appropriate responses to him from the fact that things are, and happened, thus and so? Very often they found it difficult to discover methods for answering this question, particularly in periods or areas in which figurative exegesis was at a discount. In his book *From Bossuet to Newman*,[18] for example, Professor Owen Chadwick has described fascinatingly the logical shifts to which some of them were put in the later part of the period we are considering; they were driven to devise logical techniques of great subtlety in order to show what were the implications for their life and times of the various statements in the Bible, regarded as timelessly valid and true. Fr George Tyrrell, among others, makes clear the vital consequences of all this. Since the implications, if validly deduced, were *necessary* implications of revealed and infallible statements, they carried the same binding authority as the statements from which they were deduced. With regard to such implications Fr Tyrrell writes:

> these, as well as the revealed basis, are considered as organic parts of the entire theological system. And, therefore, so far as all (its) parts are knitted together syllogistically, those that were divinely authorised entail the assumption of the rest under pain of constructive heresy . . . If any one principle or admission possesses a certain grade of authority, the whole system of its necessary antecedents and consequences possesses the same.[19]

The extent to which the whole contents of the Bible were taken at their face value can be gauged by anyone who considers medieval carving or stained glass. We look, for example, at the innumerable biblical figures which stand in the stained glass windows and carved doorways of Chartres cathedral; it is obvious that, though they carried important theological and typological overtones, they were seen as real people who had played a real part in the real past. Even the portrayal of the act of creation over the north door at Chartres shows by its form and position that the creation was conceived as a specific event, or series of events, comparable to the call of Abraham or the victories of King David.

The main things of importance which emerge from this survey will, I hope, already be clear, or will become clear later in the lectures. All I wish to do now is to emphasize three inter-related points.

The first is that in the cultural context in which biblical study was traditionally carried on the aim of such study seemed self-evident: to elucidate the meaning of the various passages in such a way that dogmatic theologians or conciliar authorities could put them together in due order and proportion so as to produce a coherent system which would enshrine *the* meaning of the Bible. It is true that since every definition or formulary was produced in response to some specific issue or controversy, no definition was more than a partial statement relevant to the particular controverted question which called it forth. But in principle, presumably, the ultimate objective, even if it was not consciously formulated, was a comprehensive statement which would set out *the* meaning of the Bible as a whole.

The second point is that this meaning was conceived as the literal meaning, in the sense that every statement and figure in the Bible was thought to have, or to have had, a factual counterpart. There *was* an act of creation; there *are* angels; Christ's death *was* a ransom for sin and a victory over the demonic powers.

Thirdly, being a Christian was understood to mean accepting the biblical truths as set out in the formularies of one's particular period and denomination, and living in a way appropriate to the situation and demands revealed. In order to do that one needed to understand the situation to the height of one's bent, and that gives a clue to the character of a great deal of traditional theological activity. As we have seen, the great divine acts of creation, redemption and so on were taken, more or less at their face value, as fixed data. The endeavour was to understand more fully the workings, or if you like the 'mechanics', of them so as to be able to respond more sensitively. What effects had such and such a divine act been intended to produce, and how? Why had just that divine action been necessary in order to attain a certain end? Anselm's atonement theology is an obvious case in point. It starts from the fact that there had *been* a *deus-homo* (God-man) as an unquestioned and unquestionable datum and then seeks to expose the mechanics of atonement, to list the reasons why that particular unique being was *the* being — the only sort of being — through whom the problems raised by human sin could be solved. It was broadly in that sense that the theological enterprise based on the Bible in the classic period was *fides quaerens intellectum*; and the criterion for judging the orthodoxy of any theological system was that it should 'save the phenomena' in the sense of doing justice to the 'literal' truth, in Donne's sense, of the Bible *in toto*, or of all the relevant biblical passages.[20]

Such are some of the main items in our biblical heritage from the distant past. Whether it proves a *damnosa hereditas* depends on our attitude and reaction to it. Which brings us to our present situation.

3 Two previous solutions

The analysis in the last lecture was undertaken with the aim of beginning to test the thesis that a set of writings which were handled for centuries in a way essentially correlative to one type of cultural situation, have now to be handled in a cultural situation if not totally, at least very substantially, different.

Since the role I am assuming is that of analyst rather than historian, I am fortunately under no obligation to attempt a comprehensive account of the new situation or how it arose. What I have an obligation to do is to make sure that the patient is aware that the present situation is novel and just how novel it is. Forgive me therefore if I repeat the telling phrase of Charles Galton Darwin that 'London in 1750 was far more like Rome in A.D. 100 than either London or Rome in 1950' (See above, p. 55), and let me commend you to the admirable survey in the first chapter of C.S. Lewis's book *They Asked for a Paper*,[1] and recommend the first paper in the *Speculations* of T.E. Hulme, the writings of Professor Basil Willey, of Professor Arthur O. Lovejoy and other writers in the History of Ideas school, and above all the voluminous works of Ernst Troeltsch (1865–1923), who, though until recently so grievously neglected, yet perhaps more than any other single man has made this subject his own, at any rate in its bearing on religion.

These and similar writers will make you unmistakably aware that a movement of cultural change which began perhaps as long ago as the thirteenth century and gained momentum in the so-called Renaissance has, since the Enlightenment of the eighteenth century, attained what can only be described as revolutionary dimensions and produced radical changes in men's attitude and outlook in every sphere of life.

Not only the extent but the modernity of this change need to be emphasized. C.S. Lewis was quite right to insist that the widely recognised changes of outlook at the Renaissance, important though they were, are almost as nothing compared with the changes of the recent past. Change in a really radical form is so recent that Lewis could at any rate *affect* to regard himself, with his conservative temperament and very traditional education, as a dinosaur or a Neanderthaler surviving from before the flood.

It is my impression that theologians have on the whole been insufficiently seized of the full extent and implications of this change, or have deliberately sought to minimise them, as Barth was inclined to do, at any rate in his earlier period. Yet in the light of the last lecture even to describe the main motif of this cultural movement is to make clear its vital importance for our subject. Essentially it has been a movement which demands autonomy for every discipline and is opposed on principle to 'authorities'.

It is significant, for example, that as long ago as 1662, when the Royal Society received its charter, it took as its motto the words *nullius in verba* which might, I suppose, be paraphrased: we refuse to be bound by the words of any authority, however venerable or sacred. Men have learned instead to base their statements and convictions solely on experimentation and on what can be empirically verified, whatever the appropriate method of empirical verification may be in any particular discipline. It is by now inconceivable that in any branch of study a conclusion grounded on sound empirical evidence should be contested simply because it does not accord with the *dicta* of some authority or with what Christians have traditionally been accustomed to believe.

Perhaps this is the moment at which to repeat, and enlarge on, a point made briefly in the last lecture. The new cultural situation is important for us not only because various disciplines as practised within it bring in question some individual statements and passages of the Bible and cast new light on others. It also provides a completely new set of coordinates for the handling of the Bible as a whole, and in so doing makes clear that the coordinates within which the Bible was traditionally handled were in fact particular and contingent, and not, as they seemed at the time, part of the givenness of things, in the way that the law of gravity, for example, is for us. T.E. Hulme and R.G. Collingwood, among others, have some pertinent things to say about how habitual assumptions — 'doctrines felt as facts' — can seldom be identified by those who make them; they become clear — and even then not without great effort — to men of later generations. What is happening to theology today is that it is just becoming aware what some of the important habitual assumptions of earlier theologians were, and just how contingent, and even arbitrary, they appear from our perspective, once we have isolated them.

This is the more important in relation to the Bible because in the traditional view the Bible and the cultural coordinates in terms of which it was studied came to be treated as an integrated and indivisible whole; and thus the coordinates came to be regarded as being derived from the Bible and as possessing biblical authority. An example will show how easily such a feeling arose. If the Bible spoke of angels, and these were interpreted in what then seemed the only way possible, as a group of *hypostases*, or entities, with their own appropriate place in the great chain of being, then it could easily seem as if the existence of the chain itself was a part of the biblical revelation, or at any rate an indisputable deduction from it.

I shall have more to say later about the character of the cultural revolution, but before that I should like to look briefly at the reactions of theologians to it in its earlier stages, that is, in the past century or two, in order to see, so to speak, how the patient himself has sought to adjust to the situation before the analysis. There have of course been innumerable responses of various kinds, but for our purpose it may be possible to divide them *in a rough and ready way* into three groups.

The first questioning of the traditional position, according to the popular view at any rate, came from the side of the natural sciences — in the sixteenth and seventeenth centuries in connexion with the discoveries of Copernicus and Galileo, and more seriously in the nineteenth century as the result of the work of geologists, evolutionary biologists, astronomers and other natural scientists. In confirmation of Dr Hodgson's contention that the traditional Christian view generally regarded the statements of the Bible as authoritative on all subjects, it is instructive to notice the extent to which, both in the sixteenth and nineteenth centuries, the immediate and passionate reaction of the Church was to try to defend the statements of the Bible in every sphere. Everyone knows of the efforts of Bishop Wilberforce and Philip Henry Gosse; and earlier in the nineteenth century John Keble had already written that 'when God made the stones he made the fossils in them', presumably in order to test the faith of nineteenth century scientists!

However, by the nineteenth century the cultural revolution had already established itself, and it soon became clear that the way of flat denial was a 'no thoroughfare'. The debate focussed understandably enough on the early chapters of Genesis, and it was increasingly recognised that a definite breach had been made in the customary tradition of interpretation. However, men's instinct was not to write off these chapters, but rather to assume that if they did not convey scientific truth they conveyed some other sort, and to ask what they are about and what sort of information they convey. After a period of anguished debate scholars settled down with surprising speed and unanimity to the view that what these chapters give is 'true myth', but they did so, I suspect, without seeing the full implications of what had happened. For this there were a number of reasons. For one thing, it seemed for some time as if only a small part of the Bible, and that entirely confined to the Old Testament, was involved; it was not immediately recognised that if the biblical account of the first things was 'myth', something similar must be said about the account of the last things and a good deal else, in the New Testament as well as the Old. Secondly the question of the meaning of the Genesis 'myth' did not reveal its full difficulty. This was at least partly because the rest of the Bible — all the passages not directly put in question by the discoveries of natural science —

continued to be interpreted in the traditional way. The Genesis myth was thus interpreted in terms of the traditional picture of God, men and their relations, and in that context it seemed fairly self-evident what it meant. The meaning of the myth was defined under the influence of orthodox dogma in the way described in the previous lecture. Thus the word 'myth' tended to be used without any very deep exploration of its meaning; and for some time the question was not raised how the biblical writers knew that this particular myth, interpreted in this particular way, was the appropriate vehicle for truth in this connexion.*

Thus, without making any accusation of complacency, we might perhaps say that from some points of view the Darwinian controversy and other scientific challenges to the truth of biblical statements, acted as a sort of inoculation which prevented many biblical scholars from getting the disease. Certainly large parts of the Bible, especially the central core of the New Testament, continued to be interpreted for the most part along the customary lines.

The reason for all this may have been partly that this first questioning of the exegetical tradition had come from the side of the natural sciences, and it was quickly sensed that this was not where the nub of the matter lay. The Bible itself seldom emphasizes its statements on scientific matters nor does it often appear to suggest that vital religious issues hang upon them.

Nevertheless there are important lessons to be learned from this type of response. First, a great deal turns on the precise way in which it is formulated. You may say: 'The statements in the early part of Genesis cannot be accepted as a true account of what they purport to describe and yet they can prove highly illuminating and suggestive to a sensitive, meditative and informed Christian of today.' Or you can say: 'The early chapters of Genesis are not really about matters of cosmology or pre-history; they are really concerned with the

---

* These remarks refer principally to the English scene. Were it a historian's and not a psychoanalyst's rôle that we have assumed, we should have had to discuss the debate on the meaning of *myth* set going in Germany by the publication of D.F. Strauss's *Life of Jesus* in 1835–6. See the brief, but illuminating, discussion in the Rylands lecture delivered by Prof. M.F. Wiles on 5 May 1976.

world's total dependence on the creative activity of God.' Or you can even say: 'The statements at the beginning of Genesis were never intended as a factual account of the origin of things; they were intended from the first as a vehicle of religious truths about man's relation to his maker.' About the last I confess I have reservations; it suggests a consciousness of distinctions of which I suspect men had not at that stage become aware. However, I am not really competent to judge; the matter is one for Old Testament specialists.

In any case the distinction between the different ways of expressing the point may seem a fine one; if it is, it is also a very important one. The second way of putting the matter involves all the difficulties which Professor Ninian Smart has pointed out about such language. Anyone who claims that a document 'really' means something different from what it appears to say must be careful to ask himself how he knows and also what he means by the word 'really'. (Much virtue in your 'really'!)

On the other hand it is important to see why this second way of putting the matter has been so attractive to a great many people. If it is justifiable, it can be extended to any passage which may cause trouble to the modern mind when taken at its face value; and it thus provides a way of maintaining a doctrine of biblical inerrancy. *If properly understood* – in the sense it 'really' bears – every statement in the Bible can be claimed as true. Allowing for the element of caricature which brevity necessitates, we may say that this is the line which has been followed in a great deal of Roman Catholic theology. For example, it seems to underlie even a work as liberal in many ways as the book by the Jesuit Father, Luis Alonso Schökel, referred to above. It received authoritative expression in the papal encyclical *Divino Afflante Spiritu* of 1943, especially in paragraph 39, which begins, significantly enough: 'Frequently the literal sense is not so obvious in the words and writings of ancient oriental authors as it is with the writers of to-day.' Pope Pius XII urged Roman Catholic biblical scholars always to establish the *genre* of any passage before attempting to expound it – perfectly sound advice of course, but in the context clearly intended to suggest that, once its true *genre* has been discerned, every biblical passage will be found inerrantly true *in the mode appropriate to that genre*.

The amount of room for manoeuvre afforded by such a position is shown by the fact that an upholder of it could quite logically say of any biblical passage: 'we cannot in present circumstances be sure what it means; but we can be quite sure that if we could discover what it meant, what it says would be infallibly true'. As is clear from the words of the Encyclical quoted just now, this is in fact a resuscitation of the traditional view that every passage has a literal meaning, its *sensus literalis*, and that the literal meaning may often be a figurative meaning.

The drawbacks of such a position are obvious enough. It demands a quite staggering act of faith in the Bible as a set of writings wholly different from any others ever known, and a correspondingly rigorous, if not mechanical, doctrine of biblical inspiration. Even greater difficulties in it will emerge later. True, it has the quality of logical invulnerability. It cannot be disproved; but it is not clear how much that commends it at a time when logically invulnerable positions, such as no conceivable evidence could prove or disprove, are increasingly coming under suspicion.

One is almost tempted to the irony of quoting some words of G.K. Chesterton against a predominantly Roman Catholic position: 'If you argue with a madman', he writes,

it is extremely probable that you will get the worst of it; for in many ways his mind moves all the quicker for not being delayed by the things that go with good judgment. . . . The madman's explanation of a thing is always complete, and often in a purely rational sense satisfactory . . . the insane explanation, if not conclusive, is at least unanswerable; this may be observed in the . . . commonest kinds of madness. If a man says (for instance) that men have a conspiracy against him, you cannot dispute it except by saying that all the men deny that they are conspirators; which is exactly what conspirators would do . . . But if we attempt to trace his error in exact terms we shall not find it quite so easy as we had supposed. Perhaps the nearest we can get to expressing it is to say this; that his mind moves in a perfect but narrow circle. A small circle is quite as infinite as a large circle; but, though it is quite as infinite, it is not so large.'[2]

Perhaps we should all benefit from asking ourselves how far in our use of the Bible in study or teaching or preaching, we exhibit this type of response, and if we do, how we should justify it if challenged to do so.

The second type of response I want to discuss was essentially a response to questioning of the Bible from the side of the historian. When doubts began to be cast on the historical statements of the Bible, theologians reacted with great seriousness. As we have seen, such scientific statements as the Bible contained, if indeed such a phrase is not impossibly anachronistic in this context, were comparatively peripheral to its central concerns. With its historical statements the situation is different. Many of these were given great prominence in the Bible, and it was felt that they form the heart of the matter inasmuch as it is in and through the events they report that God principally revealed himself and established his redemptive relationship with the world. Consequently, as I say, when the historical statements of the Bible came under fire, theologians reacted with great seriousness, and a great deal of attention was concentrated on them.

To understand the form it first tended to take it is necessary to know something about the character of historical study as it was understood at the time, that is to say in the nineteenth century. We cannot too often be reminded how very modern the critical study of history, as we know it, is. Its foundation is often attributed, with as much truth as such a generalisation can ever have, principally to two German scholars, Barthold Georg Niebuhr and Leopold von Ranke, whose dates were respectively 1776–1831 and 1795–1886. Without taking that attribution too seriously, we may note the great influence both men had, and remember Lord Acton's story that von Ranke was set on his career as a founding father of modern history by noticing the discrepancy between the account of Louis XI in Scott's *Quentin Durward* and that in the contemporary chronicler, Philippe de Commynes.[3] At any rate, the story has symbolic truth; it became von Ranke's aim to uncover the past, as he put it in a much quoted phrase, *wie es eigentlich gewesen,* 'as it actually happened', in distinction, that is, from the embroideries and tacit interpretations of it in the later sources.[4] In historiography as he and his like understood it, there was a high premium on the discovery and identification of the earliest sources and the discounting so far as possible even in them of all elements of elaboration and *Tendenz*.

When it soon became clear to most people that the accuracy of the historical statements in the Bible could not in all cases be defended, the achievements of secular historians such as we have mentioned led theologians to copy their methods in dealing with historical criticism of the Bible.* When such methods were applied to the Bible, inaccuracies in the writers had to be admitted and their works came to be treated critically, just like other historical sources, in the service of an attempted reconstruction of the past; in this respect at least, the advice which is said to have originated from J.A. Turretini in the early eighteenth century that 'the Holy Scriptures are not to be expounded differently from any other books' came fully into its own.[5]

The ways in which this historical activity was related to the religious significance of the Bible may be pinpointed with the aid of a dictum from A.N. Whitehead: 'Christ gave his Life. It is for Christians to discern the doctrine.'[6] The revelation, it was said, was given in events, ordinary, actual unrepeatable happenings not in principle different from other historical events. What was necessary therefore was to establish the precise historical truth about these events, and it would then be possible to draw from them their revelatory content in a form appropriate to the present time.

---

* That way of putting it involves a serious oversimplification which, however, does not affect our argument. A further discussion of the matter will be found in the volume of the Cambridge History of the Bible entitled *The West from the Reformation to the Present Day*, (ed. S.L. Greenslade, 1963) or, more briefly, but very instructively, in C.F. Evans, *Queen or Cinderella* (published by the University of Durham, 1960), especially pp. 6 ff. Note his statement: 'It is widely supposed that the specifically modern scientific study of history was first elaborated on its own, and was then later applied, not without considerable reluctance, to the Scriptures . . . The matter seems to have been both more complicated and more interesting than this.'

Under the influence of this sort of view a great deal of learned exegesis became almost indistinguishable from historical criticism, but a great deal of very valuable and scholarly work was undoubtedly done. Indeed assured results, as they were called, were often claimed and it is at this point that the limitations of this sort of response begin to appear.

These have been frequently discussed and there is no call to delay over them now, but certain points of interest for our subject emerge. Under the influence of philosophers as unalike as David Hume and F.H. Bradley, the theologians we are discussing worked on what is sometimes called 'the principle of analogy', the principle, that is, that nothing should be believed to have happened in the past of a kind which is never experienced in the present. To anyone working on that principle a great deal in the Bible narratives was bound to appear so legendary that the establishment of the historical truth about it was almost impossibly difficult; and it is notorious that many of the allegedly 'assured results' of the biblical scholarship of the period were achieved only as the result of filling up yawning gaps by an unconscious process of reading into the texts contemporary attitudes and motivations. In the classic case of the life of Jesus, that has been definitively documented by Albert Schweitzer. As a result, the historical reconstructions of many of the biblical events produced in this period are apt to appear in retrospect over-confident, speculative and often, to be candid, faintly ludicrous.

What it comes to is that, given their assumptions, scholars of this sort were excessively naïve, or optimistic, about the possibility of reconstructing the biblical past *wie es eigentlich gewesen*. Either in many instances it could not be done, in which case large parts of the Bible had no religious significance at all on this view; or it was done by reading into the biblical accounts traits and motivations derived from contemporary culture, in which case the biblical history and its religious significance were in practice derived in large measure not from the Bible, but from the modern mind. There may have been the germ of a real insight here, but if so, the scholars of this period were not consciously aware of the insight they had glimpsed. When Harnack looked down Father Tyrrell's well[8] what he *thought* he saw was not 'the reflexion of a liberal Protestant face' but the face of the historical Jesus.

All this is widely recognised; what has not, so far as I know, been marked is the assumption which underlay and motivated the whole enterprise, namely that if the biblical events could have been reconstructed 'as they actually happened', they would have proved to have a privileged religious status, to be religiously revealing and illuminating in a unique way. We may well wonder why men as hard-bitten as many of these nineteenth-century scholars were, should have worked on such an assumption, especially as a number of them were well-versed in the comparative study of religion and so familiar with other sacred books; and also since they did not accept for the most part the religious interpretation which the Bible itself placed on the events. No doubt they themselves, if challenged, would have pointed first to an important gap in the account I have so far given of their position. A lot of the biblical material, they would have said, is not historical at all in the obvious sense of the word; the prophetic books, for example, or the Gospels and epistles in the New Testament, consist very largely of direct teaching and exhortation. There is an obvious truth here, and one which, as we shall see later, has sometimes been lost sight of; though it must be added that the scholars we are discussing were often over-confident about discovering which teaching ascribed to a given figure actually originated from him, and generally about their ability to identify the original historical setting of the biblical teaching and so to place the correct historical interpretation upon it. This teaching, these scholars would have said, was the work of what they used to call 'religious geniuses', men who towered so far above others in their insight into the nature and ways of God that that insight, if allowance is made for the outdated mode of its expression, is still illuminating and authoritative today. If we had asked why it should be accepted and in what its authority consisted, the answer would have been broadly the same as in the case of the historical events of the Bible as critically reconstructed. In both cases, they would have said, what was propounded or narrated in the Bible 'found' them; it validated itself in their experience and that of their predecessors and contemporaries. It was just a brute fact that the words, events and personalities of the Bible, and especially the person and activity of Jesus as so far recovered by unbiassed critical study, had proved to speak for themselves, to be lastingly true and timelessly attractive.

In claiming such timeless authority and attractiveness these scholars would have revealed how far they still were from having grasped the full extent and implications of the cultural revolution; and are not we in a position to see the cause of their blindness? Was it not the influence of the traditional approach to the Bible, with its unquestioning assumption that the Bible itself contained 'the essence of Christianity', as Harnack put it, or at least data so extensive and so firm that Christianity could be constructed on the basis of them without there being any real room for dispute about its nature or contents?

From this point of view the first and second types of response I have distinguished have at least one vital thing in common, despite their great differences. They certainly were very different, not least in their estimate of the biblical writers, the first group treating them as writers of divinely guaranteed infallibility, the second regarding them, where history is concerned, as at best honest, but simple-minded and ill-educated, primitives, and at worst, as in the case of St Paul, serious, if unintentional, distorters of the truth, whose accounts had to be heavily discounted in any attempt at historical reconstruction.

Nevertheless both groups had this in common that they wanted, in the new cultural situation, still to be able to find in the Bible the essential content or basis of Christianity, and to find it in a form which should be invulnerable to criticism. We have already discussed that in the case of the first group. So far as the second is concerned, it can hardly be doubted that what attracted them about historical events, as those were understood in current historiography, was their satisfying air of irreformability. If a thing happened, it happened, and no amount of development in philosophical or scientific thought could alter that one jot or tittle. The historical statements of the Bible thus seemed to offer the interpreter an unshakable base from which to conduct his operations.

If the events which could be recovered with any assurance proved so meagre as to form the basis of a much reduced gospel, at least that gospel was believed to be invulnerable to criticism from the historical side; and the reduction of its content also reduced its vulnerability to criticism from any other side, that of the scientist or the metaphysician, for example. In that invulnerability lay its attraction.

4 The solution of
biblical theology

The third type of response I want to discuss is more difficult to deal with adequately for a number of reasons, not least because in one form or another it still largely holds the field and we are all — I, no less than anyone else — in large measure the products of it. So it is fortunate that once again I am under no obligation to give a comprehensive and balanced account of it and its origins.

There can be no doubt that it arose partly out of dissatisfaction with the second type of response I have described. According to that view, once the facts had been established about the historical events lying behind the Bible, and the words of the great biblical geniuses understood in their context, they would speak for themselves, which meant in practice, as we have seen, that each theologian would interpret them for himself against the background of his own beliefs and assumptions; and that again meant in practice that where the contents of the Christian faith were concerned, it was very much a case of *quot homines tot sententiae*.

Whatever the interpretation, however, it always seemed to assume that neither in biblical times nor at any other did God ever go beyond the activity of relevation. He never actively intervened in the world to effect changes, or at any rate outwardly observable changes; he always confined himself to revealing himself or disclosing timeless truths about himself and his relations with the world. Even that perhaps is overstating what seemed possible, and the sort of criticism to which this position gave rise is well exemplified in the following account of it taken from a lecture by Professor T.W. Manson.[1]

A 'message about God and the good' marked by purity and strength. It is to be noted that it is a message *about* God rather than from God. Its purity lies in the fact that it can be reduced to the simplest terms — 'the kingdom of God, God as the Father, and the infinite value of the human soul, and the higher righteousness showing itself in love'. The strength of the message lies in the power of the personality behind the words.

If we ask how, on Liberal presuppositions, we are to conceive these pure and simple verities, the answers available are not very satisfactory. The Kingdom of God ought to mean an effective control of events by God and a genuine exercise of royal authority by God over his subjects. The difficulty is that any interference on God's part in the settled order of Nature is barred; and so is any direct action in human affairs by way of special revelations. In short, the essential thing about God's sovereignty is that it should be acknowledged by men: that the believer should believe that somehow or other God is king, though for all practical purposes he appears to be a *roi fainéant*. . . . The effect of this is to establish a thick plate-glass window between God and the world. The eye of faith can see through the window and observe that there is a God and that he appears to be benevolently disposed towards men; but nothing more substantial than signals of paternal affection and filial trust and obedience can get through.

As would be expected in the light of these words, the third movement of thought to which I refer was very much a movement back to the Bible which shows God actively doing things in the world to guide history and save men, and offers authoritative interpretations of his actions instead of leaving each man to be his own interpreter. This movement sought to give full weight to its observation that in the Bible historical statements and theological interpretation go closely together. The typical biblical statement, it was argued, is logically of the form: 'Such and such an event occurred, and it constituted a divine intervention in this world by which God's redemptive work was carried forward in such and such a respect.' It is significant that one of the best known expositions of this type of view in English bore the title *The Bible from Within*,[2] and that the old slogan: 'the revelation was in events or in a person', was extended by William

Temple and others in such a way as to include within the scope of revelation the terms in which the Bible interpreted the person and events in question.

This third type of response has taken so many forms that in the interest of manageability it may be well to start with one reasonably typical form, that advocated by Karl Barth. During the first world war Barth felt strongly, as Manson was to do in the second, the inadequacy of the previous type of position. In the face of the terrible holocaust which Barth could actually hear going on just over the Swiss border, the liberal theologians seemed to have nothing to say except for protestations of a generalised love on the part of God which never expressed itself in any particular salvific action. The more Barth thought about it the more he came to feel that this dumbness of the theologians was unnecessary, the result of an unnecessary bondage of biblical scholarship to the canons of current historical study. And that study itself, he felt, so far from having achieved autonomy, was in bondage to the prejudice that the course of events is always completely uniform, that nothing ever happens for the first time and that nothing can be allowed as having happened in the past of a kind which is not experienced as happening in the present.

True, it is difficult to see how ordinary historical research could be carried on without some such assumption. How, for example, could a historian evaluate even such a simple thing as a statement in some record that ten thousand well-trained and well-armed troops routed a rabble of one hundred unarmed peasants, if he had to allow for the possibility that some supernatural intervention occurred at the time in virtue of which every unarmed peasant was more powerful than two hundred armed soldiers?

On the other hand, suppose that the Bible were at least to some extent what it purported to be, an account of certain divine interventions in history, occasions when God — who, after all, if he exists, must be complete master of his own universe — had for sufficient cause infringed the 'laws' by which he normally deals with his creation and intervened in an exceptional and decisive way. If that supposition were even partly correct, historians working on the normal historical assumptions were bound to do disastrous injustice to the biblical text.

About the time of the first war such a supposition about the Bible chimed in well with a current of opinion which, though still a minority current, was increasingly popular. No doubt the standard historical position was related to the idealist outlook of Hegel and others, which, in sharp contrast to the supernaturalist dualism of the *philosophia perennis* (cf. the analogy of the iceberg introduced on p.51) saw the whole of reality in more monistic terms as a single integrated system. Even those of this way of thinking who believed in God and the supernatural, as many of them passionately did, nevertheless thought of the supernatural and the natural as so integrally related (for example the natural might be thought of as the 'self-realisation' of the Absolute) that the inter-workings between all the elements could be rationally grasped; all the relationships within the whole were described as 'intrinsic' and could be understood from 'this side', as it were, of the God-world relation.

In the nineteenth century, however, Søren Kierkegaard in Denmark had strongly contested this entire way of looking at things and had argued for what he called 'the absolute qualitative distinction between time and eternity', the natural and the supernatural. Just after the turn of the century his views were becoming more widely known outside Denmark and they seemed to supply a context in which to take the Bible at something more like its face value without any *immediate* sacrificium intellectus.

What was needed was to provide a conceptual framework in which the matter could be worked out and applied to the Bible. In Germany this was attempted by introducing a distinction between two hitherto synonymous words for history; the little-used *Historie* and the common *Geschichte*. *Historie*, and its cognate *historisch*, were to be confined to the ordinary course of events, historian's history, events conceived of as all on a horizontal plane, each one – the French Revolution, the Crimean war or whatever – capable in principle of being exhaustively understood on the basis of its lateral relations with other historical events. *Geschichte* on the other hand was to be used for a way of seeing the past which was also believed to be grounded in reality but which saw events as having vertical, as well as horizontal, connexions; saw them in their relationship of total dependence on, and guidance by, active supernatural agency.

In England an appropriate conceptualisation has often been sought through analysis of the idea of interpretation in relation to history. Secular historians, it is suggested, normally interpret the past in an unnecessarily limited way, relating historical phenomena only to what went before and what came after on the horizontal plane. If they could only free themselves from what is no more than a positivist prejudice, they could themselves be brought to see that in certain cases at any rate, such as Jesus' resurrection or the events of the Exodus, any interpretation which does justice to *all* the evidence, reviewed without bias, would have to allow for a vertical dimension in which history depends on, and is actively influenced by, transcendent being.

Whichever way it is put, the aim is clear. These theologians are no reactionaries in the fundamentalist sense. They seek a conceptualisation which on the one hand will enable them to do full justice to the genuine achievements of *Historie* and the historians, including the new light it has shed on the biblical text and the inaccuracies it has revealed in it; and on the other hand will enable them to keep open the possibility that *some* biblical events at any rate were, seen from God's side so to speak, due to his direct initiative — direct interventions by him designed to push history in a certain direction and achieve certain results in it.

Diagrams may perhaps help to make the matter clearer.

(*a*) History as *Historie*:
   (*i*) In elevation

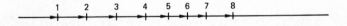

The numbered marks represent events seen as dependent on previous historical events and on nothing else. The arrowheads imply that each epoch leads on to the rest; they imply no overall direction to history.

(*ii*) In plan

Crosses represent events within the stream of history in their complex but wholly intra-mundane relationship.

(*b*) History as *Geschichte*, in elevation:

The space above the top line represents the heavens from which God acts, first, at point A, to create the world and then at innumerable points (the dotted lines) to guide and push his creation towards the goal which he has planned for it and will eventually achieve by a second direct and unmediated intervention (O). The subsequent state of affairs which this final intervention into history will introduce is represented in bold hatching to indicate that it will be radically different from all that has gone before, a wholly 'new creation'. (The bold vertical lines with arrows above the hatching are meant to indicate the continuous direct mutual contact expected to exist between God and his creatures in the new age.) It will be noted that historical, as contrasted with divine, life has a definite beginning and end.

However, any diagram which helps to make the point clear also serves to show that there were some questions to be asked.

If certain past events were in fact interventions of God in a special sense, how are they to be recognised as such? On this there is some difference of opinion. Barth and others in the Lutheran tradition, with its strong emphasis on faith and its doctrine of the divine *incognito*, were inclined to say that these *magnalia dei* are recognisable as such only by the eye of faith. Some periods of history may perhaps have the character of craters or dry river-beds which betray, though only by implication, the previous existence of volcanoes or rushing streams; some past events may even appear as 'entrances' or 'presences' of God; but if so, they are veiled presences or entrances not discernible by ordinary *historisch* vision any more than the crater-like or wadi-like character of certain historical periods.

Other scholars are less hesitant about claiming for the historical events in question, at any rate when taken together, some outward signs of being divine interventions, or about claiming that they produced subsequent situations such as even on empirical grounds are best accounted for as being the results of special divine intervention. 'The resurrection is needed in order to explain the transformation of a frightened band of disillusioned disciples into the early church' is a characteristic example. Dr Alan Richardson, for instance, has been a champion of this last position.

One special aspect of the matter deserves mention. Some of the past events narrated in the Bible, among them some of the most important, cannot be called historical at all in *any* plausible sense of the word; for example, the virgin birth or the resurrection and exaltation of Jesus. Even if we accept to the letter the biblical narratives of how Mary conceived without human intercourse or how the body of Jesus was seen by many outside the tomb and finally watched by the disciples rising into the sky, the interpretation of those events as a conception by the Holy Ghost or a divine incarnation, or as Jesus' exaltation to God's right hand in heaven, takes us right outside the realm of history. Yet the theologians we are considering, Barth most emphatically, insist that they actually happened, that they are events of the past every bit as much as the Battle of Hastings or the Battle of Britain.

Of that more later; meanwhile our diagram suggests a further question. If God intervened in the suggested way, what precisely was he seeking to achieve? Here again there is some difference of opinion, or at least of emphasis. Barth, although he encourages us, in a process he calls *meditatio*, to use our wits, and any philosophical categories we may find useful, in an effort to answer this question and make sense of what God was after in his carefully planned and interrelated series of interventions — to investigate the 'why' of the divine actions — nevertheless closely limits the scope of any such activity and insists that *meditatio* must start from, and never be at odds with, the interpretative categories of the Bible itself. Just as the occurrence of God's mighty acts is recognisable only by faith, so is the understanding of their meaning and purpose. And in his own *meditatio* as revealed by the *Dogmatics*, he works very largely not only with biblical categories, creation, incarnation, covenant and so on, and not only with the categories of the general interpretative tradition of Christendom, such as the Trinity and the Incarnation, but with such rather *recherché* categories as the *communio naturarum*, the *communicatio idiomatum* and the three 'offices' of Christ traditional in Lutheran theology. Indeed in reading the *Dogmatics* one gets an impression of a very determined attempt by a twentieth century writer to make sense of biblical, and traditional ecclesiastical, categories at all costs.

Others of the same general way of thinking are content to allow fuller rein to our wits in this connexion. In the case of some of them, I believe I can detect a significant tendency; they tend to be happier with the Old Testament in this matter than they are with the New.

As I view the works of such theologians as Richardson, Dodd and Wheeler Robinson for example — and incidentally such names remind us how artificial is the distinction between the second and third positions I am trying to identify — they seem to tell a quite plausible story about the Old Testament. They find no difficulty in accounting quite intelligibly for God's reported actions in choosing a particular people, rescuing them from Egypt, helping them through the prophets to moralise and desacralise their religion and their conceptions of himself, rescuing them from their Babylonian captivity and so on; they explain all this, after the manner of the Bible itself, as the setting of the scene for the appearance of Christ. But when the Christ appears on the scene, these writers' accounts of what exactly God was doing through him seem to me to become much more vague, confused and unconvincing; and if I am right about this phenomenon, it is, as we shall see later, very significant.

In the remainder of these lectures I shall frequently have occasion to advert, directly or indirectly, to this type of response again, and to expound and assess it further. Meanwhile I should like to say certain things about it at once. The general drift of it is clear enough. As Luther commanded and taught us, we are to be bold enough, even in the twentieth century, to say: 'Let God be God'. If we say that, and really mean it, we cannot possibly presume to dictate to God, or allow the *Zeitgeist* or modern historical method or anything else to dictate to him, what he can, or cannot, have done in and for a world of which he is *ex hypothesi* complete master and supreme controller. If we assert the absolute transcendence and sovereignty of God in Kierkegaard's sense, it is part of what we mean that we have to allow that he may from time to time have intervened in ways essentially 'incalculable and unpredictable' which make certain stretches of the past discontinuous with, and transcendent over, neighbouring stretches and events. We shall have to allow for the possibility that certain periods of the past will exhibit what Barth calls an element of 'sacred incomprehensibility' such as the historian does not normally take account of, or need to take account of.

There is real truth here. There is no reason why anyone who has a well-based belief in God and his relations with his creatures should allow any positivism, whether the positivism of the historian or any other, to rule out *a priori* the validity of his belief. So far as this movement is a vigorous and extremely well-informed counter-attack against the false pretensions of groundless positivism, we in English universities who have continually to defend the reality of *any* belief in God and the supernatural against the positivism of the philosophers, should be fully sympathetic to it.

Nevertheless, there is another side to the matter. Just as we have no right to dictate to God what he *cannot* have done, so we have no right to dictate to him what he *must* have done. We may only believe that he has intervened in history in certain exceptional events if he has given us good ground for thinking he has done so.

So the question arises, to borrow the terminology from Dr Van Harvey: What positive warrants have we — what warrants, that is, satisfactory to a person of integrity in the twentieth century — for supposing that God has intervened in times past in a way different in principle from any we know now?

We are asked by the theologians we are considering to accept two things:

(*a*) that some of the events recorded in the Bible happened more or less as they are represented, and

(*b*) that the biblical interpretations of them, or, if you prefer, the biblical insight into their meaning, are true, or at least capable of being reformulated in a way which is still acceptable and illuminating.

You notice I say we are asked to accept *some* of the biblical events in this way; we are not asked by the members of this group to accept all the biblical narratives in this way; for example, they do not insist on the story of how the sun stood still for Joshua and the interpretation placed on it in the Bible.

However, in the case of some more 'central' events, especially events connected with the life and ministry of Jesus, we are asked to accept that they happened more or less in the manner reported in the Bible and that they carried more or less the significance there attributed to them. On this view the biblical writers are seen neither as guaranteed purveyors of infallible truth, as on the first view, nor as indifferent reporters, ideological distorters or religious geniuses, as on the second. They are seen as 'witnesses', that is, writers who simply in virtue of the time and place in which they lived, were in a privileged position, able to bear testimony to what they, or their fairly immediate predecessors, had witnessed; and, in view of their proximity to the events, they were able to draw out their significance in a way that no subsequent generation can ever do. It is largely from their character as witnesses that their authority is seen to derive. Language of this type is so common in contemporary theological writing, especially about the New Testament, that it serves to emphasize the wide dominance of the third view now under discussion.

So the question is even more pressing: what are the grounds for our acceptance of these historical reports? Here there is a considerable variety of opinion. As I reminded you just now, the threefold classification of approaches to the Bible with which I am working is an artificial and largely arbitrary one; and so far as this particular matter goes, it would not be easy to say of many English theologians whether they fall into the second or the third group.

In some moods, some of the exponents of this type of response go so far as to say that nothing distinguishes the biblical events outwardly from many, or all, other events. What gives them their character as acts of God in a peculiar sense is not so much that God was active in them in a peculiar way as that there were witnesses present to understand and disclose the divine initiatives which lay behind them. On such a view, the divine initiative lies behind some, or even all, other events in a similar way, but it is only because the biblical writers, or their predecessors, divined and disclosed it behind the events of their day that it can be recognised behind others. Even such a view, which of course makes the Bible essentially a medium of *revelation*, involves the 'scandal of particularity'; for whatever some of these theologians may imply to the contrary, we can hardly suppose that Socrates and Plato, for example, were men of markedly less integrity and insight than, let us say, Isaiah and Jeremiah; and so we must presumably attribute the ability of the latter pair to descry the divine hand behind history in a way the former pair could not, to some special divine grace or election. And if the answer is suggested that the Jewish prophets inherited the only interpretative tradition in which the necessary insight could find expression, that only pushes the problem a stage further back.

However, it is doubtful if any theologian relies entirely on that line of thought. Dr Alan Richardson, for example, is probably typical, if not perhaps entirely consistent, in combining with it the view that certain past events have been *per se* divine acts in a peculiar sense. This view, however, is usually combined by English scholars with the assurance that we are not expected to accept the occurrence of the events in question unless there is good historical warrant for doing so. It is mainly on this ground that they would distinguish Joshua's sun-miracle, for example, from the resurrection of Jesus.

The question here is what exactly is meant by the word 'historical'. If it implies, as it often appears to do, that we need accept only events on which a majority of practising historians would pass a favourable verdict, irrespective of their religious beliefs or disbeliefs, that surely implies a drastic minimising of *credenda*. For historians will not lightly confer the accolade of historicity without having had an opportunity to 'torture the evidence' as Collingwood put it, that is, to sift and analyse the sources and compare them with other sources and relevant data, in fact do everything possible to make them yield their true meaning and ensure that the explanation offered is the simplest, in the sense of involving the least departures from the normal way of things. And, according to Collingwood, unless the material is capable of being fruitfully cross-examined in this sort of way, we should not raise historical questions about it.

If the biblical narratives are submitted to such procedures, we can certainly expect many affirmative verdicts, but we can also be sure of many negative ones, and of still more verdicts of 'non-proven'. Few of the events with which we are concerned are reported in more than one independent source and there is seldom any corroboration from extra-biblical sources or remains; and many of these events — and those some of the most vital — are precisely of the miraculous kind which, as we have seen, puts the historian out of business and prevents his offering any verdict other than 'non-proven'.

Paradoxically, the Old Testament records might in some ways come off better than those of the New; for they deal very often with large-scale events such as have left their mark on world history and enjoy a measure of corroborative testimony from pagan sources and remains. The New Testament narratives by contrast, although drawn up comparatively soon after the events to which they refer, report events so largely private and unrelated to the public history of the period, and withal so frequently miraculous, that there is little independent basis on which to evaluate what the historian, *qua* historian, will regard as their initial implausibility. It is thus easier in the case of the Old Testament to satisfy the historian about the occurrence of the main events which the Bible interprets as divine interventions than it is in the case of the New. Which perhaps partly explains why, as I suggested just now, the type of theologian whose position we are discussing sometimes gives the impression of having a surer touch with the Old Testament than with the New.

Nevertheless the English scholars I have in mind insist that all the biblical events they propose for our acceptance, in the New Testament as well as the Old, are well attested. If by that they mean that no logical impossibility is involved in their having occurred, they are of course right. It may also be possible to deploy a cumulative argument in favour of some of the New Testament events, for example some of the miraculous events in the Gospels, while remaining sceptical about Joshua's miracle or the bleeding hosts of medieval chronicles, by saying that you would expect the advent and career of one such as Jesus to be accompanied by exceptional events.

Nevertheless, if I am asked to say of many of the events both in the New Testament and the Old, including some of the most central events, that they are historically well-attested, I think most historians would agree that I am being invited to use the word 'historically' in a somewhat unusual sense. It is surely difficult to resist the opinion that, consciously or unconsciously, the theologians of this school are giving these stories the benefit of a number of doubts because they occur in the Bible. As Professor John Knox, himself to some extent a supporter of this view, puts it: because these events are reported in a sacred source, the *onus probandi* tends to be placed firmly on those who would deny, rather than those who would assert, their historicity.[3] Which is to say that these theologians are, in their own way, treating the Bible as an *auctour*. One is perhaps a little reminded of Dr Johnson's verdict on Bishop Burnet, the author of the famous *History of His Own Times*: 'He was like a man who resolves to regulate his time by a certain watch; but will not inquire whether the watch is right or not'.[4] The judgement is no doubt partly a personal one, but I can only record the fact that this is the impression that is made on me by a great deal of English biblical scholarship from about the time of the first world war until very recently. Clearly the temptation is bound to be very strong for the scholars I have been describing, since their position stands or falls by the historical accuracy of certain specific narratives.

I am the more confirmed in my analysis of the position of these scholars because Barth, who seems to me here to be more clear-sighted, takes a rather different line. In the case of the life of Jesus, for example, he denies outright that there is any point in letting the historian as such (*Historie*) loose on it at all. If it is investigated in a *historisch* manner, he says, in abstraction from its *geschichtlich* character, then the result will inevitably be a false abstraction of the most misleading kind. Even in his later period he could write: 'the history of Jesus which is central is the testimony of the biblical texts themselves. They provide us with a sufficient portrayal of the history which is the concern of faith. Indeed they give us the only portrayal which can legitimately play a normative role in dogmatic thinking, for they contain the initial testimony to Jesus *in his existence as the Christ* . . . the one who fulfils and actualises the covenant between God and man'. [Italics mine.] And again: 'There is no need to 'dig out' the so-called 'historical' facts.' 'Jesus Christ is present to us and speaks to us in the *logia* that have been handed down. He acts among us to-day in the *records* of his miracles, the *story* of his passion, the *accounts* of his resurrection on the third day.' All this is more significant because it is so reminiscent of Martin Kähler and a whole tradition of scholarship in Germany.[5]

One can see what Barth means, but just consider what his position commits him to. He is saying in effect: certain events of a *geschichtlich* character occurred in New Testament times; whatever the situation may have been considered from the purely *historisch* point of view, it does not, and cannot, affect that assertion. Barth himself says, in discussing his concept of *Sage* [the German form is retained because the English word 'saga' has connotations which make it a very inexact equivalent], that what is needed is a way of

penetrating behind the 'purely historical' facts and relating
them to the all-important *unhistorisch* dimension. You need
'a means of portraying the *reality* of history by imaginative
and poetic means'.[6] So I take it what he is saying about the
history of Jesus is that the 'reality' of it was the *Geschichte*
portrayed in the New Testament and that *historisch* investigation of it would not be of any value, because even if
we could discover the Jesus of history, he would be bound to
be whatever he needed to be for the *geschichtlich* Christ to
have existed. To any historian who replied, 'but my
investigations at the *historisch* level prove that he was *not*
such as to be a plausible basis for the *geschichtlich* Christ',
Barth would presumably reply: 'You have not the gift of
faith; if you had, you would see things in a different light.'[7]

Again one can see what sort of claim he is making. It is as
if a man were accused of having failed to perform some duty
as the result of criminal negligence and a court of law found
against him. His wife, out of her deeper knowledge of the
man, might be able to believe, indeed to be certain, that he
had in fact fulfilled his obligation. Her peculiarly intimate
knowledge would perhaps enable her to place a correct,
though otherwise surprising, interpretation on evidence
which had naturally led the court, not possessing her
knowledge, to a negative verdict.

Obviously the analogy is not exact. What corresponds to
the woman's peculiar knowledge of her husband is faith, and
Barth would be the last to suggest that faith gives the believer
privileged access to the inner mind of the 'Wholly Other'.
What it does do, however, is to make possible a true
appreciation of certain past events as *Geschichte* in a way
that would be impossible without it, rather as the wife's
achievement of the correct interpretation would have been
impossible without her special knowledge of her husband.
Moreover, since the divine activity in past events is essentially
a *supernatural* intervention, the faith which descries it is not
a *historisch*, psychologically explicable, phenomenon, but
itself a purely supernatural gift, the result of an illumination
of the mind by the exalted Christ or his spirit. Normally it is
granted through hearing the biblical narratives expounded by
preachers. On this view preaching is the characteristically

Christian or churchly way of using the Bible; the biblical narrative is essentially *kerygmatic*. It is preaching material and only in the process of being expounded in preaching does it normally yield its true meaning. We might almost speak here of a quasi-sacramental view of preaching in the sense that only as the bread of the word is broken and distributed in the preaching does it have its intended effect. The fact remains, however, that not all who hear the preaching become believers, and so any believer may have a more just appreciation of the biblical events than the most brilliant and painstaking non-believing historian, who is rather like the judge in our analogy.

The sort of thing Barth says about the occurrence of the biblical events he also says about their meaning in their biblical setting. Often that meaning is conveyed in terms and categories, such as sacrifice, covenant, or victory over demonic forces, which are no longer in current usage and may not even be intelligible to the 'natural' man of today (i.e. the man who is not a believer). In the light of faith, however, the abiding meaning of those categories and their relevance for today becomes clear, and once again their being made intelligible and acceptable is the result of supernatural illumination.

A further point of a similar sort arises. The biblical understanding of events sometimes involves belief in the occurrence of certain past happenings of an entirely super-historical kind; for example the resurrection and ascension stories of the New Testament presuppose the occurrence of Christ's ascent to the right hand of the Father and his taking his place there as Lord. Faith is able to assert the occurrence of such events in the past which on principle could never have been discovered or verified by human observation or historical investigation; and it is only in the light of these events that the rest of history, both biblical and non-biblical, can be understood and responded to in its true meaning and unity. As we have seen, Barth is insistent that these super-historical events were just as real as other past events. '*Sage*', he writes, 'points to real historical occurrences which took place at a certain point in space and time . . . It is sheer superstition to suppose that only things which are open to *historisch* verification can have happened in time.'

Although it is from Barth that I have tried to document this position, it is by no means peculiar to him, or indeed to the continental protestant traditions. A position in some ways similar appears to be held, for example, by the Roman Catholic scholar, Bishop B.C. Butler who writes:

> As a historian I am indeed 'inclined to believe' that Christ was virginally conceived and rose corporeally from the dead . . . But as a Christian I 'believe' these mysteries on the authority of the *kerygma* of the Church, and therefore with a certainty that historical investigation can never give me. So far as I can see, supernatural faith in the articles of the creed implies the absolute authority of the word of Christ upon the lips of the contemporary Church.[8]

In practice, as we have seen, Barth, even more than some other theologians of the third group, is heavily indebted to the categories of traditional, post-biblical orthodoxy for his understanding of the biblical events. And although he is selective in his use of traditional categories, and seeks always to show that those he uses are genuine interpretations of the biblical material, it is clear in fact that his enterprise of biblical exposition would have been impossible without them and that in practice many of the writings of traditional orthodoxy are *auctours* for him and, in varying degrees, for the other exponents of this type of view.

It should now be clear why Barth so willingly makes his own Anselm's slogan *fides quaerens intellectum*. He uses it in fact in very much the same general sense as Anselm did. *Intellectus* certainly has a preparatory role; for example the *intellectus* of the historian and the philologist are indispensable in determining the historical context in which the various books and passages were written, the sources on which they were based, the relevant linguistic data, the ancient events and customs the text presupposes and so on. The exercise of the intellect in these areas is referred to by Barth as *explicatio*. Yet in the last resort what *intellectus* has to take as its starting point is not, as in the previous view, the historical events behind the biblical text *wie sie eigentlich gewesen*, but that *Geschichte* which faith alone can recognise

as having 'encompassed' the *Historie* of the biblical period —
the language is Barth's own.

In the case of this response, as is obvious, not only the
essence or basis of Christianity, but virtually the whole of it,
is to be found in the Bible. Thus Oscar Cullmann, for
example, can describe Christ's life and ministry as having
constituted God's decisive victory over all forces opposed to
his will, and speak of all subsequent divine activity till the
end of time as just so many 'mopping up operations'. On this
view, all relations between the natural and the supernatural
are related to, and subsumed under, God's relations with the
world in the biblical history, and must be understood in the
light of them. Barth claims that the only true account of any,
or all, history is a 'Christological' account.

Equally obviously, this position, in its Barthian form at
least, approximates to logical invulnerability. For from
whatever quarter objections may come, it is always possible
to reply that they are purely at a *historisch* level, and that in
the light of faith things would look different. Here, however,
as we have already noted, (cp. p. 79 above) Barth is by no
means entirely representative. He seems content to say
simply that at the *historisch* level events in biblical times
must have been whatever they needed to be if they were to
form the substructure of the *Geschichte* which is the object
of Christian faith. But many exponents of a view otherwise
similar would not only admit, but insist, that their position is
vulnerable to historical criticism of the normal type. They
admit the possibility, at any rate in principle, of a de-
monstration on the basis of *historisch* investigation that the
biblical events were not such as to admit of the *geschichtlich*
interpretation Christian faith wishes to place upon them; and
they believe that if that were to be shown, the Christian faith
would be invalidated. Indeed they would claim that it is of
the essence of Christianity as a historical religion that it
should stand or fall by the relative accuracy of certain
historical records and the occurrence of certain alleged
historical events.

One difficulty here is to know just what, or how much,
this means, in view of the fact, as I take it to be, that the
positions which would *decisively* count against the faith on

this view — Christ-myth theories for example — are on any sober historical assessment simply not tenable.[9]

There are of course some less radical opinions current which might nevertheless be thought negative enough to tell against such a position; but these are commonly dubbed by the holders of this view 'unnecessarily sceptical', and there is so much room for legitimate difference of opinion about what constitutes unnecessary scepticism that it is difficult to see what could possibly count as a decisive refutation of this position. Given their lax definition of 'well attested', and barring the emergence of some relevant new evidence such as it is very difficult to envisage, the upholders of this view in its non-Barthian form seem *in practice* likely to remain as invulnerable as Barth himself.

There is a further group of comments on this position I should like to make before I leave it. As we have seen, it claims to offer a form of Christianity which reproduces 'the Bible from within'. If it lived up to any such claim, that would hardly be the point in its favour it is sometimes taken to be. For is it conceivable that after two thousand years of cultural change, much of it extremely radical, it could be right, even if it were possible, to handle the biblical material on its own terms?

In fact, however, it may be doubted if this position lives up to the slogan even to the limited extent which is claimed. There is first the obvious point that it discounts a great many of the biblical statements as being historically inaccurate or theologically irrelevant or outmoded. Less remarked is the fact that the doctrine of transcendence with which it operates is not that asserted, or even implied, in the Bible, but an essentially modern doctrine evolved in the course of polemics against Hegelianism; indeed so far as it speaks of God as the 'wholly other', it is saying something which many of the prophets and others among the most profound biblical writers explicitly denied. (For example, one of the main concerns of the 'writing' prophets was precisely to insist that, morally, God is *not* wholly other than man. In face of the tendency before their day to think of God's behaviour as in no way subject to the sort of standards which govern human morality, the prophets insisted that no conduct could rightly be attributed to God which would not win our unqualified approval in a human agent. When Abraham is represented (Gen. 18:25) – no doubt under prophetic influence – as asking 'Shall not the Lord of all the earth do right?', the last word means exactly what it would as applied to a human agent.) Closely connected with that is the point emphasized by Professor Barr that the 'mighty acts of God in history' receive less stress and have a less exclusive place in the Bible than they do in this type of biblical interpretation. Furthermore, as we have already seen, *all* historical events were in some sense acts of God for the biblical writers, and so for them the 'mighty acts of God' (if that is what *megaleia tou theou* means in Acts 2:11) did not differ from other historical events in the unique qualitative way suggested by the biblical theology school. This links with a point which I have made elsewhere:

> Even so far as biblical writers did see things in terms of a series of 'mighty acts of God in history' . . ., modern exponents of this view seem to me to be involved in a 'scandal of particularity' quite other and greater than they were. For the New Testament writers, God had been active in a *heilsgeschichtlich* way throughout the world's history from creation day to Doomsday; for remember that, to a man, they believed that, whatever else God had done in Christ, he had brought very close the end of this world and of history as we know it. For modern exponents of this view, on the other hand, *Heilsgeschichte* did not begin until millions of years after the original creative act, and it finished, in the full sense, at least 2,000, and possibly many million, years before the close of human history. This is a 'scandal of particularity' indeed, and it seems to give to long periods of history what I might perhaps call a certain vacuous character.[10]

There for the present I should like to leave this view. It would be as impertinent to deny the deeply Christian concern that lies behind it as it would be to deny the immense ability and the devoted care that have gone into the evolving of it. Nevertheless I sense that there is increasing dissatisfaction with it among many people who believe they are, and certainly want to be, Christians. A good proportion of them are lay men and women who find it difficult to articulate their thoughts in theological terms, and meanwhile feel guilty for harbouring doubts about what are constantly put before them as positions essential to being a Christian.

I suspect their feelings centre mainly on two related points:

(a) Despite all that has been said by Barth and others, they wonder about the historical basis of this view; they are not persuaded that they have sufficient justification for accepting the occurrence of certain historical events — still more of certain supra-historical events — with as much conviction as they are expected to do.

(b) They are concerned about the obligation which seems to be laid upon them to be more certain about the occurrence of certain past events in their capacity as Christians than they could ever hope to be in the capacity of historians, however learned or acute (cp. Bishop Butler as quoted on p.89 above).

They are puzzled about a God who makes, if not salvation, at any rate present reconciliation and communion with Himself, dependent on ability to answer certain relatively vexed historical questions in a particular way. Their concern may in some ways be akin to Lessing's doubt whether 'accidental truths of history can ever become the proof of necessary truths of reason', but it is not identical and not, I think, liable to the accusation of 'latent obscurity and confusion' which is brought with some show of justice against Lessing by Dr Henry Chadwick.[11]

On their behalf as well as my own, I should like to ask whether there may not be some alternative way of relating to the scriptures which may qualify for the description 'Christian'.

5 The 'Cultural Revolution'

Our discussion of current approaches to the Bible has taken us so far afield that perhaps I should remind you of the question about the Bible from which we started. It was whether and how far responses already made in the Church to the problems raised by the modern cultural revolution have been satisfactory.

It would not be altogether surprising if they had not, because, as I have already pointed out, the historical side of the cultural revolution, which is one of the most important for our subject, has been one of the latest to develop. Yet once it did develop, it has proved to be of the greatest significance, as witness the words of two writers as different as Friedrich Nietzsche and F.R. Tennant. Tennant writes: 'this historical movement has exerted a determinative influence upon thought and investigation comparable in importance to that of Newtonian science and the Copernican revolution. It has done so by furnishing us with two potent ideas, both of which are involved in the current notion of revolution. The one of these is the idea of continuity and the other is that of emergent novelty, epigenesis.'[1] Nietzsche went so far as to say that in the nineteenth century mankind developed, or recognised, a sixth sense, the historical sense.[2] This is fighting talk and it refers to far more than the fact that historians now give significantly different accounts of certain historical events from those accepted by their predecessors. It envisages even more than the change in method which lies behind the new accounts, important though the new methods are. As we have seen, modern historians start with a deliberate preliminary scepticism about the evidence at their disposal and seek by every means in their power to wring from it all the information it has to give about the past, which is often something very different from its overt meaning or obvious significance. For example, some ancient account of the origin of the world may tell us nothing of value about its ostensible subject but a great deal about the mentality, religious beliefs and views on astronomy and cosmology of, let us say, an Indonesian tribe in the twelfth century B.C.

As I say, however, there is more to Nietzsche's sixth sense than that. Perhaps I can highlight something of it if I remind you that as recently as the eighteenth century thinkers could regard human beings in all ages as just so many members of a single group, distinguished from one another by relatively superficial differences of appearance and customs. It is only on such an assumption that the doctrine of the noble savage, for example, makes sense. 'Homo sum; humani nil a me alienum puto.'[3] True enough in a sense, as we shall see, but today we cannot help being aware that the savage — primitive man as he really was — differed so much from us in his understanding of himself, his gods and his world that it is at least as misleading as it is illuminating simply to lump us both together under the category 'human beings'. (This is not to claim — and I should like to emphasize this — that we are *better* than he was; it is difficult to know against what scale of goodness such a claim could be measured. It is simply to take note of the fact that we are different.)

If we enquire in what the difference consists, we are brought up against a question I have so far only skirted, the question of cultural change; and it is time to say something more, however briefly, about the rather *cliché* expression 'cultural revolution' I have used more than once. (If some of what follows seems to repeat things said in the Introduction, readers are asked to remember that there was nothing corresponding to the Introduction when the lectures were originally delivered. It seemed best nonetheless to leave this lecture substantially as originally given.)

The context of this metaphor is the constant process of change which goes on in the ideas and knowledge-ranges of any human community. If the basic ideas of the community change significantly in a short time, if there is a rapid increase or decrease in the range of its knowledge, then a quite new situation is quickly produced in that community and the analogy of a political revolution naturally suggests itself.

There is more to the metaphor than that, however. Political revolutions — at any rate successful ones — usually involve a change of sovereignty, and there is something comparable in the cultural sphere. If the imagery is not over-pressed, it is fair to say that every age, or every community in a particular age, is dominated by certain interests or groups of interests. In fact it is largely the dominance of a particular set of interests that gives a particular epoch its characteristic flavour, as Renaissance or Enlightenment or whatever it may be.

If we enquire into any cultural revolution, we shall find that the changes in ideas and knowledge are accompanied, not to say caused, by a major transference of interests. When a change of interest occurs, people begin to ask different questions, both questions about subjects previously neglected as uninteresting and also questions of a different sort about every subject, questions that is, which require a different sort of answer to satisfy the questioner. It may help if I quote again here an example already given in the Introduction. The Middle Ages were a period dominated to a large extent by religious interests. Men tended, therefore, to be satisfied with answers to their questions which clarified in some way the relation of the subject under discussion to the divine. Thus, if questions were raised about the motions of things for instance, even the most acute thinkers were satisfied with answers which spoke of things in a state of potentiality seeking to actualise themselves, that is, to exercise fully a divinely implanted potency; or of their seeking the place or direction proper to them, 'proper', that is, according to God's intentions for them. Such explanations satisfied because they were consistent with the contemporary world-view, with its intense religious interest.

Galileo typified the growing changes of interest characteristic of his period when he ignored such explanations in his study of movement, because, however true, they shed no light on the manner in which bodies move in space and time, how one natural state precedes, and leads up to, another; and that was precisely what interested Galileo. In order to answer *his* questions and satisfy *his* type of interest it was necessary to devise experimental techniques and this in turn led to a further set of interests and enquiries.

All this in its turn could easily lead to the discovery of many more 'secondary' causes, some of which might account completely at the natural level for phenomena previously thought to require special divine activity for their explanation.

Such secondary causes, or natural explanations, once established, were not logically incompatible with the earlier type of explanation – it is characteristic of the differences between cultural situations that they seldom involve strict logical contradiction – but so long as interest focussed on the natural realm, explanations in terms of primary causality ceased to be necessary and therefore ceased to be interesting, until we get Laplace waving aside the existence of God as a quite uninteresting question on the grounds that, as he said to Napoleon: 'we have no need of that hypothesis'. Not, you notice, it is not true or logically compatible; it is not necessary.

Meanwhile not all men ceased to be interested in religious questions and relationships; however, those who remained interested in them naturally found themselves on the one hand pondering the old explanations, and on the other driven to modify and reformulate them in the light of more recent interests and discoveries. It was thus that the theological successors of the medieval schoolmen had different explanations even of divine activity or supernatural causality.

As a further example may make clear, it is only another way of putting the same thing to say that in different cultural *milieux* different things are taken for granted. As soon as we ask: What does such and such an explanation amount to? we are already demanding an explanation of the explanation and putting some of our predecessors' basic assumptions to the question; we are questioning an explanation which seemed quite satisfying before. The explanation which satisfies us will in its turn depend on certain assumptions, 'doctrines felt as facts', but in the nature of the case it will prove extremely difficult to detect what these are.

The example, very briefly, is this: we saw earlier that at one time historical interest centred exclusively on the events reported in the available authorities, these last being taken as more or less undistorted and undistorting windows on to the past.[4] There came a time, however, when the interest of historians centred as much on the source as on what it reported. Who had written it? When? In what interest? On the basis of what evidence; and what in turn were the sources and value of that evidence? When this sort of question began to be asked, once again new techniques, diplomatic, palaeographical and so on, were devised; and as a result of the critical study which they made possible, a quite new view was often taken of the reports in the sources, and a new picture formed of what happened in the past. As a consequence, men came to a different understanding of their origins and their relations to their past, and so of themselves. Thus once again, a great cultural change took place, and one of the greatest importance for our subject.

One way of emphasizing the point at issue would be to say that in different cultural situations a given phenomenon, for instance a particular disease such as epilepsy, or a given document such as the Donation of Constantine, may be seen as having quite different origins and character, scientific and historical, and therefore, very often, as having a very different place in the scheme of divine-human relations, if any such are envisaged. That will be taken up later.

Meanwhile this phenomenon of cultural change is far more complex than has been so far suggested, and in order to expound the matter more fully I will make use of terminology derived largely from Ernst Troeltsch; but though the terminology may be peculiar to him, the general ideas, so far as we shall be making use of them, would command pretty general assent.

It is by a happy — or should I say inspired? — instinct that historians have long taken as their objects of study not isolated incidents, comparable to the separate elements on which the natural scientist concentrates, but slabs, or blocks, of the past. Such blocks must have a measure of internal coherence, but, given that, they may be past phenomena of various sorts, for example a person, a class, a nation, a trade union, or a period.

Such blocks, or areas, of the past are called by Troeltsch individual totalities, or more briefly, totalities or (historical) individuals. As we have seen, these totalities will always in part have been conditioned by their environment, geographical, climatic, ecological, human and so on. Yet each will be peculiar; it will, as Schleiermacher insisted, always be an individual — not, as in the case of scientific elements, to be exhaustively described and explained in terms of any general laws. The reason why totalities are the appropriate object or unit of historical study is given in this (I fear rather characteristic) sentence from Troeltsch: 'They are magnitudes which have already coalesced . . . in which an abundance of psychical elemental occurrences, together with certain natural conditions, are already clustered together in a unity of life or totality.'[5] The point is that in any totality men's actions and beliefs, whether individual or corporate, their attitudes and their ways of understanding and responding to their environment are always closely related to other elements in their totality, including their material environment as well as other human activities. Consequently a full understanding of one element is only possible when it is seen in relation to the rest.

The significance of this insight is immense even though it should not be exaggerated; meanwhile perhaps a single illustration may help to make it clearer. Some years ago when I first read Sir Richard Southern's book on the making of the Middle Ages,[6] one of the things which came across to me very clearly was the extent to which the affairs of medieval people — and particularly, I noticed, their legal and constitutional arrangements — were affected by the paucity and poverty of the means of communication. For example, it was because travel to centralised courts was impossible that the circuit system and the variety of local jurisdictions obtained; and it was for the same sort of reason that all the various legal ways of attesting facts grew up. The point is obvious enough; you cannot really understand medieval life — especially, in this example, on its legal and constitutional sides — without taking account of another element in the medieval totality, its slow and scanty means of communication; and if you stop to think about it, those in their turn were obviously connected with other aspects of the totality, its comparative ignorance of matters chemical, physical and metallurgical, itself a result of the lack of interest in experimentation and experimental techniques and so on. It was a consequence of many interrelated elements in the medieval totality that almost all the conditions were lacking necessary for the discovery of steam power and the invention of the loco-motive. And the results of that were not confined to the legal and constitutional sphere; anyone, for example, who has read Sylvia Townsend Warner's novel *The Corner that Held Them* will have been made vividly aware what profound and varied effects lack of communications, and the consequent isolation of communities, had on the thoughts and feelings of medieval men and women in every sphere, including, for example, the kinds of guilt they felt.

That will help you to see, at least dimly, I hope, the sense in which at any given stage everything is tied up together in the bundle of life. Troeltsch of course did not suggest that historical totalities are ever, in any real sense, isolated from one another. They change gradually, paving the way, and eventually making way, for subsequent totalities which take over many of their cultural features, but in the process restructure or replace them, understanding and synthesizing them in such a way that they fit in with whatever elements of novelty differentiate the new totality from the old.

Totalities, as Troeltsch put it, link with one another, and merge into one another, in what he called 'a continuous connexion of becoming'[7] — notice once again the deliberate choice of neutral language to avoid any suggestion of automatic improvement or progress. Troeltsch has a com-plicated analysis of this process which need not concern us now. Suffice it to say that though he would have been the first to admit that from one point of view totalities are abstractions from a continuous connexion of becoming which is the very stuff of life in history, he would have insisted that they are abstractions vital to a proper under-standing of the past. For it is only in the context of its totality — that coherent group of past events in which it originated and had its *raison d'être* — that any human action or system of thought or belief can be understood. That is why it is the sign of a good historian that, by what Troeltsch calls 'intuition' — based of course on a wide knowledge of the facts and sound judgement — he can distinguish genuinely coherent totalities and characterize their dominant interests, traits and motifs, thus enabling himself to place the objects of his study in their true, and therefore illuminating, context. To study them in any other would be, in a measure at least, to misunderstand them.

Because totalities are linked together in a continual 'connexion of becoming', no totality is entirely opaque to any other, not even the totality of very primitive men to our own; though, as that instance shows, it may sometimes need great historical knowledge, a good historical imagination and a readiness for what Coleridge in another context called 'the willing suspension of disbelief'[8] on a considerable scale, if we are to have any clear idea of what the life and thought of a previous totality was really like. Even then, it is doubtful how far it is possible to enter fully into the mind of another age. Lionel Trilling, it will be recalled, puts it in the form that: 'To suppose we can think like men of another time is as much of an illusion as to suppose we can think in a wholly different way.' (See p. 39 above.)

The last words of that quotation are of course as important as the first. Because of the way totalities are continuously linked, the words, ideas, and feelings of one totality can often speak directly to the condition of later totalities. A case in point is Vergil's line: *sunt lacrimae rerum et mentem mortalia tangunt*, though even there, as readers of John Wren-Lewis* will know, it is possible seriously to conceive a situation in which the apparently perennial pathos of Vergil's words will no longer make a direct impact but will have to be recaptured by an exercise of the imagination.

However it may be with individual lines or ideas, it seems clear that any considerable body of action or thought *must* be understood in relation to its cultural context. Plato's

---

* See e.g. *Faith, Fact and Fantasy*, ed. C.F.D. Moule (Fontana Books, 1964) pp.9ff., and *What Shall We Tell the Children?* (Constable, 1971). Now see also Ann Faraday, *The Dream Game* (Temple Smith, 1975).

thought, for example, makes full sense and holds together with full coherence only in the cultural context of ancient Athens; one can say today that one is a Platonist, or embraces Platonism, but only in the sense that one finds one's understanding of reality in one's *own* totality illuminated and moulded by Plato's understanding of it in *his*.

Or, if we want a negative example, when liberal theologians expounded Jesus' teaching about the fatherhood of God, on which they so much concentrated, there can be no doubt that they often seriously misrepresented it by neglecting its context in the psychological, educational, ethical and other aspects of the totality, so different from ours, in which Jesus' teaching was delivered and meant to be understood.

For the present that example, which will later need some modification, may at least serve to emphasize an obvious corollary of what I have been saying. If the elements of a totality cohere, as they do, then to handle any one in isolation is in all probability to mishandle it, in some respects at least. That is what lies behind the encouragement given to every theological student always to set a biblical verse or passage in its correct *Sitz-im-Leben* (situation-in-life) before seeking to interpret or expound it. The interesting thing, as we shall see, is that those who give that advice unhesitatingly about individual passages of the Bible seem not to realise that it applies equally to the contents of the Bible as a whole.

How then, if at all, is it possible to bridge the gap between one totality and another? The fate of an experiment in literary criticism, not without some parallel to Barth's theological experiment, may perhaps forewarn us against one possible false-start. It is said to have been the American John Jay Chapman who in 1927 (a date interestingly close to that of Barth's earliest writings) first led a revolt against what he denounced as 'the archaeological, quasi-scientific and documentary study of the fine arts'. What he was rebelling against, not without justification, was the virtual substitution of the history of literature for the study of literature, 'scholarship' for 'criticism' as it is often put. (Readers of the biblical commentaries of fifty years ago will know what he meant!) The impulse of Chapman and his numerous and influential followers was precisely to make past works of art more immediate and real, to confront them in their immediacy, in the conviction that between now and then there is no essential difference, the spirit of man being one and continuous. In view of the parallel at which I have hinted between this movement and Barth's, it is interesting to note that in the view of most critics, salutary though this movement was, and great the gain it has brought, in the end it will not do. Lionel Trilling, for example, lists among the faults of the New Critics 'that in their reaction from the historical method they forget that the literary work is ineluctably a *historical* fact, and, what is more important, that its historicity is a fact in our aesthetic experience'.[9] In Troeltsch's terms, you cannot derive full and proper satisfaction from a work of art of the past without appreciating, and allowing for, its origins in a totality different from your own.

Since I find that this sort of point is generally rather unfamiliar, may I come at it another way, drawing this time on a discussion by R.G. Collingwood? As most of you will no doubt know, Collingwood insisted that the historian's task is not confined to the discovery and recording of the various remains left by the past, nor even to reconstructing on the basis of them the outward course of past events, for example the route by which an army reached the site of a battle or the composition of a conference or council. It is a further, and quite essential, part of the historian's task, according to Collingwood, to discover *why* the various actors acted and reacted as they did, and *what they had in mind* in following the policies they did. 'Historical knowledge', as Collingwood himself expressed it, 'is the re-enactment in the historian's mind of the thought whose history he is studying'.[10] There has been some criticism of this as a general account of the historian's task; luckily I do not need to discuss that now, but I should like to quote, without prejudice, a further passage from his *Autobiography* in which Collingwood illustrates what he had in mind; acquaintance with it is necessary for the understanding of a point of his I do wish to stress. He is recalling a time when, as a boy, he sat in his father's study pondering the story of Nelson's refusal to remove his decorations at the battle of Trafalgar. He writes:

When I understand what Nelson meant by saying 'in honour I won them, in honour I will die with them', what I am doing is to think myself into the position of being all covered with decorations and exposed at short range to the musketeers in the enemy's tops, and being advised to make myself a less conspicuous target. I ask myself the question, shall I change my coat? and reply in these words. Understanding the words means thinking for myself what Nelson thought when he spoke them: that this is not a time to take off my ornaments of honour for the sake of saving my life. Unless I were capable — perhaps only transiently — of thinking that for myself, Nelson's words would remain meaningless to me.[11]

Such a degree of identification is obviously not easily achieved, if indeed it is achievable at all. If we are *really* to understand Nelson's thoughts after him — if, for example, we are to know whether his words were a declaration of courage or foolhardiness or maybe an empty show of bravado, we shall need to know a great deal about Nelson's general character and also need to know as much as he did about contemporary muskets and how far they could be used with accurate results at the sort of distance within which early nineteenth century men-of-war could approach one another.

It is often said that such a degree of identification is neither necessary nor possible. Be that as it may; Collingwood thought it was and that makes his subsequent remarks all the more significant. He thought the identification could be so complete as to raise the question what the difference is between Nelson's original thinking of the thought and his rethinking it, and he tells us 'No question in my study of historical method ever gave me so much trouble'.[12] It took him years, he says, to find the answer, and here, in his own words, it is:

The difference is one of context. To Nelson, that thought was a present thought; to me, it is a past thought living in the present but (as I have elsewhere put it) incapsulated, not free. What is an incapsulated thought? It is a thought which, though perfectly alive, forms no part of the question-answer complex which constitutes what people call the 'real' life, the superficial or obvious present, of the mind in question. For myself, or for that which at first sight I regard as myself, the question 'shall I take off my decorations?' does not arise. The questions that arise are, for example, 'shall I go on reading this book?' and later, 'what did the *Victory*'s deck look like to a person thinking about his chances of surviving the battle?' and later again, 'what should I have done if I had been in Nelson's place?' No question that arises in this primary series, the series constituting my 'real' life, ever requires the answer 'in honour I won them, in honour I will die with them'. But a question arising in that primary series may act as a switch into another dimension. I plunge beneath the surface of my mind, and there live a life in which I not merely think about Nelson but am Nelson, and thus in thinking about Nelson think about myself. But this secondary life is prevented from overflowing into my primary life by being what I call incapsulated, that is, existing in a context of primary or surface knowledge which keeps it in its place and prevents it from thus overflowing. Such knowledge, I mean, as that Trafalgar happened ninety years ago: I am a little boy in a jersey: this is my father's study carpet, not the Atlantic, and that the study fender, not the coast of Spain.[13]

The point is so important that it is worth spelling out a little further. An 'incapsulated' thought is one which a historian, in the present, thinks after some character of the past; he thinks it vividly, entering into its full flavour and individuality, but it is incapsulated in the sense that it cannot tie up in the same immediate way with the rest of the historian's circumstances and experience as it did in the case of its original thinker.

It will be clear how Collingwood here links with Troeltsch. Nelson's thoughts, words and action belonged to a past totality; although by a sufficiently willing suspension of disbelief and a vigorous exercise of the imagination it may be possible to think his thought after him, that thought must remain 'incapsulated': it cannot be taken over as it stands into the present totality.

The relevance of all this to our present enquiry will, I

hope, be obvious. If the historian may not treat any element of a totality apart from its context; if an incapsulated thought may not overflow into our present life as it stands, or be moved across the equation without the signs being changed in some way, there seems no reason why the same should not apply to the Bible and the religion of the Bible. The biblical material comes to us from more than one totality; the Bible as a whole, if we include the New Testament, comes to us out of a single totality, that of the Early Church, in which, for example, the earlier material was related to the later by means of categories indigenous to that totality — fulfilment, type-antitype, and so on. And to talk of the biblical material is to talk of the faith, or faiths, enshrined in the Bible.

That, however, is by no means all. In the process of transmission from its original totality to ours, the Bible has been interpreted in the context of various totalities, none of them, it is true, anything like as different from the original as ours, but nonetheless differing from it in subtle but significant ways. Perhaps even more important is the fact that most of these post-biblical totalities, including those which are classic for the interpretation of the Bible, have been very largely non-historical in their outlook. Precisely one of the things that differentiates our totality from any previous totalities is the radically historicizing attitude to the past it not only takes but cannot help taking. That is to say, our totality cannot help being aware, as previous totalities were not, that the thoughts, beliefs, words and actions of any culture are essentially related to the other elements in it and cannot be understood, let alone actively reproduced, except in the context of that culture.

Because people of earlier cultures were largely unaware of this, they were free from a problem which is bound to arise for us in an acute form. Christians of earlier totalities could believe it both possible and right to try to assimilate the whole of biblical religion, essentially unchanged, in their own formulations and practice. Although the attempt was never entirely successful, the belief has become so ingrained in the Christian consciousness that we find it difficult to think of any other way of using the Bible, or of any way of understanding Christianity on other terms.

Yet other ways may have to be found, for at least two reasons. On the one hand, our awareness of the fact of cultural relativity means that we know that it is unlikely to be of any use attempting to lift the biblical religion, or any of the interpretations of it adopted by our predecessors, and make them our own as they stand. Secondly, it is simply a fact about our cultural outlook that it is for the most part orientated towards the future rather than the past. A modern advertiser proclaims, not that his firm was established two hundred years ago — that would merely make us suspect it of being out of date — but that he 'makes today the cars, or refrigerators, of tomorrow'. The example is trivial but it is symptomatic of a very deep feature of the outlook of us all. To borrow Troeltsch's words, whereas for earlier outlooks 'all the foundations of culture were complete, *we* are essentially future-orientated; the world is to be changed, truth is to be guaranteed only by the inner necessity of the human spirit, not by deference to past authorities'. The point is documented, a shade wistfully perhaps, by Professor J.H. Plumb in his book *The Death of the Past*,[14] and although Karl Marx was no doubt being deliberately one-sided in his eleventh thesis on Feuerbach, the thesis, if we ponder it, will tell us a good deal about ourselves and our outlook. 'The philosophers', he said, 'have only interpreted the world . . . .; the point, however, is to change it'. *Our* point is not that the balance struck nowadays between the attitudes to the past and the future is necessarily the right one (or that the contrast drawn by Professor Plumb covers all aspects of human experience), but that we should be aware what it is, so that we understand the 'doctrines felt as facts' in terms of which most of our contemporaries approach the Bible. For the reasons explained in the Introduction (see especially pp. 31—3), it is also important that we should become clear how far we ourselves share in the current attitude on this matter and how far we feel obliged in integrity to do so. If, in some measure at least, we find that we do, that is a fact of considerable importance for our subject.

This is perhaps the point at which to say how acutely aware I am of the inadequacy of what I have been saying. To mention only one point, the need for brevity has made my treatment too exclusively intellectualist; differences between totalities embrace the emotional and imaginative, as well as the more specifically intellectual, sides of human nature. Marshall McLuhan, among others, brings out, and documents well, both how extensive and how profound are the differences between human beings of different totalities in all aspects and levels of their humanity.

However, we are now perhaps in a better position to ask how it stands in this regard with the three modern approaches to the Bible we considered earlier. The question can at least be raised whether, from our present perspective, they do not all three attempt the impossible.

So far as the third, and most modern, is concerned, it could be argued that it is precisely an attempt to lift, not exactly the religion of the Bible, but something as nearly as possible 'the Bible from within', out of its original totality in order to offer it, more or less neat, for assimilation by our totality. If so, the various difficulties we noticed about it in the previous lecture would be so many aspects of the fact that an element from a past totality, or series of totalities, cannot be transplanted into another, any more than one person's heart can as yet be transplanted into someone else's body and fully or permanently assimilated. And the problem is compounded to the extent that this modern approach seeks, as we saw in the last lecture it does, to interpret the Bible in categories derived from post-biblical totalities almost as alien to our own as that of the Bible itself. As one test whether this approach is genuinely compatible with a contemporary outlook, it is a revealing question to ask how far any version of it views the relations between Old Testament and New Testament material in categories genuinely indigenous to our own totality and not just taken over, unassimilated, from others.

The categories in question will be theological, but the same sort of question may be raised about some of the historical connexions suggested in the Bible. As you will all know, the Old Testament interprets the Babylonian captivity of the Jews as divine punishment for the idolatry and syncretistic worship of the preceding centuries. However much we may deprecate that idolatry or appreciate the prophetic protest against it, are we tied — can we with integrity be tied — to the causal explanation invoked in the Bible? What if some scholar in the new edition of the Cambridge Ancient History should declare that the causes of the Exile were clearly discernible as political and economic, and would have produced the effect they did whatever the purity of Israel's Yahwism? Are we under any obligation to assert that if the Israelites had avoided idolatry they would also have avoided captivity? Would not attempts to refute the historian's view on any but its own scholarly grounds be attempts to import the outlook and categories of one totality into another, quite different, totality?

The question to be asked about any version of the response to the biblical problem we are discussing is whether the modifications it advocates in the biblical faith, and the classic interpretations of it, are the right ones, adequate to ensure that the resultant Christianity is a faith genuinely tenable with integrity in the context of our totality.

That question we shall take up later; meanwhile it should be clear by now that, and why, it will not do to try cutting the Gordian knot simply by saying: 'If the modern totality cannot assimilate the gospel in one or other of the forms suggested by the third type of approach, that just shows that there is somthing radically wrong with the modern totality.' Of course it is never right to be dominated uncritically by the *Zeitgeist*; as Dean Inge said, 'He who marries the spirit of the age will soon find himself a widower.' Yet all the versions of our third response, including Barth's on inspection, are attempts to tailor the gospel to our condition. If they do not entirely succeed, it is absurd for their authors to say: 'It's the man who's the wrong shape, not the suit'!

The second, or 'liberal', type of response can be seen as attempting to ignore the problems raised by cultural relativism at a vital point, namely in its assumption that any figure or teaching from a long past totality can be attractive or illuminating in a completely new totality in exactly the same way that it was in its own. Albert Schweitzer put his finger on the point unerringly so far as the figure of Jesus is concerned, and it is interesting to notice how strongly his words bring out that Jesus is a stranger to us as he was understood in his own totality (and, no doubt, as he understood himself), and also a stranger in a different way as he was understood by previous post-biblical totalities, though the point will need refining in the light of what is said later. Schweitzer writes:

> The historical Jesus will be to our time a stranger and an enigma. The story of the life of Jesus has had a curious history. It set out in quest of the historical Jesus, believing that when it found Him it could bring Him straight into our time as a Teacher and Saviour. It loosed the bonds by which He had been riveted for centuries to the stony rocks of ecclesiastical doctrine, and rejoiced to see life and movement coming into the figure once more, and the historical Jesus advancing, as it seemed, to meet it. But He does not stay; He passes by our time and returns to his own.[15]

The point is clear: both the Jesus of the New Testament and all the Jesuses of subsequent ecclesiastical totalities, because they belonged essentially to their own totalities, are equally, though in very different ways, strangers or enigmas to our time. And the Jesus of History, you notice, is — surely rightly — not excluded from the judgement.

By way of contrast, the wrong attitude is exemplified by some words of the late Bishop Kirk on the subject of marriage and divorce. Arguing for a rigorist position he wrote: 'Our Lord's teaching has the same value, authority and application to-day as it ever had.'[16] Assuming that Kirk meant his words to be confined to Jesus' teaching on the particular subject under discussion, we might conceivably defend them on the ground he himself advances[17] that in this particular matter the situation is broadly identical in our totality with what it was in that of Jesus. The grounds Kirk goes on to adduce, however, strengthen the suspicion that his words were meant to be interpreted in a wider sense. 'In this matter more than any other', he wrote, 'our Lord surrounds his teaching most firmly and definitely with the atmosphere of "rule" or "legislation".'[18] Kirk's error lies in supposing that, however great the authority of Jesus' words when spoken, or however complete his divinity, they, or anything else, could suffice to give words a meaning, or commands a validity, in isolation from their original context, and relevant to every context; as we shall see, that is something which even God cannot do without negating the historical character of his creation. It is important to see that the words, activity and self-understanding of Jesus were as much affected by the fact of cultural relativism as those of any biblical writer. There can be no question of exempting his teaching or self-understanding from the general principle that such things are always relative to the cultural context in which they occurred.

It hardly needs to be added, I hope, that this in no way settles the question of the rightness or wrongness of Kirk's general view on the matter of divorce. It says only that the very nature of the problem in our day will depend on its context in our social situation; and the words spoken about it in a quite different social situation, where, for example, polygamy was still in principle, and occasionally in practice, accepted, cannot by themselves determine what our attitude and practice should be.

The first of the three responses I have distinguished fails to take account of the cultural relativist problem in its assumption that a form of words composed in the context of one totality can bear a sense which will not only be meaningful, but bear the same meaning, for all subsequent totalities. And it is worth noting that no doctrine of inspiration, however high, will dispose of this difficulty. As we have just seen, even God cannot alter the fact that the meaning of words is essentially related to their cultural context, so long as he takes seriously the essentially historical existence he has created, and works in terms of it. [The sense of this rather bald statement, and some justification for it, have been given in the Introduction. Spheres of discourse such as mathematics or physics may seem at first sight to require some modification in the generalisation and perhaps they do. But it is interesting that Troeltsch, writing in his last book and summing up a lifetime's reflexion on the matter, could say:

What was really common to mankind, and universally valid
for it, seemed, in spite of a general kinship and capacity
for mutual understanding, to be at bottom exceedingly
little, and to belong more to the province of material
goods than to the ideal values of civilisation . . . . Indeed,
*even the validity of science and logic seemed to exhibit,
under different skies and upon different soil, strong
individual differences present even in their deepest and
innermost rudiments.*[19]

As we saw in the Introduction, philosophers, especially in
England, have shown themselves curiously reluctant to take
account of such truths. R.G. Collingwood, who did full
justice to them, was very much a 'lone wolf' among the
English philosophers of his time, though cp. now the work of
Sir Isaiah Berlin. The matter has recently been discussed by
R. Trigg in *Reason and Commitment.*][20]
It was precisely because of the fact of cultural relativism
that previous ages had to apply figurative modes of interpretation to the biblical text in order to extract from it
meanings intelligible or relevant to their circumstances. Their
error (as it must appear from our point of view) lay in
supposing that any meaning they found was part of *the*
meaning it originally bore, and not meaning which they
found (often perhaps quite legitimately — we shall discuss
that later), in a sacred book which their orthodoxy forbade
them simply to find irrelevant and their stage of cultural
development prevented them from contextualising historically.
If we ask why the exponents of all the three views we have
discussed have tended to ignore our problem or sought to
circumvent it, does the answer not lie in the influence upon
them of the hitherto unchallenged assumption that Christianity must be a phenomenon, in its essential character at any
rate, identical in every totality — 'the faith once and for all
delivered to the saints' — and identical moreover, in the sense
that some one form of words will serve as an adequate'
expression of it for generation after generation, totality after
totality?
As a tail-piece to this lecture it may be pertinent to ask

whether the same influence has not been at work on Bultmann's solution of our problem. Whatever may be thought of Bultmann, it must surely be to his lasting credit that he above all has seen and tried to solve, the problem raised by cultural relativity, confronting it clearly and with courage. As everyone knows, his way of conceptualising it has been to designate as 'myth' everything in the culture of past totalities which is incompatible with the cultural outlook of our own. In view of what was said earlier (see e.g. pp. 6 and 30 above), he may perhaps fairly be criticized for over-confidence about our ability to grasp the essence of our own totality and define the *differentiae* of its culture exactly enough to be able to say confidently and distinctly what is, and is not, myth. I doubt if he can fairly be criticized for failing to say, what he undoubtedly realises and *does* in fact occasionally say, that the culture of our totality will seem mythical from the perspective of the future. That is no doubt a general truth* and recognition of this may serve to keep us humble; but it is not very helpful, for in the nature of the case we cannot know what characteristics of our cultural synthesis will make it look mythical to our successors.

No one, I imagine, wants to deny the great insight and value in Bultmann's existentialist way of dealing with the problem, but certain features of it are significant from our present point of view.

In his discussions with Fritz Buri, Schubert Ogden and others, Bultmann insists that the process of demythologizing must have limits, and he is quite right in so far as he means that human language about God must always involve a vital element of myth or 'story' of some sort. In view of that, Bultmann feels justified in talking of 'miracle' and of God's

---

* And it is what lies behind the advice so often given to substitute *remythologization* for Bultmann's *demythologization*. The trouble with that advice is that it risks obscuring the fact that myth in the sense in which it applies to *our* talk about God differs in a vital respect from myth as Bultmann uses it. As we have seen (cp. p. 36 above) the language we use about God, even if we call it 'myth' in order to emphasize its non-literal character, should never be in flat contradiction with any truth of which we are firmly persuaded. It is precisely incompatibility with such truth which constitutes myth in Bultmann's sense.

'acting' uniquely in Christ. It is true that for him God's action was not confined to the life and work of Jesus in isolation from the response of his first disciples and the creative interpretation of his person and work they were led to give in the Jewish, gnostic and Greek philosophical categories appropriate to their totalities. Nor, on Bultmann's view, was it the purpose of God's action to produce effects in or upon 'the other world' or to settle accounts with the devil. All such language is the language of myth. What God was concerned to do was to introduce that self-understanding in virtue of which men can live out of the future and cope with the otherwise intractable problem of the inauthenticity in their condition and behaviour, which all serious human beings have always recognised.[21]

Yet when all is said and done, the Christian gospel is for Bultmann the proclamation of something God did once for all in the early decades of our era. It was not done *ex opere operato* and men must appropriate ever anew the self-understanding that it made available; the fact remains that God produced it once for all for them to appropriate. For Bultmann the Christian commitment is to a single, once for all, divine action, and one that can be specified and its 'mechanics' worked out in twentieth-century, Heideggerian terms much as Anselm worked them out in the medieval terms of his day (see above, p. 59).

Bultmann and his school have, as is well known, given a great deal of thought to the problem of biblical interpretation. The motive has been their belief that if only the appropriate hermeneutic techniques can be discovered and employed, the New Testament will be found to yield, in a form fully intelligible and acceptable today, an account of that once for all divine intervention which has been the *articulus stantis aut cadentis ecclesiae* for all Christian totalities from New Testament times onwards, and was the very core of the faith of Luther and the Reformation.

Once again we have the *sola scriptura*, the conviction that the Christian faith is to be found *in toto* in the Bible, or more precisely, where Bultmann is concerned, in the New Testament. (The measure of Bultmann's confidence that the New Testament *kerygma* as discovered by his hermeneutic is the sole and sufficient *articulus stantis aut cadentis ecclesiae* is that he, a Lutheran, is prepared to jettison even the Old Testament because on his reading it is incompatible with it.)[22] All that is needed is the right hermeneutic key to undo the lock.

6 The Old Testament

A simple analogy may help to make the transition to the next stage of the discussion. Suppose that some member of this audience were unfortunate enough to fall forward from his seat, thrash about on the ground for a few moments and then become completely unconscious. What should we do? Assuming him to have fainted, we should perhaps loosen his collar and tie and clear a space around him; or if we suspected an epileptic seizure, we might put something between his teeth to prevent his biting his tongue. If he did not regain consciousness fairly soon, we should send for a doctor. The doctor would examine him and then, learning perhaps from a friend of the patient or his usual doctor that he suffered from diabetes, he might diagnose a diabetic coma. He would then inject an appropriate amount of sugar or insulin, as the case might be, and before long the patient would no doubt regain consciousness and soon feel little the worse for the incident.

Now suppose that a precisely similar incident had occurred in first century Palestine; what would people of that time and place have said and done? I suppose they would have thought that the patient was possessed of a devil, and perhaps they would have loosened any tight band round his neck to make the exit of the devil easier. They would certainly have fallen to prayer over the man, and if the devil did not respond, they would have diagnosed a particularly stubborn devil, or a whole legion of devils, and sent for someone known to be skilled at exorcism. He would have prayed over the man and performed appropriate ritual actions, with what result we cannot tell; though we may guess that short of a miracle, there would have been little chance of success in a case of diabetes.

Now suppose that an identical incident had occurred in the early seventeenth century; what would have been said and done then? I am not sure, but I imagine the by-standers would have said: 'Ah, poor fellow, the balance of his humours is disturbed'; and if he did not quickly recover, they would have sent for a chirurgeon who would have come with one of those fearsome articles known, I believe, as a cupping-glass, or with some leeches, and let a good deal of blood, with what result again we cannot say, though the chances of success would surely have been small.

By A.D. 2500 we may venture to hope that diabetes will somehow have been eliminated, or at least that prophylactic measures will have been discovered which rule out the sudden onset of diabetic comas; if not, we cannot tell how exactly people of that date will respond to the occurrence of a diabetic coma, except for being sure that, whatever they do or say, it will not be what we, or any of our predecessors, have said or done in the same situation; and probably it will be more effective.

The point will be obvious enough — a precisely identical incident, due to exactly the same physiological condition; yet the interpretation and treatment is quite different at different epochs. And in view of what was said in the last lecture, you will not need a detailed analysis by me to help you see that the understanding and treatment of this particular phenomenon in any culture links closely with the contemporary understanding in that culture of almost everything else, things chemical, medical, psychological, astronomical, theological, and so on.

That analogy may perhaps help to focus some of the questions with which the last lecture was concerned; but it has also been chosen in the hope that it may help to clarify the way most modern biblical theologians try to solve the problem with which thinkers such as Troeltsch have presented them.

According to these theologians, the situation with regard to Christianity is on all fours with the medical case in my analogy at any rate to this extent: Christians of one cultural totality may express their faith differently from those of another, but all alike are responding, in the way

appropriate to them, to identically the same thing. To be a
Christian in any generation is to respond, in the way
appropriate to your culture, to that self-same situation to
which the earliest Christians responded with the words of the
New Testament and the actions and attitudes they describe.
It is the identity *of that to which they respond* in their
different ways which provides the continuity between Christians of different generations.

These theologians concede that however faithful or traditional a Christian you may be, you cannot speak or act
exactly as the New Testament Christians did; but what you
do say and do as a Christian should be the best response *you*
can make to the situation to which *they* reponded in the way
appropriate to *their* totality, the way revealed in the New
Testament.

If so, it obviously becomes an important question just
what it was to which they were responding. Bultmann stands
rather apart among those who adopt this general approach,
because he is content to say that the object of their response
was a proclamation. Everyone who became a Christian in
New Testament times had listened to what Bultmann calls
the *kerygma*; that is, they had all heard a series of words
spoken by some preacher, and through faith had been able to
discern in the human words a word from God himself, a
demand for authentic living and a promise of the possibility
of it for all those who responded in faith, a promise which
had proved itself in experience. According to Bultmann, the
reason why the proclamation and the response take the
precise form they do in the New Testament is because they
were conceived in the categories of a combination of cultural
totalities, Jewish, Greek and gnostic, all very different from
our own. (In his view, as we have just seen, there was a
further, distorting factor; New Testament Christians attempted what he regards as the impossible task of trying to give a
positive valuation to much in previous Jewish religion,
whereas they should have rejected the Old Testament faith *in
toto*.) As for the historical events which gave rise to the
proclamation, Bultmann regards them as largely irrecoverable
and in any case not particularly interesting. For it was the
proclamation, on his view, not the events which led up to it,

which was the essential medium of revelation and salvation; and, if suitably demythologized, it can still constitute such a medium when men respond to it in faith, whatever events did, or did not, lie behind it.

Over the last point, at any rate, Bultmann's view has been questioned even by most of his own disciples. The more general view is that it is both necessary and possible to uncover the general course of the events witnessed to in the *kerygma*; and that when this has been done, it becomes possible to see that the faith of the early Christians was, not of course the only possible response to them, but a perfectly reasonable response — even, it is sometimes claimed, the *only* fully reasonable response.

Opinions differ about how much of the biblical material this approach will cover, but English-speaking theologians in particular often extend it to cover a good deal of the Old Testament material, suggesting that here too it is possible to recognise the occurrence of events to which the response evinced in the Old Testament was broadly the right and reasonable one.

It is pointed out that the occurrence of events which deeply and permanently affect a community's understanding of itself and the world is by no means confined to the biblical narrative. Whitehead wrote that: 'rational religion appeals to the direct intuition of special occasions, and to the elucidatory power of its concepts for all occasions. It arises from that which is special, but it extends to what is general.'[1]

Scholars such as H. Richard Niebuhr have taken up this idea, and the expression 'paradigmatic events' has been coined to describe the sort of events envisaged. For the definition of a paradigmatic event we may go to Professor Van A. Harvey, who in the relevant section of his book *The Historian and the Believer*[2] leans heavily on Niebuhr and quotes from him. A paradigmatic event is

an event that so captures the imagination of a community that it alters that community's way of looking at the totality of its experience. It is an event that strikes the community as illuminatory for understanding all other events. Just as we are sometimes perplexed by a complicated argument in a difficult book and suddenly come across a luminous sentence from which we can go forward and backward and so attain a comprehension of the whole, so revelation may be understood as an event that makes other events meaningful. . . . To say that certain events impose their own categories is to say that these events have the power to demand a consideration on their own terms, so to speak, that there are some ways of interpreting them less eccentric than others. They intrude certain questions and images upon us because they seem to touch human experience and feeling at some primordial level. They speak to our hopes and fears. Consequently, they provide us with the symbols and parables for the interpretation of our existence. . . . Whitehead, especially, makes a distinction between the concrete image cast up by the event and the concepts that are abstracted by the reason. The imagination is dominated by the image, but the image may be rationalized because it contains the universal in the particular.[3]

Paradigmatic events can be significant in different ways and with varying degrees of generality and comprehensiveness. An example Professor Harvey quotes, from the American angle, is the assassination of President Kennedy, with its challenge to the self-understanding of Americans, both as individuals and as a group. If an example is wanted of an event of this type from European history, one might cite the French Revolution, with all the questioning and reassessment it has meant, both among individuals and communities inside and outside Europe, both among friends and opponents of the Revolution, about issues of sovereignty, liberty, equality and so on; and the part it has played in moulding the assumptions and self-understanding of modern western man on both sides of the iron curtain.[4] An example cited by Richard Niebuhr was the voyage of the Pilgrim Fathers, with all that it has meant for the formation of American self-understanding both individual and corporate. As he says, no one is an American until that part of history has become part of his or her history.[5]

The concept of a paradigmatic event provides a model in

terms of which to understand the relation between history and faith in biblical religion. No one familiar with it need have any difficulty in principle in understanding or accepting such a statement as that of Professor G.E. Wright that 'the Hebrew mind was trained . . . to view the historical scene as the arena of God's primary self-disclosure, whereas by contrast the polytheist looked to the mythical happenings behind the natural order, in the cultic celebration of which he experienced his religious exaltation.'[6] Although, out of context at any rate, such a judgement may seem somewhat sweeping and we may wonder, for example, whether 'the Hebrew mind' had been trained in this way at the time when it expressed itself in the beliefs and cultic practices prevalent in the courts of David and Solomon. (The question is more than a pedantic aside. Fashions in scholarship are always apt to lead to one-sided emphases, and it is a real question whether the modern fashion in biblical scholarship has not exaggerated the historically based character of biblical religion and underestimated how much it owed, even in its developed form, to general beliefs and influences in the ancient near-East, including myths based on the natural order.) Nevertheless as a judgement on the Old Testament as a whole and on the developed Jewish faith it can very well stand.

The idea is that by the direct will of God certain of the events described in the Bible were paradigmatic events. They played their part in moulding and changing the Jewish, and later the Christian, community's self-understanding and its relation to God; they produced the situation which threw up the biblical traditions and writings; and they each helped to set the scene for further paradigmatic events. Viewed from the divine side, so to speak, they were what the Bible calls them, 'mighty acts of God' in history; and Christianity consists in responding appropriately to them. Although we today shall respond in our own way, our response will be guided by the biblical interpretation of them as an inter-related series through which God's saving policy for the world was worked out.

Professor Wright is confessedly an exponent of biblical theology and this view of Christianity as essentially a faith-response to certain great acts of God in history, and of the Bible as a record of these acts and an authoritative guide to their general meaning, is clearly a version of the biblical theology movement discussed in chapter four.

It allows, however, that we must respond to the biblical events in our own way, and, as we have seen, in the twentieth century, part of our way of responding to any alleged past events is to examine their credentials. We must therefore examine the credentials of the paradigmatic events in the Bible; but before doing so we need to remind ourselves of a point already discussed in the Introduction. It is this.

In the period before the rise of the modern type of historical study, attitudes towards, and motives for, the recounting of the past were very different from what they are today. Nowadays it is axiomatic that in any serious account of the past the absolutely overriding consideration is the greatest possible degree of accuracy; to that everything else is subordinate. In the past things were different. For one thing, the kind of accuracy we take for granted as a requirement of any historical or biographical work presupposes conditions which did not exist in earlier times, for example the existence and availablity of accurate records and the means of communication which make it relatively easy to consult them or have them investigated.

In the second place the purpose of recording the past used to be very differently understood. Very often the aim was not simply to disclose the past *wie es eigentlich gewesen*, but to exhibit it as an edifying tale which would promote deeper faith and purer morals. As recently as the eighteenth century, a man of the intelligence of Bolingbroke could describe history as 'philosophy teaching by examples', and even Schleiermacher could be accused by Troeltsch of viewing 'history as a picture book of ethics'.[7] We might perhaps put it that whereas for us, in our history writing, accuracy comes first and edification nowhere, for earlier ages edification was frequently a value in history writing which stood alongside, and very often high above, accuracy. That is something which will be recognised alike by students of the books of Chronicles, or, say, eighteenth-century British historians; and it is not a matter for moral disapproval, but just one of a difference of outlook. It may be worth quoting in this context an illuminating passage from one of our leading medieval historians. Sir Richard Southern prefaces his discussion of the so-called Donation of Constantine in his volume on the medieval church with these words:

> It may seem odd, and even repellent, to begin a discussion of the greatest of all ecclesiastical institutions with a forgery. To put this matter in perspective it is important to understand the importance of forgeries as vehicles of ideas in this early period. They did not have the vulgar associations of modern forgeries. The primitive age had few records, but it had clear ideas of the past. These ideas were based on accumulated traditions, legends, pious fabrications, and above all on a reluctance to believe that the past is largely unknowable. Hence even learned and critical men easily believed that the past was like the present, only better; in a word that it was an idealized present. *Documents were therefore drawn up in which the theories of the present were represented as the facts of the past.* . . . The forgeries, which are a conspicuous feature of the age, provided documentary proofs for claims which, in the minds of those who made them, scarcely needed to be justified. The pen corrected the corruptions of nature and restored the gross imperfections and injustices of the world to a primitive excellence. . . . the authors believed that they enforced truths which could not be abandoned without grave danger to their souls.[8]

(The Donation of Constantine is a document which purports to be a letter from the emperor Constantine to Pope Sylvester I written on 30 March A.D. 315, but was in fact written in the eighth century or later in order to provide the title-deed for the theory of ecclesiastical primacy and church-state relations which prevailed at the time.)

No one of course would want to suggest that conditions in biblical times were exactly what they were in eighth or ninth century western Christendom; I quote Sir Richard Southern only as showing that in earlier cultural totalities men of faith could write about the past in a way quite impossible for a man of faith and integrity today. If we bear that in mind as we look at the events reported and treated as paradigmatic in the Bible, we shall be prepared at least for the possibility that some of them may turn out to have been 'theories of the present represented as facts of the past'.

It may come as a surprise to some readers to be told that the first paradigmatic event in the Bible is the creation event. Yet on the definition of a paradigmatic event given above, that must surely be the case. Creation was certainly an event for the Old Testament writers, even if it was a complex event which extended over a period of days; and it was clearly an event which struck the Jewish community 'as illuminatory for the understanding of all other events' and 'made other events meaningful'. Equally clearly it 'provided them with the symbols and parables for the interpretation of their existence'. Indeed it did all these things to an extent not fully recognised until lately. One of the results of recent Old Testament study has been to show that the Jews had, and probably acted out in the ritual of their New Year festival, a far richer understanding of creation than had previously been recognised; and that this understanding controlled their other beliefs and attitudes to a hitherto unsuspected degree. Yahweh's creative purposes were held to have involved him in bitter conflict with various forces of evil and chaos which were identified with, or located in, the waters of the sea (cp. Bible dictionaries and commentaries, e.g. under *Rahab, Tiamat* and *Dragon,* and see below). These had to be vanquished before the act of creation could be effectively carried out, and to a considerable extent Jewish confidence in Yahweh was based on the victorious power he had displayed in these conflicts and the subsequent act of creation.

Again and again the faith in Yahweh, and the confidence in his ability and willingness to save, displayed by the Jewish liturgy and the Jewish prophets, is based on the disclosure of his power and glory in the act of creation, and the ability it revealed to overcome the most powerful forces opposed to him. To quote just two examples:

Awake, awake, put on your strength, O arm of the Lord,
    awake as you did long ago, in days gone by.
      Was it not you
who hacked the Rahab in pieces and ran the dragon through?

Was it not you who dried up the sea,
the waters of the great abyss (*Tehom*, cp. *Tiamat*)
and made the ocean depths a path for the ransomed?
  So the Lord's people shall come back, set free,
and enter Zion with shouts of triumph,
    crowned with everlasting joy;
    joy and gladness shall overtake them as they come,
    and sorrow and sighing shall flee away.

O Lord God of Hosts, who is like thee?
Thy strength and faithfulness, O Lord, surround thee.
  Thou rulest the surging sea,
  calming the turmoil of its waves.
Thou didst crush the monster Rahab with a mortal blow
  and scatter thy enemies with thy strong arm.
Thine are the heavens, the earth is thine also;
the world with all that is in it is of thy foundation.
Thou didst create Zaphon and Amanus;
Tabor and Hermon echo thy name.
  Strength of arm and valour are thine;
thy hand is mighty, thy right hand lifted high;
  thy throne is built upon righteousness and justice,
true love and faithfulness herald thy coming.

Happy the people who have learnt to acclaim thee,
who walk, O Lord, in the light of thy presence!
In thy name they shall rejoice all day long;
  thy righteousness shall lift them up.
Thou art thyself the strength in which they glory;
  through thy favour we hold our heads high.
  The Lord, he is our shield;
  the Holy One of Israel, he is our king.[9]

It would appear that the sculptors of Chartres, in depicting
the act of creation as an event on all fours with the later
magnalia dei were closer to the mind of the biblical writers
than many modern commentators. In the eyes of the biblical
writers the creation was a paradigmatic event, a real
occurrence at a particular point in the past and one which
played a large part in producing and moulding the Jewish

people's faith in God and its understanding of its relation to him.

What then are we to make of the fact that this intensely paradigmatic biblical event was entirely mythical, was not an event at all in our sense of the word? We may well react, as we have seen most critical scholars have done, by taking the creation story as the Jews' way of stating the fact of the world's total and continual dependence on God. If so, however, the realisation of that dependence will not have come to them as the result of any specific event; there were no witnesses present at the creation event to hand on an account of it! In this case there is in fact no event for us to respond to, in our own, or any other, way. All that we can respond to are the beliefs, or the theories, arrived at by the Jews as the result of we know not what experiences and questionings on the part of different groups and individuals at different times. There is no reason to think that these were in principle different from the questionings and concerns about the origin of things which led to the appearance, and gradual refinement, of creation mythologies and theories among other peoples. In Israel, as elsewhere, reflexion on various facts and puzzles of experience led to the formation of doctrines which in this case certainly came to be represented as facts, the supposed facts of the creation story.

This case has been laboured at such length because, apart from its intrinsic interest, it makes clear that one way in which 'the Hebrew mind' *could* work was to borrow from what Professor Wright calls 'the polytheist' and then, after working over the myths or doctrines it had borrowed, to 'represent them as facts of the past'.

Nor is this an isolated example. When we come to the Fall and the Flood, much the same must be said. The 'fall' in particular was very much a paradigmatic event which moulded subsequent belief and self-understanding, if not in earlier Old Testament times, certainly for Jews and Christians of the New Testament period. ('O Adam what has thou done to all those who are born from thee?' (2 Baruch 48:42f.) 'Christ the second Adam', and so on.) Yet the very form of the story shows in part the sorts of questions and puzzlements — about the distinction between the sexes, the need for laborious tilling of the earth, the pangs of childbirth and so on — which gave rise to it, or at any rate helped to give it its present form; and, as in the case of the creation story, they were questions and puzzlements common to most cultures.

To take less significant examples, the observance of the sabbath, a central feature of later Jewish religion, was not in fact a response to the 'event' described in Gen. 2:3; and the equally important, though again by no means distinctively Jewish, institution of circumcision, did not arise out of the alleged events of Gen. 17:9ff.

By the exponents of biblical theology such examples, so far as they are significant enough to attract their attention, are usually treated as exceptions which prove the rule. They are said to be retrojections on to a particular point in the past of doctrines which *did* arise as responses to genuinely historical paradigmatic events. Thus God's victory over the forces of evil at creation, for example, is seen as a retrojection into the cosmic past of his historical victory over his enemies at the Exodus.

However it may be with regard to this last suggestion, biblical theology is certainly right in regarding the Exodus as the paradigmatic event *par excellence* in the Old Testament. In and through the Exodus the Jews believed they had been chosen by their God as his peculiar people, admitted into covenant relationship with him, and given the Law, the possession of which was one of their special glories (e.g. Ps. 147:19—20) and the observance of which was a key factor in keeping them unified and distinct, for example during their Babylonian exile. If any event in the Old Testament deserves to be called paradigmatic, this was surely it, especially in view of the way it was used by later biblical writers, for example by the Deuteronomist, by Deutero-Isaiah as the basis of his confidence in his people's eventual return to Palestine, and by St Paul and other New Testament writers. (e.g. Deut. 30:1ff., Is. 52:4, 1 Cor. 10:1ff., Heb. 12:18ff.)

The Exodus is usually understood as comprising everything from the birth of Moses at least to the making of the covenant and the giving of the law at Sinai. So highly complex and controversial an event cannot be discussed fully here, but our argument demands that certain things should be said about it.

Almost all competent authorities now agree that, in the form in which we have it, the Exodus story is a cult epic, that is, a story told during the course of an act of worship — in this case a cultic celebration dating from a relatively late period — to explain and justify what was being done. Pedersen, for example, describes the Exodus story as 'not a simple history, compiled for history's sake, but a "cultic glorification", a celebration of God's great victory by the worshipping people in the paschal festival. Its object is not to describe ordinary events, but to describe events of a different character, exploits in which God is glorified and a people made great.'[10] Other scholars agree with Pedersen that 'everything is transmitted and refracted through this usage', including the account of the Sinai covenant.

To call a story a cult epic is not of course to deny that it has its roots in history, but in this case the question has inevitably arisen whether the epic gave rise to the cultic celebration or *vice versa*. How far did the cultus simply use and refract a pre-existing narrative on which it was itself largely based; or how far did the need to legitimate and explain the cultus and the beliefs which it expressed give rise to the epic?

To a considerable extent the latter alternative seems the more likely one. If we take first the third element we have distinguished in the Exodus story, the giving of the Law, historical research shows that the ascription of the whole Law to Moses was simply the Jewish version of the habit we have seen to be common among primitive peoples of ascribing the law under which they lived to some ancient lawgiver believed to have acted under divine inspiration (see p. 23 above).So far from having been delivered on a single occasion, the Jewish law in fact grew up over centuries, a great deal of it dating from many generations after Moses. Whether or not we accept Albrecht Alt's theory of the difference in derivation between the casuistic and the apodictic elements in Jewish law, it seems clear that much of it consisted originally of tabus and cultic regulations derived from, and shared with, other peoples; while much originated from judicial decisions on individual cases, given, very often, as the result of procedures such as the casting of sacred lots or the observation by local priests or priestesses of the movements of the leaves of sacred trees. We must therefore conclude once again that what was seen in the Old Testament as the fruit of a single paradigmatic event was in fact the fruit of innumerable responses to innumerable individual situations no longer recoverable by us.

The Exodus cannot even have been the *origin* of Jewish Law since many of the provisions date from an earlier period. It may of course be that some incident at Sinai gave a special direction to the Jewish observance of law and contributed significantly to the later Jewish habit of ascribing the whole Law to Moses. Scholars quite properly try to isolate and reconstruct some such event. Their findings, however, are speculative and diverse; and even if we are convinced by some of them, we cannot with any confidence describe the incident to which they point as a paradigmatic event. For we are far too uncertain about its occurrence and character to know how large a part it played relatively to other factors in giving rise to the Jews' later interpretation of the origin of their Law; and we are obviously in no position to claim that that interpretation was 'less eccentric than others' (cp. p. 120 above).

With regard to the other elements in the Exodus story, the same sort of things must be said. Martin Noth and other scholars distinguish the story of the Exodus proper from the story of the making of the Covenant, and give reasons for thinking that they were originally independent epics, each derived from a number of sources and attached to a different cultic celebration, their fusion to form the present single account of a unified 'event' being a relatively late development.

So far as the Exodus proper is concerned, it is generally agreed that not more than two of the later tribes were originally involved in it; and the passover story, which forms such a central element of it, appears to have been a historicizing 'legitimation' of a ritual already known and practised long before any date to which it is plausible to assign the lifetime of Moses. This ritual, which appears to have contained elements of moon worship and apotropaic magic, as well as a dissuasive from eating uncooked carcases, blood, bones and all, seems to have originated among nomadic peoples outside Israel and was possibly connected with the lambing season. (Cp. the comment of Wellhausen: 'the Exodus is not the occasion of the festival, but the festival the occasion, if only the pretended one, of the Exodus'.)[11]

The story of the making of the covenant is also the subject of a great deal of controversy. Older critics were convinced that the relationship of the Israelites to their God was originally a 'natural' one, Yahweh being little more than the symbol of the tribe, as with many other tribes and their gods. According to these scholars, it was only in the time of Amos and his successors that this natural relation was historicized and came to be thought of as deriving from a covenant initiated by the God. More recently this has been questioned. One group of scholars, for example, claims to discern parallels between some of the covenant language in the Exodus story and the forms of certain suzerainty treaties, mainly of Hittite origin, dating from the late bronze age. It may therefore be that the Jewish belief that its relation to God originated partly at least from a covenant may go back to the time of the Exodus. It must be stressed, however, that such theories are by no means universally accepted; and even if they should establish themselves, we should still have no means of knowing what the events were which led to such a reinterpretation by the Jews of their relationship to their God and whether or not their understanding of those events was 'eccentric'.

Nothing in all this puts in question the general validity of Professor Wright's distinction between the conviction of the Hebrews that their beliefs and their relationship to God originated largely from historical events, and the non-historical religious outlook of many of the groups who surrounded them. Clearly *some* event or experiences must have occurred to account for this distinctive Jewish attitude; and on the principle of 'no smoke without a fire', the event and experiences in question are located by many scholars in the Exodus. It is pointed out that descent from a group of oppressed slaves is not something sufficiently creditable for a people to have commemorated unless the events involved had been regarded as significant from some other point of view. Certainly it is clear from the form of the Exodus narrative that it was preserved in order to perpetuate and reinforce a certain understanding and practice of relations with God, rather than pride in the secular history of the Jewish people; and though it is speculative, there may well be something in the contention that the Exodus events were regarded from an early date as having profound religious significance. The fact remains, however, that scholars differ widely in their reconstructions of what originally happened at the Exodus and the initial response to it; and undoubtedly many of the beliefs and practices which the Old Testament writers describe as having originated at the Exodus in fact originated on quite different occasions. Whether the original events were such as to make it plausible for the Jews to allow them to dominate their subsequent interpretation of their relations with God to the extent they did, we have no means of knowing for certain, if indeed this question is an intelligible one, a point to be discussed later. All that is in fact available in this connexion for our inspection and response is not an event, but an understanding of the relation between God and his people derived in fact from innumerable events and experiences beyond our power to recover, and 'expressed' – in large part erroneously from this historical point of view – 'as a fact of the past'.

Perhaps even so cursory a glance at the immensely complicated situation in contemporary Old Testament scholarship may suffice to establish one thing. All attempts to reconstruct the Exodus event are widely recognised to be highly speculative; and of late that recognition has grown stronger rather than weaker, until now most scholars would agree that any chance of ever being able to recover or describe the event with sufficient precision for us to know how to respond to it, apart from its immeasurable influence in producing the Law and the Jewish attitude to it, is infinitely remote. It must be admitted that much of the biblical account of the Exodus comprises insights or interpretations – call them what you will – based on innumerable and irrecoverable experiences on the part of later individuals and groups. Belief in a special relationship between a particular people and some warrior god devoted to protecting its interests was common enough in the ancient near east, and it is difficult to believe that some such primordial belief was not the original basis for Israel's eventual understanding of its relation to Yahweh. The significant thing was the shape that understanding came to take under the influence of various events and experiences by no means confined to the time of Abraham or Moses.

Another obvious example of the paradigmatic event in the Old Testament is the exile to, and return from, Babylon, in view of the influence these happenings exerted on subsequent Jewish faith and practice, and of their interpretation, at the time and later, as in some sense a re-enactment, or fulfilment, of the Exodus.

Here questions of a different sort arise. In this case we are indubitably dealing with an historical event, and the Bible furnishes material for a fairly, though by no means fully, complete and accurate reconstruction of it. Such a reconstruction, however, would be unlikely to reveal anything which differentiated the incident in any essential way from other historical incidents. As already hinted (see p. 109), it would be perfectly possible — indeed it would be natural — for a modern scholar, writing, let us say, in the new *Cambridge Ancient History*, to be fully satisfied with an account of the events which presented them as a quite normal instance of the working of political, economic and other 'natural' factors. He would be unlikely to find anything which eluded explanation in such terms, or demanded interpretation as the direct upshot of divine intervention. He would be unlikely to trace any specific causal connexion between this incident and the syncretistic religious beliefs and practices current both in northern and southern Palestine during the preceding centuries, or to suggest that if such practices had been less prevalent, events would have turned out differently from the way they did. To say that is not to deny all truth in the biblical interpretation, or even to say that a modern scholar would deny it. What it does suggest is that there was nothing about the event itself which demanded that it should be interpreted paradigmatically in the way the Bible interprets it. In fact that way of interpreting it depended on its being linked in a special fashion with other events. It was only when the various earlier paradigmatic events, including the creation, fall and Exodus, to which the Jews traced their existence as a people and their present relationship with God, were linked together into a developing story, and the Exile and return were seen *as the latest episode in that story*, that these latter could take on the paradigmatic character accorded to them. It is when seen as part of that sequence — as an episode in a super-historical story — that this genuinely historical event could become for the Jews 'elucidatory for all occasions' and paradigmatic; and it is only within the context of that story that it can be an object of religious response. So the status of the story becomes a matter of the utmost importance.

Before taking that point any further I should like to recur to another fact about the Old Testament to which I have already alluded, the fact, namely, that the Old Testament does not purport to be confined to descriptions or interpretations of paradigmatic events. As Professor Barr, for example, rightly keeps reminding us, there is much material in the Old Testament which can be fitted into that sort of description only by a fairly violent *tour de force*. The prophets, for example, appear to speak more of the future than the past, and, to judge from their own account, although they based part of what they had to say about the present and the future on a reading of the recent or distant past, they relied principally on specific communications direct from Yahweh. 'Thus hath said Yahweh' is the characteristic preface to a prophetic oracle.

Indeed from a modern point of view we might perhaps feel that the rise of prophetism, with its moralising of the Jewish understanding of God and its desacralising of Jewish-Canaanite religion, is more aptly described as a paradigmatic event than any of the events so regarded in the Old Testament itself.

However much truth there may be in such an idea — and it implicitly underlies a good many modern books on Old Testament religion — there is also need for caution:

(*i*) In the first place recent study surely suggests that

prophetism was not so sudden or homogeneous a phenomenon as earlier critical scholarship sometimes supposed.
The roots of the so-called 'great' prophets go deep into the
Jewish past; and what is more, many an utterance which
appears in the great prophets — with or without the formula
'Thus hath said Yahweh' — was in fact a piece of traditional
lore or a truth otherwise arrived at by means we can no
longer discover, and then attributed to the prophet speaking
under direct divine inspiration.

(*ii*) Secondly, we shall want to apply to any formula such
as 'thus saith the Lord' the type of critical analysis that
would naturally be applied in our totality to any such
formula in an ancient religious document. We shall have to
discuss in the terms natural to us the psychological and other
processes by which the Jewish prophets became convinced of
the truth and divine origin of what they said. Anyone for
example familiar with the English romantic poets and with
modern studies of them — or indeed with the work of such
scholars as Mowinckel on the prophets themselves — will
recognise that the question how the prophets came to speak
as they did is a very complicated one. It should not too
lightly be assumed that their motivation or inspiration were
in principle different from those of some other writers,
especially as we have to bear in mind the widespread
moralising of religious and philosophical beliefs in the Greek
world and elsewhere at about the prophetic period.

Have we not once again, in prophetic inspiration, an
example of new insights, beliefs and experiences, arrived at in
various ways we can no longer exactly determine, but which
need not essentially be mysterious (or at any rate more
mysterious than the workings of grace must always be),
projected back and seen as the result of direct divine
interventions in a series of separate, minor but vital,
paradigmatic events?

If so, much the same sort of thing might obviously be said
about the Wisdom literature, in fact the fruit of international
experience and enlightenment, but so largely ascribed in the
Old Testament to the supernaturally wise Solomon; or about
the Psalms and their attribution to King David. Such
examples remind us, however, how artificial many of our

distinctions are; the Wisdom writings in particular lay little outward stress on the great paradigmatic events of the past or their interpretation in story; yet there is no doubt that the God of whom Jewish wisdom speaks is assumed normally (but ? Job) to be the God of Abraham, Isaac and Jacob, that is, the God of the story.

It may well be that the whole question how biblical writers knew what to say is one which deserves more attention than it often receives, a possiblity which was vividly brought home to me some years ago when I watched a play about St Paul written by a former pupil.[12] In one scene the apostle was portrayed having supper with the Christian family with whom he was staying, after making the speech in which he had for the first time nailed his colours to the mast on the subject of the entry of gentiles to the church without circumcision. His hosts were shown as Christians of the conservative type and they freely expressed considerable doubts about the position he had taken up. In the next scene we saw Paul, after the household had retired to rest, pacing up and down outside the house and asking himself whether he had been right. How did he *know* that Gentiles could become Christians without first becoming Jews, and that justification was by faith alone? The scene is one I have pondered many times, asking myself whether (and if so why) modern Christians should expect to be any less troubled by such questions in connexion with their beliefs than the apostle was in connexion with his. I venture now to offer it to you to ponder, in connexion not only with Paul, not only with other biblical writers, but also with the many anonymous people whose faith, traditions and insights the biblical writers transmit to us.

Before we pass to a discussion of the New Testament, however, it may be well to summarise the drift of what has been said in this lecture. You will remember how this phase of the discussion arose: from the suggestion that since the words of the Bible were uttered, like all other words, as a response to something, the way to use the Bible is to discover what it was the biblical writers were responding to and then to respond ourselves in a way which, while being entirely appropriate to our own cultural situation, reproduces the biblical response as far as possible.

At first blush, the Old Testament may seem to offer an admirable opportunity for such an approach. No doubt, as Professor Barr says, the extent to which Old Testament writers saw their words as responses to certain specific *magnalia dei* has been exaggerated by most exponents of 'biblical theology'; but the fact remains that in large measure the Old Testament does purport to communicate understanding of, belief in, and response to God *as revealed in certain specifiable mighty acts* performed in history, and certain revelations made directly to the prophets.

The point of my analysis has been to show that in their attitude to the past the Old Testament writers and their sources approximated fairly closely to Sir Richard Southern's medieval authors; and that their account of the origins of their beliefs and teaching cannot be taken at its face value to anything like the extent often suggested.

Some of the events on which they believed their faith to rest, for example the creation or the fall, were not events at all in any sense acceptable to us; so we have to ask on what the faith supposedly based on these events was in fact based. One common answer is that it was based on − or should I say, extrapolated from? − certain divine interventions which we *can* still assert to have taken place in Israel's history, and which, it is suggested, gave rise to some elements in the Jewish faith directly and to others indirectly. For example, as we have seen, it is often held that the supposed victory of God at creation was a projection into the cosmic past of his historical victory over his enemies at the Exodus.

Our soundings, however, such as they have been, have suggested considerable reservations even about that; for on analysis, some of the events generally put forward as key divine interventions have themselves proved to be what I may call constructions-out-of-faith, that is, imaginative reconstructions by the later Jewish community of what, given their assumptions, *must* have happened in the past for their relationship to God in the present to be what they believed it to be.[13] In part their reconstructions may sometimes have been guided by fact or by historical memories and traditions; but having in mind the results of our analysis, and remembering Sir Richard Southern's warning about how the primitive age was in the habit of representing the theories of the present as the facts of the past, we shall probably want to be rather cautious about the possibility of poking a stick into the moving stream of the Jewish religious tradition at certain points and claiming: 'Here we have bedrock; *this* moment or event really was historical and was also paradigmatic in the sense that here God was uniquely active in an action which we can isolate and interpret correctly and then respond to in a way appropriate to our situation.'

Instead, I suggest, we have to take the Old Testament religion in its various aspects and stages as a whole, for what it is, the developing religious tradition of a community which belonged to a totality or totalities other than our own. Its accounts of the past events, natural and supernatural, to which, without differentiating at all sharply between the two types, it ascribed its present condition and faith, will have to be distanced and accepted as part of a past totality, just as much as its rituals and moral and religious beliefs, which it believed to be derived from those past events.

Of course, we may — indeed if we want to keep our integrity, we must — attempt to unravel the true course of events with all the tools and methods modern scholarship makes available. We must isolate and date sources and strata and seek to understand how all the various factors and forces, Jewish and non-Jewish, converged to produce the result they did. In the process we may hope to be illuminated and edified. For example, the present Dean of Durham, (the Very Reverend E.W. Heaton,) if I understand him correctly, finds the source of some of the most valuable later developments in what he calls the 'gritty', prophetic, moralising influence, deriving from Egypt and other non-Canaanitish sources, which helped to desacralise and moralise a religion heavily influenced by Canaanitish beliefs, and to emancipate it from trust in holy places and magic rituals.

He may well be right; but, however valuable and fruitful-for-the-future such an influence may have been, it cannot be absolutised. It too belonged to, and was conditioned by, a particular cultural totality. It cannot *be* the truth of God or the will of God for any other totality, however much it may help other totalities to see the will of God for them. We may be enlightened by it; we cannot be bound by it.

You will of course have noticed that in this lecture I have been talking almost exclusively about the Old Testament, or at least pre-Christian Judaism, and perhaps you are wanting to say: 'The New Testament writers *do* surely rest on, and bear witness to, a paradigmatic event.'

Provided the word 'event' there is given a sufficiently wide definition, the statement seems to me indisputable. In the New Testament you have a new, almost compulsive, urge to write and an upsurge of vigour, confidence and enthusiasm which contrasts pretty sharply with much of what we know of Judaism in the preceding period; you have evidence of a new quality of life and faith. This phenomenon must have been due to *some* event, and that event deserves to be called 'paradigmatic' if only because of the remarkable results it produced.

On purely historical grounds it seems to me implausible to deny that an important element in this event was the life and activity of one, Jesus, who lived in Palestine in the earlier part of the first century of our era. What is not so clear to me is just what the connexion was between the life and activity of Jesus and the result produced; and whether by now it is possible to establish the nature of the connexion.

7 The New Testament

In view of what was said in the last lecture, the general character of my uncertainty and of the grounds for it will be clear enough; but the question at issue is so important that it must be explored in at least enough detail to make clear why the argument seems to me to lead in the direction it does.

The New Testament writers are for all intents and purposes our only authorities for the events of Jesus' life and for the connexion between them and the life and faith of the early Church.[1] For all these writers the life, death and resurrection of Jesus constituted a paradigmatic event not only in the sense that it gave rise to a new understanding of the entire situation but also in the sense that it had produced an entirely new situation to be understood. It is in fact with this new situation and its understanding that the New Testament writings are chiefly concerned. They would not have been produced had it not been for an urge to spread the good news of the existence of this new situation and to make clear the right way of understanding it and reacting to it. Of course the occurrence of the events which gave rise to the new situation is everywhere *presupposed*, but the Gospels,which are the only documents in the New Testament to deal directly with them, occupy considerably less than half of the whole, and even they, as we shall see, take a basic knowledge of the events for granted* and are designed to bring out the religious significance and upshot of what Jesus was and did, rather than to give any comprehensive and connected account of the course of his life *wie es eigentlich gewesen*.

---

* For example in Mk 1 it is assumed that the identity of John the Baptizer and of the locality of 'the wilderness' will be known. Similarly in Mk 15:1 readers are assumed to know who Pilate is.

What then was the new situation and way of looking at
things which Jesus had produced and which made his life the
paradigmatic event *par excellence* the New Testament Christians took it to be? If we stand back from the traditional
christian definition and interpretation of it and allow the full
range of the New Testament accounts to make its impact on
us, we are likely to be struck by the variety and strangeness
of them.

At one level, to be sure, the element of variety is not very
obvious. The New Testament is pervaded throughout by a
mood of joyful triumph and release, release from the various
forces which had been making men's lives a misery and
separating them from God and one another. There is a feeling
that the great distance which had seemed to separate God
and men had been annihilated and, despite the writers' full
recognition of their sinfulness, they betray a sense of an
intimacy with God at least as close as any that Abraham,
Moses or the old Hebrew prophets enjoyed. God is no longer
primarily king or judge, but father.* There is everywhere a
consciousness of a spiritual presence, a presence which puts
an end to fear and loneliness and gives full confidence in the
face of all enemies, both natural and supernatural, including
death. This presence gives outward tokens of itself in various
ways; it occasionally manifests itself in exceptional ecstatic
experiences and activities, it regularly gives to anyone who
enjoys it a sense of being a new person, capable in a quite
spontaneous way of conduct which would previously have
been a great effort, if indeed it had been possible at all. 'If
any man is in Christ, he is a new creature; the old things are
passed away.' 'The fruit of the spirit is love, joy, peace,
patience, kindness, goodness, fidelity, gentleness and self-
control.' (2 Cor. 5:17; Gal. 5:22.)

However, as soon as we look closely at individual New
Testament writers and the way they articulate their feelings
and their understanding of the new situation, the elements of

* This is highly significant, even though it is impossible to go all the way with
J. Jeremias's thesis in the first chapter of his book *The Central Message of
the New Testament* (SCM, 1965).

variety and strangeness become much more apparent, and it becomes clear that the variety derives from the fact that the writers have come from a variety of backgrounds, each with its own mythology and terminology, each dominated by its distinctive religious outlook, fears and aspirations.

All the very earliest Christians came from a Jewish background of some sort and it was widely believed in certain Jewish circles at the time that God would shortly intervene dramatically, either in his own person or through some intermediary, to bring the course of world history to a close and introduce what was variously described by such titles as the 'age to come' or 'the reign of God'. By such terms was meant a blessed condition to be shared by God and his elect, from which all evil and suffering would have been banished and in which everything would have been brought eternally and unchangeably into accordance with God's will. (This is the real meaning of the phrase usually translated 'kingdom of God'. The noun is in fact a verbal noun (effective control by God) and the primary meaning is a state of affairs which would have been brought about by God and in which his will would be the sole and unhindered controlling factor. Needless to say, it would be a condition of total happiness because that was God's will for his elect. We should not interpret too literally the rather grossly materialistic symbolism by means of which this happiness was often depicted.)

That being so, it is not surprising to find many early Christians interpreting the new situation along the lines that Jesus had been the divine intermediary in question and that what he had essentially done was, if not actually to introduce the kingdom of God, to bring its arrival very close. With a degree of unanimity seldom recognised by most modern readers of the New Testament, primitive Christians believed the life of Jesus to have meant that the kingdom of God would arrive in their own lifetime or, at the latest, within that of the generation which followed. It would not be too much to say that a great many early Christians, including St Paul, lived with their

ear permanently cocked for the sound of the last trumpet.*
And, as that imagery suggests, there is no reason to suppose
that the pictures the early Christians had of the kingdom
differed in any important respects from those current in the
Jewish groups from which they came. For them the kingdom
of God signified not a further period of history, however
different from previous history, but a totally supernatural
state of affairs whose arrival would *ipso facto* mean that life
in this world as we know it had come to an end. If we are
even to begin to understand the mind of the early Christians
it is essential to recognise that in the eyes of the majority of
them, history had at most a generation and a half to run.
They believed that right from the moment of creation God
had intended history to last for only a limited, and in
practice a relatively brief, period — brief at any rate in
comparison with our calculations in terms of light years —
and for reasons known only to him, the age in which they
lived had proved the appropriate one in which to bring it to
an end.† As St Paul put it, theirs was the period in which the
ends of the ages met (1 Cor. 10:11); that is to say, 'this age'
— what we should call the course of history — was coming to
its close, and was being met at its end by the incoming
'future age' the totally new and transcendent state of affairs

---

* Cp. e.g. 1 Thess. 4:15, 1 Cor. 7:29 and 10:11, Rom. 13:11, James 5:8, 1 Pet.
  4:7; and for evidence that Jesus was believed to have predicted the nearness of
  the end Mk 9:1,for example, or 13:30. Such an attitude was quite compatible
  with taking life in the world seriously so long as it lasted. For example, Paul
  (or whoever wrote 2 Thess.) deprecated the attitude of those early Christians
  who, presumably on the ground that there was no point in providing for an
  earthly future which would never come, refused to work. See 2 Thess. 3:6—7
  and 11; the words rendered 'walking disorderly' in AV are now known to
  mean 'living without working'. Nevertheless Paul fully expected to be alive
  himself when the trumpet sounded, and the time-scale involved is important
  for the full understanding of his thought. In 1 Cor. 15:50 ff. he could even
  wrestle with the question how he and his fellow Christians who would be
  going about their ordinary business, normally clad, when the trumpet
  sounded, would be transformed into a condition suitable for entry into the
  kingdom. Obviously 'flesh and blood could not inherit the kingdom' just as
  they were! See p.29 above.

† Compare e.g. Mk 1:15a which might be paraphrased: 'the time allotted by
  God for the duration of world history is now complete and the appropriate
  moment for the introduction of the kingdom has arrived.'

which God had begun to usher in through the life and activity of Jesus.*

It hardly needs stressing that this was good news indeed to many. To the slave, for example — and many early Christians were slaves — it meant that the days of his slavery were numbered; he would soon be redeemed indeed! For the Jewish Christian it meant that the domination of his people by the hated pagans would not last much longer; to those oppressed by ills of any other kind, natural or supernatural, it meant light at the end of the tunnel. Whatever distresses the Christians suffered from, they would soon be swallowed up in what St Paul called 'an eternal glory which outweighs them far' (2 Cor. 4:17, NEB).

We must not blink the fact that the near approach of the kingdom of God in more or less the normal Jewish sense was one of the most widely pervasive elements in the various pictures the early Christians formed of the situation created by the life of Jesus; belief in it should be assumed as the constant background to all the rest of what most of them had to say. Yet even those of them who believed most vividly in it were conscious of other important elements in the situation. Jesus' life and activity had had further consequences which improved the condition of his followers in this world and ensured their having a share in the blessedness of the next. (For according to what he was believed to have taught, that blessedness would by no means be for all. Cp. e.g. Matt. 7:13–14.)

How these further beneficial results of Jesus' life were conceived by any particular group of early Christians depended once again on what the religious preoccupations, fears and aspirations of the members had been in the period before their conversion. In very many cases the chief thing had been fear of the demonic. It is almost impossible to exaggerate the extent to which people of all races in the time of Christ were hag-ridden by fear of evil spiritual powers —

---

* The (literally) interminable scholarly debate about whether Jesus' appearance on earth was thought to have ir.troduced, inaugurated or only presaged the kingdom is fortunately unimportant for our purposes, as is the question whether Paul meant in 1 Cor. 10:11 that the ends of the ages had actually overlapped. Perhaps he did; see J. Weiss's commentary *ad loc* (*Meyer Kommentar* 9 Aufl., 1910).

powers which resided in the planetary spheres, in the middle air where demons were thought to roam, and in the cities, villages and above all woods and desert places of the earth. Before their conversion many early converts had felt themselves threatened or dominated by these powers, which could not only bring illness, madness and ruin to them and their families, but could make their lives abhorrent to God and cut them off completely from him. To such converts the chief feature of the new situation was that the power of this whole demonic realm had in principle been broken, and that meanwhile in the period until the kingdom came, divine help was available to deal successfully with any attempts the demons might still be able to make to produce suffering and separation from God. In this connexion the spiritual presence of which they were so much aware was indeed a very present help in time of trouble.

To Paul on the other hand and other early Christians of his way of thinking, the situation appeared rather different. Paul had been convinced before his conversion that the only way to find acceptance with God and win admission to his kingdom when it came, was through total and willing obedience to his demands as laid down in the Jewish law (or, in the case of Gentiles, expressed through their consciences and what they knew of the law of nature). On the other hand, his own experience, and what he had observed of others, convinced the Apostle that there was that in human nature which makes such obedience impossible for any human being. Humanity, wherever it was found, was vitiated by a weakness, or rather a compulsive urge to sin, traceable to the sinfulness of Adam, which Paul, along with many other Jewish thinkers of his time, conceived as having been passed on to his descendants rather in the way that we conceive a hereditary disease as being transmitted. The result was universal disobedience to God's will; and since God was a god of justice, the inevitable consequence of that was hostility and anger on his part and refusal to admit men to his presence or kingdom.

Viewed from that point of view, the essence of the new situation was that the path to acceptance by God was no longer obedience to any law, but something well within the capacity of any human being, Jew or Gentile — namely recognition of the death of Jesus as a sacrifice which atoned for the guilt of all previous disobedience, and acceptance of the total and unconditional reconciliation with himself God was now able to offer. Meanwhile Jesus, by his perfect obedience during his earthly life, had forged a new humanity free from the weakness and sinful compulsions of the old, a humanity which turned as spontaneously to righteousness as Adamic humanity had turned to sin. After his resurrection this humanity was no longer confined to Jesus' individual person — others could be incorporated into it through faith and baptism. So long as they continued to share in it, believers found the fulfilment of God's will which had been impossibly difficult before, not only possible but spontaneous.* By Paul the spiritual presence which all early Christians experienced, and of which he was particularly vividly aware, was interpreted as communion with the risen Christ, the head or animating principle of the new body, or new humanity, the availability of which was, according to his gospel, one of the key elements in the new situation. In this sort of sense Paul could speak equally of Christians being in Christ or of Christ dwelling in them. To describe the new relationship to God Paul used the metaphor of adoption, but it scarcely sufficed to convey all he wanted to say. It was almost as if a Victorian child, condemned to a life of misery and an early death from consumption because he came of poverty-stricken and disease-ridden parents, should not only have been adopted into a rich and healthy family, with all the wealth of opportunity that implied, but should actually have been enabled to share in the inheritance of good health the natural children of his new family derived from their parents.

On such a view of the situation Jesus had inaugurated, there was clearly no logical basis for supposing that the Jew had any advantage over the Gentile, though the influence of Paul's early training was too great to allow him ever to admit

---

* In fact their conduct and outlook were Christ's own. As Paul himself put it, they 'had the mind of Christ' (1 Cor. 2:16 cp. Phil. 2:5). In practice of course their participation in it was only intermittent and needed to be renewed ever and again. Hence the frequent exhortations in Paul's epistles and elsewhere for Christians to 'become (again) what they were'.

that Jews and Gentiles were *quite* on all fours with regard to salvation.

At the opposite end of the spectrum from Paul stood a group of early Christians who not only differed from him in their interpretation of the new situation, but regarded his interpretation as positively and dangerously mistaken. (Cp. e.g. Matt. 5:19–20.) What the coming of Jesus had in fact meant, according to them, was not the abolition of the Law as a means to God's favour, but the possibility of keeping it in a new, and much more radical and all-embracing fashion. Jesus had by no means abrogated the Law; indeed he had insisted on the duty of keeping not only every jot and tittle of the Law itself, but also the scribal elaborations of it. (Cp. e.g. Matt. 5:18, 23:23 and 23:2–3.) What he had also done, however, was to set the Law in an entirely new perspective, showing that its provisions were so many indications of the true way to love God and one's neighbour. Complete love of God and the neighbour was the ultimate principle underlying the Law and hence also the key to any uncertainties to which its interpretation might give rise. (Cp. e.g. Matt. 22:34f. and especially v.40.)

Having thus by his teaching and example made clear the true bearing of the Law, Jesus had promised after his resurrection that during the short period before the parousia (i.e. the appearance of Jesus in his final glory,) he would be present with all those who were baptized into his Church; he would thus enable them to keep the Law in the way he had shown it was meant to be kept, that is, in such a way that the love which was the principle of the Law was also the principle of their lives and characters and expressed itself in their inner attitudes and impulses, as well as in their outward behaviour. (Cp. Matt. 28:19–20 and 5:21–48.) In the meantime, according to some at least who were of this way of thinking, Christians should share news of the new situation only with Jews, for whom it alone was meant; they should not 'take the road to any Gentile lands' or even approach the Samaritans. The parousia would occur before they had time to share the good news even with all their Jewish brethren. (Cp. Matt. 15:24 and 10:5–6 and 23.)

If this picture of the new situation is to be discovered

mainly in St Matthew's Gospel and the sources on which it drew, the Lucan writings (i.e. Luke's Gospel and the Acts of the Apostles) offer yet another distinctive understanding of the matter. One of the most notable features of this understanding is that it included no belief in the proximity of the parousia. More or less alone among New Testament writers Luke not merely fails to emphasize the proximity of the kingdom of God; he consciously and deliberately rejects it. Luke expected history to continue for an indefinite period; he gives no indication of the sort of time-scale he had in mind, though it is unlikely he envisaged anything approaching two thousand years! What the advent of Jesus had done, in his submission, was not to introduce the kingdom but to ensure that it would come at some stage in the future; and the exceptional circumstances surrounding the earthly ministry had given some indication of the glorious character it would have when it eventually arrived.

For such as Luke, the basic problem in the period before their conversion, so far from being a compulsive urge to flout the known will of God, had been a feeling that they did not know enough about the nature of God, or the gods, to be sure how he or they should be approached or worshipped. Jesus by his teaching and example had made plain the true way in this connexion. A great deal of his teaching about God and the way to relate to him had been given during the forty days following his resurrection, and then, at the end of that period, he had been taken up to heaven where, as Lord and Christ, he had been endowed with spiritual power which he imparted to his followers rather in the way that God had imparted supernatural power to him during his earthly life. (Cp. e.g. Lk 4:1 and 5:17, Acts 2:22.)

This power enabled those who received it to tread the true path in their dealings both with God and men; it was appropriated through repentance and baptism, and those who availed themselves of it found themselves members of a particularly close community in which they could rely on the sympathy, support and practical help of their fellow members, and also on spiritual guidance and help from God, when occasion demanded. The practice of communal prayer and the celebration of the eucharist played a large part in the mediation of the supernatural power on which the community relied. This power was referred to as the Holy Spirit, but although it was 'the spirit of Jesus' (Acts 16:7) in the sense that the exalted Jesus was the source of it, the evidence suggests that it did not carry the intense sense of personal communion with the exalted Christ which played so large a part in Paul's understanding of the new situation Jesus had created. So far from any priority being ascribed to the Jews on Luke's view, it was only as the Church turned *away* from the uncomprehending Jewish people to the Gentiles, who often proved a sympathetic audience, that it found itself and spread its message effectively. It was not without the will of God that the course of the gospel had been from the centre of the Jewish world in the temple at Jerusalem to the centre of the Gentile world in the emperor's palace at Rome.

Although the Johannine picture is different yet again, it is too subtle and complex, and also of too uncertain interpretation, to be summarised here. Fortunately, that does not matter for our purposes which do not demand an exhaustive catalogue of New Testament views. What has already been said will have been enough to make clear that different, and often formally incompatible, understandings of the situation created by Jesus were current in the New Testament period. That point is not in any case one which modern New Testament scholars would want to dispute, as is shown, for example, by the widespread approval extended to an important article by B.H. Streeter[2] in which he isolates seven main different types of understanding in the New Testament. What is more, his article fully recognises that important subvarieties were to be found in each of his seven types.[3] And it also issues an important 'warning against the error of treating the surviving literature as a representative cross-section of Christian opinion'.[4] Understandings of the situation created by the life and activity of Jesus were undoubtedly many and various in New Testament times.

The next point to be made follows almost as a logical conclusion from what has been said so far. If the New Testament writers pictured the situation created by Jesus in different ways, they likewise had different pictures of the way in which it had been created and of the status of its creator.

The extent of the variations in this matter is apt to escape our notice because all the New Testament writers drew to a greater or lesser extent on Jewish sources for their categories and images, and so used broadly the same terminology to express their ideas. From the fact that certain key terms were common to almost all of them, however, it by no means follows that they understood these terms in a single common sense. In fact that is very far from being the case.

If we are not to be misled by the linguistic facts at this point, it is important to realise that, although as we saw earlier, many Jewish groups of the period were 'living in expectation of the salvation of Israel' (Lk 2:25) there were almost innumerable variations in the way they envisaged this as coming to pass.[5] Some, as we have seen, expected God to intervene in his own person. Others, who believed he would work through an intermediary, commonly spoke of that intermediary as God's Son or as his Messiah which simply meant his duly appointed agent. (Literally the Hebrew word *messiah* and the word *Christos*, which is its Greek equivalent, mean 'one who has been anointed'. Since anointing was the means regularly used in Israel to signalise the inauguration of kings and certain other high officials, it came to mean a duly appointed person. Hence *the* Messiah meant the one duly appointed by God to carry out the definitive, eschatological, task.) Among those who used such language many expected the agent in question to be simply some outstanding human leader, whether prophet, priest or king, it being usually assumed in the last case that he would be the Son of David, that is, a man of davidic descent. Others looked rather for the appearance of a wholly supernatural figure who would already have enjoyed a long existence at God's right hand in heaven and so would enter the world already endowed with the power to fulfil his mission on the basis of his own resources. In this form of it, the messianic belief was a Jewish version of a belief widespread among many peoples at the time that the High God, being too transcendent to have direct dealings with the world, had long ago given rise, or birth, to a lesser divine being, a sort of heavenly companion or satellite, through whom the creation of the world was effected and divine relations with it were conducted.[6]

Not only had different Jews formed different pictures of God's agent, they differed in their expectations of how his work would be carried out. Some, for example, seem to have pictured it as being accomplished more or less instantaneously; others seem to have visualised a more long drawn out process, perhaps involving suffering for the Messiah and including an interim period of a thousand years or so during which he and the faithful among his contemporaries would enjoy a paradise on earth before the final end arrived. (For a Christian version of this belief in a thousand year interim period cp. e.g. Rev. 20:4–5.)

This great variety in the Jewish and pagan attitudes of the period is fully reflected in the New Testament.

To take Paul first: according to him Jesus had been Son of God in the sense of a pre-existent divine companion sent (willingly) into the world to introduce God's reign. Only if he had possessed such status, Paul felt, could his death have sufficed to atone for the whole vast range of human sin; only if he had had such an entirely superhuman character could he have forged a new humanity to take the place of that vitiated by Adam. Just how Paul thought the descent of this heavenly being correlated with Jesus' 'birth from a woman' (Gal. 4:4), he does not make clear. By the standards of modern logic his view should have demanded that the Son of God had become truly human and had died a genuine human death; but modern logic is not necessarily a safe guide to ways of thinking in so different a culture,* and although certain passages in 2 Corinthians, Philippians and Ephesians show that such questions had been given some thought in Pauline circles, they are too mythological and imprecise, and also too uncertain in meaning, to enable us to be sure that we understand the picture.†

---

* It *may* be significant, as J. Weiss, for example, thought it was, that in Romans 8:3 Jesus is thought of only as having come 'in the *likeness* of sinful flesh'.

† Cp. e.g. 2 Cor. 8:9, Phil 2:6f and Eph. 4:9. Ephesians is in the opinion of the present writer almost certainly non-Pauline and the Philippians passage is generally thought to have been derived from a pre-Pauline hymn, even if the epistle as a whole is Pauline; its meaning is obscure and the subject of much controversy.

Although Mark incorporates a story (1:9—11) which in its original form probably envisaged Jesus as having been adopted as Son of God at the time of his baptism, the Evangelist himself seems to have held a view similar to Paul's. He regarded Jesus as a pre-existent Son of God who had made his entry into this world in some undisclosed way, though for Mark it was not so much for the validity of his sacrifice that Jesus' supernatural status had to be posited — Mark does not lay much emphasis on Jesus' death as a sacrifice — as in order to enable him to initiate God's final victory over the demonic forces. As we have already seen, it had required all God's power at the beginning to overcome these forces sufficiently to carry through the work of creation. No one could have accomplished, or even begun to accomplish, their *final* overthrow, as Jesus had done in Mark's view, unless he had enjoyed at least the status and resources of a pre-existent Son of God.

The evidence of the Lucan writings is harder to assess in this connexion because Luke, like Matthew (and Mark; see above), was content to incorporate sources whose views differed from one another's and also from his own. Thus it appears from the birth narratives both in Matthew and Luke that Jesus was believed by their authors to have been Messiah and Son of God not in the sense that he had pre-existed his earthly birth, but in the sense that God's spirit was jointly responsible with a human being for his birth. Jesus was, so to say, human on his mother's side and divine on his father's; it was in that sense that he could be thought of as Son of God and Messiah.* Not only do Matthew and Luke thus appear to know nothing of any pre-existent Son; with that disregard for consistency in their legitimating stories which we saw in the Introduction to be characteristic of primitive cultures, they have no hesitation about including in their Gospels passages which show no sign of regarding Jesus as divine even in the sense implied in the stories of the

---

* Cp. e.g. Lk 1:35. The NEB rendering suggests the right emphasis: the Holy Spirit will come upon you; and *for that reason* the holy child to be born will be called 'Son of God'. (italics mine to bring out the intended meaning).

virgin-birth. For example, they both include in close proximity to their virgin-birth stories accounts of Jesus' ancestry,
designed to prove his davidic descent, in which the whole
case depends on his having had a normal human father in the
person of Joseph. (It is true that Luke adds 'being, as was
supposed, the son of Joseph' (3:23), but unless he was *rightly*
supposed to be such, the genealogy would prove nothing. The
innumerable ingenious attempts of commentators to circumvent this truth leave it uncircumventable.) According to the
view presupposed in these passages, Jesus was presumably
Messiah in the sense of an earthly leader descended from the
line of David.

It is therefore the more noteworthy that elsewhere in his
work Luke reproduces, and perhaps sympathizes with,
sources which portray Jesus as having in his earthly life been
straightforwardly a man; not of course just any man, but a
man specially raised up by God and endowed as occasion
required with supernatural power to teach the true way and
to 'go about doing good and healing all who were oppressed
by the devil'. (Cp. e.g. Acts 2:22 and 10:38, and Luke 4:1
and 5:17.) This he was able to do, according to Luke, not in
virtue of any inherent powers he possessed as a pre-existent
supernatural being, but because 'God was with him', and it is
interesting to notice how in Luke's gospel Jesus constantly
needs to pray (presumably for the divine assistance his work
required). According to this understanding of the matter —
and there is evidence for it elsewhere in the New Testament[7]
— it was only after his resurrection when Jesus was taken up
into heaven, that 'God made him both Lord and Messiah'
(Acts 2:36; contrast John 17:5) and endowed him with the
power to inspire his followers and weld them into the Church
(cf. Acts 2:33).

Such an understanding of Jesus would have occasioned no
difficulty for Luke since, unlike Paul, he does not seem to
have regarded the human situation before the coming of
Jesus as needing an atoning sacrifice, and he certainly did not
regard the death of Jesus as such a sacrifice. He once
described Paul as thinking of it in that way — though not,
incidentally, in terms which Paul himself would have used
(Acts 2:20, 38, cp. also 13:39). But not only does he himself

never use sacrificial language in relation to Jesus' death, he deliberately strikes out from his sources any sacrificial interpretations of the death of Jesus which they contained – even those which they attributed to Jesus himself. (Cp. e.g. Mk 10:45 with Lk 22:27 and Mk 14:23–4 with Lk 22:19; vv 19b and 20 in the older English translations are widely held by scholars to be a later addition; so e.g. NEB.) In view of his normally tolerant attitude to divergent views in his sources, that shows how strongly he felt on this matter. Luke is described by Dante as *scriba mansuetudinis Christi*[8] and certainly he seems to have believed in the kindness of God and not to have shared Paul's pre-conversion nightmare of God as being, apart from the sacrifice of Christ, a god of wrath implacably hostile to sinful man.

At the opposite pole from Luke in regard to our question stands John. For him it is of the very essence of the Christian matter that Jesus should not only have pre-existed, but should have enjoyed in his pre-existence a relationship of total harmony with his divine father. For on John's showing, a primary part of what Jesus did during his ministry was to reproduce under the conditions of human existence – what John calls 'flesh' – the perfect relationship which he had enjoyed with God 'since before the world began'. In order to reproduce this relationship, thus revealing it to others and making possible their participation in it and the eternal character of it, Jesus needed not only to have had such a relationship but to have *remembered* it and its character during his earthly life. In fact the Jesus of St John consciously carries on through his earthly life the relationship with God he remembers having had before he was born, and expects to resume after he has laid down his earthly life (17:5). He is thus conscious that his earthly life is but an interlude in a much longer, if not eternal, supernatural existence.

Whether one who enjoyed that sort of consciousness can be said to have been fully or genuinely human is a moot point. (It becomes particularly dubious in connexion with such a passage as Jesus' reference to his own death and resurrection at 10:18.) If it was not one which greatly troubled John, that would not be surprising, for the genuineness of Jesus' humanity was something about which many early Christians were much less concerned than later churchmen were to be. B.H. Streeter, for example, points out that 'strange as it may seem to a modern mind, the reality of Christ's humanity and of his suffering was flatly denied by many [primitive] Christians'.[9] Nor does it make much difference in this connexion whether John thought he was giving an accurate historical picture of Jesus' earthly life or simply bringing out in historical form what the supernatural realities of the situation had in fact been.[10] In either event he was clearly convinced that Jesus had been a pre-existent supernatural being — indeed in some sense a divine being — living for a period under the conditions of human existence. Unless he had been that, he could not have achieved what John believed he had achieved.

A recognition of what he had been was thus necessary for understanding what he had achieved and the situation he had produced; and it is for that reason that John prefaced his gospel with a prologue which explicitly asserted and defined Jesus' supernatural existence before his appearance in the world. This prologue (1:1–18) appears to be a reworked version of an already existing hymn or poetic composition of some sort. Perhaps for that reason, its language is elusive and highly symbolic, and despite the concentrated labours of innumerable scholars, there is still nothing like a consensus about what exactly John meant to convey. Since we cannot be exactly sure either of John's background of ideas or of that of the original authors of the hymn,* we do not know precisely what he, or they, meant by asserting Jesus to have been the *logos*, that is, the reason, mind or word of God; nor can we be sure of the precise nuance intended when this *logos* is described as being something between *theios*, which would have meant divine in quality but not actually God, and *ho theos* which would have meant God himself. Nor is it clear what the *arche*, or, 'beginning', is which is referred to in verse one. However, the general drift is fairly clear. Whatever the exact background of the thought here may have been, it will surely have been some version of the idea referred to above

---

* These backgrounds may not by any means have been the same; Bultmann even suggests that the original hymn was of non-Christian origin.

(see pp. 149–50) that God had a heavenly companion or satellite; and John's belief is that Jesus was this companion come to earth. He also clearly thought that this companion was identical in moral character, and very close in status, to God, though it is highly unlikely that he envisaged him as identical with God, that is *Yahweh,* himself.

How does this excursion into biblical criticism, with its strong emphasis on the variety of New Testament thought, fit into the general course of our argument? It will be remembered that in this section of the lectures we are discussing the suggestion that the right way to approach the Bible in the modern world is by using the methods of historical criticism to uncover the historical realities behind the biblical accounts of the 'mighty acts of God' and then responding to those realities in the ways appropriate to our cultural totality. So far as the Old Testament is concerned, we have already seen that that is easier said than done. In the light of what has been said so far in this lecture, what is the position with regard to the New Testament?

Perhaps we may put it like this. Suppose that a modern field anthropologist could be provided with a magic carpet which would enable him to get back to the Mediterranean world in the second half of the first century of our era. He would find scattered across the eastern half of that world small communities of religious believers distinguished to a greater or less degree from their neighbours, both Jew and Gentile, by their peculiar religious beliefs, by their distinctive moral ideals – and to some extent conduct – and by the intimacy and confidence of their relation to the single god they worshipped. These people would be fairly bursting with assurance and hope in a world for the most part conspicuously afflicted by feelings of fear, bewilderment and something approaching despair.

Although there was no single designation by which all the members of these groups were known either among themselves or to the rest of the world, and no uniformity of practice or ritual among them, our anthropologist would have no hesitation in classifying them together. They all attributed the origin of their peculiar beliefs and relationship with God

to a Jewish figure called Joshua or, if they used the Greek
form, Jesus; according to their account, he had carried on an
itinerant ministry in Palestine in the first half of the century
and had been put to death by crucifixion at the orders of
Pontius Pilate, Roman procurator of Judaea from AD 26–36;
but he was now in some sense – and the sense would vary
somewhat from group to group – alive from the dead.

If our anthropologist decided to make a study of these
believers, he would soon find himself reporting that their
beliefs and practices varied quite considerably from group to
group, but it would prove possible without doing any serious
injustice to the facts, to classify the groups into certain broad
categories. As a base line for his classification the anthropologist would probably take certain strands in the beliefs of
contemporary Judaism because the groups he was studying
all acknowledged the authority of the Jewish Bible, recognised its god as their god and took over a view of the course
of world history basically derived from it. This the anthropologist might diagrammatize as follows (see also p. 78
above under (b) for the meaning of some of the conventions
used in the diagrams):

The top parallel line would represent the existence of the
heavenly world which has no beginning or end, and the
bottom line would represent the life of this world which, in
contrast to the life of heaven, has a very definite beginning
and end, the downward line A–B symbolising the particular
moment, in principle datable, when history came into
existence as the result of a specific initiative on the part of
God. From the beginning God had a purpose for history and
a goal towards which he kept it moving by constant
interventions (the dotted lines) until, when the appropriate
moment arrived, he would intervene decisively once again,
either in person or through some intermediary (O–P) to
bring history to a close and to transform it into, or replace it
by, a new, and, according to many, timeless and wholly

supernatural, state of affairs represented in the diagram by the bold hatched band.

The anthropologist would find that the beliefs of all the Christian groups were variants, more or less radical, of this general picture. He might divide the groups broadly into two classes according as they did, or did not, believe that the appearance of Jesus had inaugurated, or at least brought very near, the point P. At any rate up to about AD 100 the great majority would fall into the former class. Divergences within this class (A) might be diagrammatized as follows:

A(*i*) Those who believed that Jesus had been simply a man 'raised up' by God rather in the way that prophets and kings in the Old Testament had been 'raised up', and then after his death taken up to heaven to be invested with the necessary power to introduce the kingdom of God in its fulness.

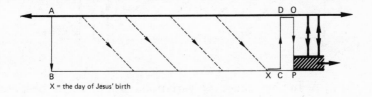

X = the day of Jesus' birth

X = the day of Jesus' birth

There may also have been some who thought of Jesus as only the herald of the kingdom and believed that it would actually be introduced by a wholly supernatural figure known as the Son of Man and quite distinct from Jesus.

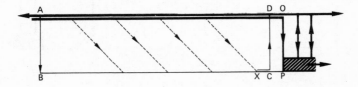

A(*ii*) Others who took a broadly similar view would, however, believe that the 'raising up' of Jesus had involved his being the product of a mixed divine and human conception;

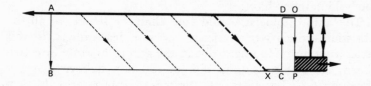

A(*iii*) Others would believe that Jesus' existence had not originated with his earthly birth but that he was a pre-existent supernatural figure of some sort (in some groups perhaps thought of as an angel) who had entered the world from above at point X;

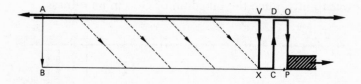

A(*iv*) A further range of variations would occur because some groups, while holding one or other of these views up to the point O expected that what would be inaugurated at O–P would not be the kingdom of God in its fulness, but an interim period of relative bliss shared by Christ and some of his elect for a thousand years;

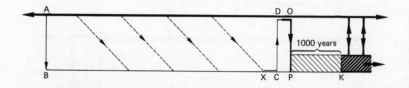

(The parousia (P) and the full arrival of the kingdom (K) would be clearly distinguished on this view.)

Christians of all these groups might well be a little puzzled why P had not ensued immediately on C; they would in any case regard the period C–P in which they were living as

essentially a short interim period. (The diagrams make clear
that the periods XC and CP were expected to be of *roughly*
equal length. Any attempt at precision was felt to be both
futile and presumptuous, cp. Mk. 13:32, noting, however,
that the Evangelist clearly envisaged definite parameters to
the area of uncertainty. 13:32 should not be taken as
implying any doubt about the *general* length of C–P. Cp. e.g.
9:1 and 13:30, 'the present generation will live to see it all'
NEB.) As a result, they might well feel that it was not worth
entering on marriage and parenthood (1 Cor. 7) or even, as
we have seen, carrying on with their jobs.

For all these Christians the imminence of the coming of
the kingdom was good news because they confidently
expected to be (among the relative minority of human
beings) admitted to it. Meanwhile during the short period
before its arrival, religious attitudes and orientation varied
somewhat from group to group. Some groups took relatively
little interest in the details of the period X–C apart from
their belief that during it Jesus had maintained unbroken
obedience to God so that his freely accepted death could be a
satisfaction for sin and his life the basis of a new humanity,
free from the compulsive influence of the evil powers. That
apart, their orientation was upward rather than backward.
They sought to live as members incorporate in the body of
their exalted lord and looked up (rather than back) to him
for the guidance and strength for which their Gentile
neighbours looked from the 'lords many and gods many' of
contemporary cults. Being 'in Christ' meant sharing his
'mind', made clear to them either by direct illumination or
through selective and meditative study of the Old Testament;
on the other hand they were quite clear that admission to the
kingdom would be entirely a matter of divine generosity
made possible by the obedience and death of Jesus, and in no
sense dependent on observance of the law or any other moral
achievement on their part. Life in Christ also brought a share
in the moral strength by which Christ had been able to
maintain obedience. It also meant for some the ability to
work miracles, and for all endowment with the appropriate
bodily form in which to take their place in the kingdom,
when the time came. It was characteristic of members of this

group that they enjoyed an experience which they interpreted as personal communion with their exalted lord, as
close — if not closer — than his followers had had with him in
the days of his flesh.

For others the whole of Jesus' activity from X through C
and D to O, or at any rate the whole of it after his baptism,
was interpreted as the final struggle by God's champion
against the forces of evil. This struggle was proving pro-
gressively successful and it was the final phase of it (which
would be achieved at O–P) which would make possible the
establishment of the kingdom. Meanwhile those who wished
to share the kingdom with Christ after P should share his
struggle aginst the evil forces during C–P and could rely on
being given the power to do so effectively. In order to
appreciate fully what this meant, a knowledge of Jesus'
activity and that of his disciples during X–C was of great
practical importance. These groups searched the past in some
detail, as well as looking upwards and forwards.

Still other groups paid even more attention to the details
of X–C; for them entry into the kingdom entailed observance of the Old Testament Law as interpreted by Jesus
through his words and behaviour during that period. However, they too looked upward, for they were sure the exalted
Lord would be with them as they sought to 'observe all that
he had commanded them'; but there is no evidence that they
interpreted his presence in terms of the close personal
intimacy the first group believed themselves to enjoy.

No doubt our anthropologist would classify and sub-
classify in much greater detail, but these examples must
suffice so far as this category (A) is concerned. As time wore
on, the anthropologist and his successors would find more
and more groups belonging to the second category (B), those
who did not associate the ministry of Jesus in any immediate
way with the coming of the kingdom. Of their beliefs we
have room for only two examples:

B(*i*) There were some who saw the essential significance of
Jesus in his having taught 'the way of (pleasing) God' and
established a community in which means of grace would be
available to ensure forgiveness of sins and ability to follow
the true way gladly.

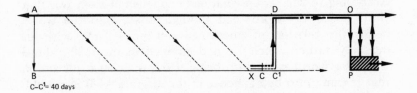

C–C¹= 40 days

These Christians did not emphasize the importance of C (the death of Jesus) quite in the way others did, and did not interpret it in sacrificial terms at all. On the other hand they laid great weight on the forty days between C and C^1 during which Jesus had taught the true way in detail, and on the ascension $C^1 - D$, which was apparently unknown to other groups as a phenomenon distinct from the resurrection. For these groups, however, it was of central importance as being the moment when Jesus was exalted to God's right hand and received the special power which he was thenceforth able to pour out on his followers. Although Christians of these groups were deeply aware of the spirit or power which they received from Jesus, and of their dependence on it, they appear to have conceived it along the rather impersonal lines on which pre-Christian Jews had thought of the spirit of God, and not in terms of personal communion with Jesus. (Contrast Lk. 24:44 with Matt. 28:20, noting that for Luke the personal presence of Jesus is something which belongs to the past.)

B(*ii*) The second group to be mentioned under this category had a very different picture which is not easy to diagrammatize. The anthropologist might attempt it somewhat as follows:

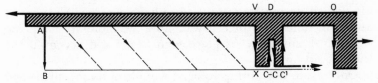

The opening C–C is meant to represent what happened to Jesus at his resurrection, as distinct from his ascension. Contrast John 20:17 and 20:2*f*, and see the commentaries <u>ad loc</u>. For O–P see e.g. Jn 6:44 and 1 Jn 3:2

According to this group what had happened at V—X was that God's *logos* or 'word' had brought down into the world below the relation of obedience and mutual love with his heavenly father which he had enjoyed in the realm above since the world came into being. (It was through his action that it came into being; hence in the diagram A—B is in bold. It should *possibly* be bold in some of the earlier diagrams as well. Note also that on this view Jesus' 'ascension' and his return took place within a very short time of one another; contrast Jn 20:17 and 20:19ff. the dotted lines are also in bold to show that God's providential guidance of the world before Christ was also exercised through the *logos* on this view.) It cost him dearly to maintain this relationship in its completeness under all the sinful urges to which life in the flesh is liable, but he had triumphantly succeeded, and as a consequence, those who recognised his true identity and the nature of his mission could be incorporated into the life he shared with the Father and partake its qualities of holiness and eternity. For those who had thus entered on 'eternal life' judgement was already a thing of the past and the moment of their own death or of the parousia was of *relatively* minor importance. It was true that the eventual character of their destiny was not yet fully clear although they were assured of it (1 John 3:2); but they were already sons of God and their eventual destiny would be no more than a full flowering of the eternal life they already shared in a form appropriate to this world. For different Christians in this group different meanings attached to the death of Jesus, but its central significance for them all was that it meant his becoming universally available. Through it he was released from the local and temporal limitations of life in the flesh; and the possiblity of sharing in his eternal life, which during his ministry had been confined to those of his own time and place, was now available to men and women of any time or place who heard and accepted the truth about him.

Once again our anthropologist would no doubt divide and sub-divide this class of believers further, but perhaps enough has been said to make clear what sort of overall interpretation he would be likely to offer. He would point out that corresponding to the various pictures he found in the different communities there were different practices and attitudes, for example different attitudes to the physical world. He would also report that, while more than one of the interpretations just described might be found side by side in a single community, there was a clear awareness on the part of the communities themselves that some of the interpretations were incompatible with others and that long and bitter controversies sometimes arose between them about which was the true one. There could be no question of treating these interpretations as simply complementary to one another and capable of being harmonized into a single coherent picture which could then be labelled 'the primitive Christian faith'. Christ's pre-existence, for example, is not an 'aspect' of someone who according to Matthew and Luke, or at any rate most of their sources, had no existence at all before his birth from Mary!

Another point the anthropologist would emphasize would be the mythological character of all the interpretations he encountered. The categories employed could sometimes be fairly closely paralleled in the writings of other religions of the same period or the same stage of cultural development, but they presupposed many doctrines which cannot be 'felt as facts' today. None of us, for example, takes first-century Judaism and its apocalyptic expectations as the base line from which we start in attempting to envisage God and his dealings with the world; and therefore we cannot adopt terms such as Christ, Son of Man or Son of God, at any rate in anything like their original meanings.

Still more significantly from the point of view of our argument, the anthropologist would insist that while the event which gave rise to all these communities must have been a very remarkable one — at any rate by the standards of the day — in order to account for their courage and confidence and sense of intimate union with God, it could not have been self-interpreting.

To put it in Van Harvey's terms, it was paradigmatic in the sense that it 'had captured the imaginations' of all these loosely unified communities and 'altered their way of looking at the totality of their experience; it struck them as illuminating for understanding all other events, it intruded certain questions and images upon them and seemed to touch their experience at a primordial level'; but, at any rate in the short run, it emphatically did *not* 'impose its own categories of interpretation' (see pp. 119–20 above). Jesus, assuming him to have been at the heart of the event, cannot have given any clear and precise account or interpretation of himself. In particular, he cannot have thought and taught about himself what later orthodoxy attributed to him. If he had, the wide variety of views about his origins, nature and work among his devoted early followers would be quite beyond explanation.

What then was the original character of the event the early Christians so variously interpreted? There can be no doubt how a modern anthropologist would respond to such a question. Being historically trained, he would try to use the historical methods familiar to him to get behind the various pictures to his own understanding of the event which they were all attempts to portray. Probably he would begin by examining such biographical material about Jesus as the various communities possessed. If so, he would soon find that, though fairly extensive in quantity, it was of only limited help to him. None of the communities would have preserved a comprehensive or consecutive account of Jesus' life, either oral or written. What each would possess would be a series of separate little stories, each one recounting a single incident or saying, and each proving on examination to be what was described in our first chapter as an aetiological story. It has been one of the contributions of form-criticism to enable us to see that these stories were preserved, mainly in the context of the liturgical, catechetical and evangelistic gatherings of the primitive communities, precisely as 'legitimations' of the beliefs and practices of those communities. If so, they would obviously be recounted in a form consistent with the beliefs and practices they were intended to legitimate. The historical Jesus 'remembered' in each community would be a Jesus who fitted in to the picture of Christian origins current in that particular community; and since those pictures varied and conflicted with one another, so would the corresponding 'memories' of Jesus. (If, when expressed in that concise form, our account appears cynical or seems to cast doubt on the honesty of the early Christians, the reader is asked to recall what was said in Chapter 1 and Chapter 6 about attitudes to the past in earlier societies; all we are in fact claiming is that Christians of the New Testament period were precisely people of that period; it is no sin to have been born before the emergence of modern historical methods and standards!) Our anthropologist's only recourse would be to seek out and interrogate survivors with personal memories of Jesus, or second-generation Christians who had known such survivors.

At that point we must part company with him, for we have no such recourse. All that remains to us are written versions of some of the aetiological stories current in the primitive communities, and we have already seen how easily in the ancient world story could modify history, especially when history was taken up into the context of an ancient religious story, as it was in the case of Jesus.

It is true that by comparing and contrasting stories from different communities we can to some extent discover, and allow for, legitimating modifications.[11] But the process will only take us a certain way and is in any case a highly speculative and subjective one. The plain fact is that no picture of the historical Jesus has yet emerged − or ever seems likely to − which comes anywhere near commanding universal, or even general, agreement. The point deserves taking a little further, if only because there are few points on which there is at present a wider gap between the study and the pew.

In one of the most important theological books of modern times Albert Schweitzer catalogued and discussed literally hundreds of attempts made in France and Germany in the last century and the earlier part of this, to reconstruct the figure of Jesus on the basis of modern historical methods. Even if we discount many of these as being unacceptably eccentric or ideologically biassed, we have to recognise that the others, produced by judicious scholars on the basis of sound methods, diverge so widely as to establish a strong presumption that what their authors were attempting to do was something the evidence does not make possible; and the progress of more recent New Testament scholarship has done nothing to alter the situation materially. Here again we may, with the majority of scholars, set aside certain views as implausible and unsoundly based, for example the views of G.A. Wells, who, as we have seen, argued in 1971 that Jesus never existed, or of S.G.F. Brandon who claimed in 1967 that he was an active member of the fanatical Zealot party.[12] Nevertheless we still have to recognise that writers whose learning and scholarship cannot be impugned diverge very widely. There is general agreement that in the first half-century of our era a Jewish figure called Jesus (hebrew, Joshua) travelled round Palestine teaching, partly in parables, and performing what he and his contemporaries regarded as exorcisms and other miracles; that he was delated by the Jewish authorities to the procurator and condemned by him to be crucified. When we come to the theologically significant questions, however, whether, for example, Jesus believed or claimed he was messiah or Son of God; whether he foresaw or provoked his death or attributed any theological significance to it; whether he regarded his activity as relating to the imminent end of the world, and if so, in what way; what precisely happened in the few days after his death, sober scholars diverge widely.

Some, for example Professors J. Jeremias and C.F.D. Moule, argue that Jesus was very like what the traditional picture suggests; others believe that he made no metaphysical claims of any kind for himself and was neither a prophet nor a teacher of wisdom but a man 'who dared to act in God's stead'.[13] Bultmann believes him to have been an ordained rabbi who called men to authentic existence in the sense of a life lived entirely 'out of the future', that is, out of God's resources, while most recently Dr Geza Vermes has also placed him firmly within the normal categories of contemporary Judaism: 'Jesus', he says, 'is to be seen as part of first-century charismatic Judaism, and as the paramount example of the early Hasidim or Devout.'[14] Yet other considerable scholars have suggested that though Jesus existed surely enough, he did not feel very sure or very strongly about his precise function or relation to God and set before himself no clearly defined function or programme.[15]

There can be no question here of attempting to adjudicate

between these various views; the point is to establish that widely divergent and incompatible views are held by writers who simply cannot be dismissed as 'wild' or unscholarly. It is true that the presuppositions which lie behind their respective views can often be pinpointed, but since none of these presuppositions is manifestly untenable and in almost all cases they are combined with a lively Christian faith, isolating them gets us no nearer the resolution of the matter, unless of course we are prepared to beg the question completely and decide to outlaw all presuppositions except those which result in the reconstruction we favour.

Needless to say, none of that prevents us from persisting in attempts to discover the historical facts, or indeed exonerates us from the duty of doing so. Anyone who is familiar with the material will rightly have formed his own conclusions about what really took place and what Jesus was really like. But if he feels inclined to insist that Christianity today means reacting to the life of Jesus as he pictures it, the recollection that others at least as able and well-informed as he is picture it very differently should surely be enough to make him realise that it could only be intellectual arrogance to raise his particular reconstruction to the level of the absolute and insist on acceptance of it as a condition of salvation.

To nothing does this apply more than to the resurrection, and in no area is it more frustrating. For to the early Christians the resurrection of Jesus was vital. Their assessments of Jesus did not rest entirely on his words and deeds in the days of his flesh. They rested at least as much, if not more, on the fact, or alleged fact, of his resurrection. Yet in what they have to say about Jesus' resurrection the New Testament writers are more divergent than on almost any other subject. The gospel narratives, which up to that point have been in at any rate relative accord, diverge sharply when they come to the resurrection. Apart from the fact that all New Testament writers believed firmly in the resurrection of Jesus, there is almost no firm ground in this area. Was the resurrection distinct from the ascension? Did it involve an empty tomb?[16] Did belief in the resurrection depend on Jesus' having 'appeared' to various people; and if so, what was the character of these appearances, to whom were they made, and what is the significance of the fact that, as reported, they were exclusively confined to people who were already disciples? Was Jesus subject to the normal physical limitations of bodily life during these appearances? To all these questions different New Testament writers return confident but incompatible answers. It is not even at all clear that they understood resurrection in the same sense.

In the face of all this, with how much confidence can a modern Christian hope to discover what the historical truth behind the New Testament narratives and references was and what the modern response to it should be? We have seen that a modern medical man might want to offer his own account of what were diagnosed in the New Testament as cases of demon-possession. Surely no modern medical man would be likely to offer any account at all, either natural or miraculous, of what happened to Jesus after his death on the basis of the inexact, fragmentary and conflicting evidence afforded by the New Testament. Once again, we must be clearly aware of all that is involved before we make it a condition of other people's salvation that they should accept *our* particular interpretation of the evidence.

These brief and inevitably controversial and ill-documented remarks will have served their purpose if they have made clear the general lines along which I should have wished, had time allowed, to mount a detailed argument for the view that any attempt to reconstruct the events of Jesus' life, death and resurrection with sufficient accuracy and detail to make them the direct object of contemporary faith is doomed to failure. In view of what has been repeatedly said before, however, I hope it will be unmistakably clear that that does not commit me either:

(*a*) to doubting that contemporary Christians have limitless truth to glean from the Gospels, or

(*b*) to believing that all reconstructions of the life and activity of Jesus are equally implausible — or plausible.

In fact I have my own fairly definite ideas and should be prepared to defend them on the evidence as I understand it; the point is that I recognise the existence of considerable areas where the evidence does not warrant any definite conclusions; and even where in my opinion it does, I recognise their relatively fragile basis and hence their inevitably controversial character.

Thus one of the cardinal differences between us and our Christian predecessors of earlier centuries is that whereas they could with integrity accept the New Testament narratives as sacred tradition and, as such, accurate in every particular, we can only regard them as raw material for investigation, material to be 'tortured', in part rejected, and used as the basis of the best reconstruction we can produce. What is more, the nature of this material and the gaps in it are such as to ensure that, unless a great deal of further evidence is discovered to supplement it — a most unlikely contingency — it will continue to give rise to a wide variety of interpretations. All but the smallest minority of modern readers would agree that in the New Testament, as in the Old Testament and various medieval documents, 'theories of the present were', to some extent, 'represented as the facts of the past'; and since there is no way of determining indisputably what that extent is, there is no chance of arriving at anything approaching unanimous agreement about exactly what happened. To construct an understanding of Christianity which presupposes that apart from a few 'extremists' such agreement already exists, or even that it is just round the corner, is simply to build on sand.

It is for this sort of reason that the American scholar Dr John Knox has long argued that if we want any certain event or occurrence as a starting-point for our understanding of Christianity, it can only be the whole event of Christ, by which he means the original events of the life, death and resurrection of Jesus, whatever they may have been, together with the known reactions to them of those who witnessed them, and the attitudes, actions and relationships into which they were led or driven as a consequence. For the Christ-event understood in this sense as a complex comprehensive occurrence, which includes all the excited reactions and speculations set up by the life of Jesus in the apostolic church, we have irrefutable evidence. For if there is one thing the facts do not allow us to doubt, it is that the New

Testament writings date from roughly the period to which they are traditionally ascribed. The Tübingen scholars of the last century, who dated a number of the New Testament books to the second century, may have had more to be said for them than has sometimes been recognised; but even if so, the latest New Testament book can hardly date from after about AD 160, the most probable date for the appearance of 2 Peter.

The wider implications of all this will be discussed later, but one matter will best be dealt with here in anticipation of that discussion. What has been said so far in this lecture is more or less certain to meet with an objection along the following lines: Your problem largely arises, it will be said, because you are working with too short a time-scale. In the long run the Christ-event *did* 'impose its own interpretation', (p.120) that expressed in the classic creeds and formularies of orthodoxy. An event as momentous and utterly unlooked for as the incarnation of the second person of the Trinity was bound to take time to assimilate. It is true that the New Testament writers differ considerably in their interpretations of it, but that is only because they were all groping, with varying degrees of insight and success, after the interpretation eventually arrived at by the Fathers and later Christian theologians.

The positive position implied in this objection is one taken by many modern theologians (see e.g. the quotation on p. 175 below), and it operates with a perfectly clear and unexceptionable model. It is quite common for an event to occur of which the significance is discerned only dimly, if at all, in the period immediately following, but becomes apparent later. Indeed it is rarely, if ever, that an event important enough to get into the history books does *not* need to have its meaning reappraised as time goes on. The question is whether the model, acceptable enough in itself, is an appropriate or illuminating one in the present context.

Before we agree that it is we must be clear what that would imply; in particular three matters must be considered. First we must be clear that if the model is used in this connexion, it is being used in a highly analogical way.

Normally the sort of reappraisal envisaged is demanded and made in the light of further *historical* developments. If an event turns out to have repercussions on the subsequent course of history which were not foreseen at first but later become plain for all to see, some measure of reinterpretation simply imposes itself. Thus, for example, Europeans alive in 1939 were bound to feel that the war of 1914–18 had had implications which their predecessors in 1920 had failed to appreciate. In the case we are considering, however, what is in question is the developing interpretation of an event in *supernatural* terms, and that clearly raises issues of a very different kind. What sort of thing, for example, would be needed to convince us that a previous interpretation of an event in *supernatural* terms was inadequate and needed modification or development? Secondly, the Fathers did not think of themselves as having independent access to the events of Jesus' life in the light of which the New Testament interpretations could be seen to be inadequate or inaccurate and in need of replacement. On the contrary, they not only accepted the New Testament interpretations *in toto*, but regarded them as directly God-given and therefore as being not so much interpretations as wholly accurate descriptions of a divine-human event. What they said in effect, though they did not consciously formulate it in this way, was: if the divine-human event A occurred, then (given our pre-suppositions) B C D . . . must also be true although they are not explicitly recognised or mentioned in the New Testament.

This places us in a double difficulty. If we are compelled to take a different view of the New Testament interpretations and to regard them as incapable of complete harmonization, and as culturally conditioned in a way which makes it impossible for us to accept them as they stand, then we do not start from the same premises as the Fathers; and even if we did, we should not argue from them on the basis of the presuppositions which the Fathers took for granted, the doctrines which they 'felt as facts'.

Thirdly, the situation which the employment of this model naturally conjures up is one in which every generation to the end of time is regarded as free to modify or discard the interpretations of its predecessors. In the case of ordinary historical events we often come to the conclusion that our predecessors overestimated or underestimated the significance of a particular incident, or that they understood its significance in the wrong way, that is, in a way no longer possible for us. What we never do in such a context is to treat the interpretation of an incident arrived at in some earlier period as definitive and authoritative in the sense that all subsequent interpretations must take it as an unquestionable datum. In view of what has been said earlier about cultural change, such an attitude would be not merely unacceptable, but virtually unintelligible.

Yet something of that sort is precisely what we are being asked to do here, and we must recognise that we can do it only if we accord something approaching an absolute status not only to the interpretations of the Fathers but to the cultural categories in which they were expressed. The doctrine of the incarnation of the Son of God, for example, demands a substance philosophy of the later hellenistic type if it is to make sense, or at any rate the sense it has traditionally been taken to have. If it is true that an interpretation arrived at in terms of those categories is *the* interpretation, that can only mean that the cultural background of the hellenistic world had a privileged status of some sort. An interpretation arrived at in terms of its assumptions is valid in a way that one arrived at on the basis of other cultural assumptions (including our own) would not be; what seemed plausible to that culture is plausible *tout court*.

The recognition of this truth is nothing new; on the contrary, the recognition of it is precisely what has lain behind the efforts of scholars like Dr Austin Farrer to vindicate for a substance philosophy such as classical theologians presupposed, permanent intelligibility and validity. This is no place to adjudicate on the success or otherwise of such efforts; our concern, as was stated in the Introduction, is simply to uncover the further beliefs to which various attitudes to the Bible commit those who adopt them. It is for them to decide whether those further beliefs are acceptable.

In order to avoid any doubt what those further beliefs are

in the present connexion, it may be well to add one further point. The position we are now discussing would appear to make those who framed the classical Christian doctrines the ultimate authority in relation to Christian belief. For it accords to interpretations in their categories superiority over interpretations couched in any other, including those of the New Testament writers themselves, (though of course it would still be true that the interpretations of the New Testament writers were the basis of the later true interpretation. In that sense they would retain their pre-eminence). Indeed in that sense it would make them superior to Jesus himself; for, as we have already seen, if Jesus had clearly taught, or even himself entertained, the interpretation of his person and work attributed to him by later orthodoxy, the variety of interpretation in New Testament times would be totally inexplicable. Thus, although, according to this view, a permanently valid interpretation of Jesus' person and work has been able to emerge in history, it emerged not directly from Jesus himself but from fourth and fifth century theologians working on the tradition about him. Traditional orthodoxy itself of course believed its own interpretation to have been that of Jesus himself; but in that it was manifestly in error.

8 History and story

The question how we should respond to the situation as analysed in the last two lectures brings us to the heart of the matter. Two types of response are possible and on our choice will depend, I believe, not only our understanding of the Bible and its relation to the Christian faith, but our understanding of the nature of Christian faith itself.

One response is to take the view that, at any rate so far as the Christ-event is concerned, the biblical writers were correct in seeing it as constituting a divine intervention of a unique and decisive kind. The very vigour with which New Testament writers of very different sorts responded to it, and the uprush of literary and other activity it occasioned, are evidence of some quite exceptional occurrence; and the unanimity with which early Christians of very varied outlooks speak of it as a unique divine intervention is at least strong presumptive evidence that they are right.

Admittedly, their versions and interpretations vary, and on occasion their evidence agreeth not together; and what they say is often mythical and impossible for us to accept as it stands. The assumption that this last is true lay, of course, behind a good deal of the last lecture. In fact it may be true on a wider scale than will at first appear to many readers. For if they have been brought up to practise the Christian religion and to regard acceptance of New Testament categories as part of what that involves, sheer familiarity, and perhaps a fear of the consequences if the opposite should be the case, may well have made many of these categories seem more compatible with the rest of their outlook than in fact they are. For example, let any morally sensitive modern person ask himself why the agonizing suffering and death of a wholly righteous person — whatever the phrase may mean in a modern context — should reconcile God to a host of unrighteous people, and he will surely find himself up against perplexities which are not easily resolved within the terms of any normal modern ethical categories. He himself, for example, would regard it as immoral to demand this suffering of a third person as the price of forgiving one of his friends. Forgiveness on such terms, he feels, would not deserve the name; it would not be the genuine article. He may of course solve his problem in this and the innumerable similar cases which could be cited simply by saying 'so much the worse for any modern categories', but some of the difficulties in that sort of solution have already been discussed (see above, p. 109) and others will be considered later. The essential difficulty about it lies in the fact that once you come to think of morality as meaning something quite different in God's case from what it means in man's, the way is open to acceptance of a God who is by any normal standards a moral monster. As Dr Austin Farrer used to ask *à propos* the extreme Barthian doctrine of the 'wholly other': 'How are you to tell God from the devil?'.

It may be said, however, that the mythical and archaic character of the biblical interpretations is explained by the considerations that the biblical writers were the first to take preliminary steps towards the understanding of a staggering new event and that their stumbling efforts were inevitably made in first-century Jewish terms foreign to us. This sort of line was taken by Dr Hodgson, for example, and is well illustrated by some words from his last book: 'The New Testament shows them trying to make head or tail of what had happened on the basis of their Jewish understanding of God and the universe. So far from having given us a full and final explanation of the meaning of our faith they were taking the first steps towards its discovery, initiating a process which under the guidance of the Holy Spirit has been continuing ever since and is still going on . . . we have to take into account how the understanding of it by the New Testament Christians has been deepened and enriched in the experience of their successors, and is still being deepened and enriched by our experience of life in the world of today.'[1]

Hodgson himself believed that a major breakthrough in

that process of understanding occurred in the patristic period with the recognition that God's intervention consisted in nothing less than his own incarnation. In a slightly earlier book he wrote: 'It is because we believe that Jesus Christ was and is God incarnate that the Bible is for us the book of books, the unique channel of God's self-revelation . . .'[2] In the same general vein Kierkegaard wrote: 'The historical fact that God has been in human form is the essence of the matter; the rest of the historical detail is not . . . important. . . . If the contemporary generation had left nothing behind them but these words: 'we have believed that in such a year God appeared among us in the humble figure of a servant, that he lived and taught in our community and finally died', it would be more than enough.'[3]

Hodgson, it will be noticed, takes a comparatively traditional line, claiming, not only that Jesus was God incarnate but that he still continues to exist after his resurrection as a distinguishable heavenly person with whom communion is still possible, and in communion with whom Christian life is to be lived. This is very close to the Pauline view as traditionally interpreted.

On this view Christianity consists in seeing the Christ-event as constituting the divine intervention the New Testament represents it as being, in seeking to understand its nature, purpose and consequences as fully as possible and living in a way which relies on its effects and is an appropriate response to it. Correspondingly, the task of the theologian is to expound its meaning and purpose as fully and relevantly as possible and to show how it enmeshes, so far as it does, with some philosophically coherent position.

The difficulty about it seems to me to be this: the notion of a final saving act of God fitted naturally into the outlook of any Jew or Christian of the biblical period, both because, as we have seen, the Jews had no distinct conception of impersonal laws of nature and thought of every event as in some sense an act of God; and also because of their belief in a *Heilsgeschichte*, a whole interrelated series of special saving divine actions, beginning with the act of creation and intended to pave the way for a culminating act which the Jews still expected in the future and the Christians believed to have happened, or at least to have begun, already.

If, as I have suggested, that general picture is hardly acceptable now, the idea of a final decisive act of God in Christ tends to stand out in isolation with no very clear point, or obvious *raison d'être*. It is also questionable how far this picture will fit into modern philosophical categories; the substance philosophy of the Fathers, which the very word 'incarnation' presupposes, is as foreign to many people's way of thinking today as the outlook of the biblical period.

I suppose I am only saying the same thing in another way if I point to the embarrassment of the modern scholar in the face of the various New Testament descriptions of what the divine intervention consisted in. Was it, he asks himself, the singling out of a man through whom portents and signs should be worked as in the speeches in Acts? (Acts 2:22). Was it the constituting of a man as son of God through a miraculous birth as in Matthew and Luke, or through his resurrection from the dead as in Romans 1:4 or Acts 2:36 or 13:33? Or was it the incarnation of a pre-existent son or word of God, as we have seen Paul and other New Testament writers hint, and John explicitly states?

Then, whatever its exact form, what was the point and result of it? The conquest of demonic forces opposed to God? Victory over Sin and Death conceived as quasi-personal powers? The provision of an effective sacrifice for sin or of a new Adam who could undo the work of the old and be raised to be a universal figure in whom all could be incorporated?

It is only by a very drastic and unhistorical treatment that modern, as distinct from ancient, theologians can harmonize all these.

Moreover, even so summary a list makes clear that none of these images, as it stands, is going to prove acceptable in our totality. It is of course possible in theory that every one of the New Testament explanations can be reinterpreted, or demythologized, in such a way that it has something to contribute towards making the divine act intelligible to us. If so, modern theologians have conspicuously failed to discover how to work the oracle and this is no doubt part of the reason why, as we have seen, theologians who take the sort of approach I am discussing frequently seem so uncomfortable with the Christ-event.

Scholars such as Bultmann, who have made a serious attempt at demythologizing the New Testament explanations, have found that the only way is to treat all of them simply as different ways of expressing a single truth — but in practice this involves disregarding a whole lot of their statements and images altogether; it is a highly Procrustean procedure.

Incidentally, it is worth stressing that essentially Bultmann is in fact an exponent of the sort of approach I am discussing, though his handling of it is very different from Hodgson's. He too believes that in Christ a decisive divine intervention took place; but in his view it was a direct and decisive address by God to man, based on no external attestation and demanding a sheerly existential response in the form of a decision no longer to live on the basis of the flesh, that is, confining one's outlook to the horizons of this world and living on the basis of natural wisdom and resources; but to live out of the divine resources, that is, in the strength and vision which God can be relied on to provide in every situation, if only men will open themselves to receive them. '(His) strength is made perfect in (our) weakness', to quote one of Bultmann's favourite texts.

This interpretation which some of Bultmann's followers claim — surely a shade implausibly — to trace back to Jesus himself,* implies no metaphysical claims, such as a doctrine of a divine incarnation, no literal belief in Jesus' resurrection; and therefore no trinitarian theology in any traditional sense. But it nevertheless claims that what happened in Christ was a decisive and indispensable divine action — what Bultmann himself calls a miracle — since apart from it, although men could recognise the inauthenticity of their lives, they could have no hope of breaking through to an authentic form of

---

* 'Implausibly' because the demand for a faith commitment which springs from pure inwardness and is not based on external evidence seems to belong to a twentieth-century, post-Kierkegaardian, rather than a first-century Palestinian, cultural situation. Cp., for example, the difficulty Bultmann has in explaining — or explaining away — 1 Cor. 15:3ff. See e.g. his *Theology of the New Testament* (S.C.M. Press, 1952), i, p. 295 and n.

existence.

It will be noticed that though Hodgson and Bultmann are in a sense both representatives of the same approach, their conclusions differ quite widely, especially as, according to Bultmann, the character of the Christ-event as a decisive divine intervention can never be grasped as a timeless truth; it is recognised only in the moment of decision by one who is resolving to live henceforth in response to it. Also Bultmann's conclusions are much less influenced, at the conscious level at least, by traditional doctrines, especially of the pre-scientific period. His aim is to bring the modern situation and the Bible into direct confrontation and it is a commonplace that for him hermeneutics virtually takes the place of dogmatics.

What is more, it is not easy to see how the differences between theologians like Hodgson and Bultmann could ever be resolved by reference to the Bible itself; for both sides contain equally competent exegetes and commentators. The differences spring not from disagreements about the meaning of the original, but from differences in philosophical and confessional background and differences about the weight to be attached to traditional orthodoxy.[4]

The difference of opinion between scholars such as Hodgson and Bultmann is the more important because it involves a different approach not only to the Christ-event, but to the rest of the Bible as well. Those who take one view of the Christ-event will be likely to take at something like their face-value the various Old Testament accounts of divine interventions, as being necessary to pave the way for God's decisive intervention. Those on the other hand who take a line similar to Bultmann's will be likely to follow him in his estimate of the Old Testament as simply a reflexion of the natural religion of the Jews, which so far from being the result of direct divine revelation and guidance, was a religion of works from which the only lesson to be learned is how *not* to regard our relationship with God. For Bultmann, therefore, as we have seen, there was only the one decisive divine intervention.

All this suggests three reflexions about any attempt in present circumstances to interpret the Christ-event broadly along the lines of the Bible itself, as a unique divine intervention in history which in principle brought to completion God's plans for the world.

First, the attraction and seeming naturalness of such attempts arises from their continuity with the traditional understanding of the nature of theology and the way the Bible should be handled. This type of approach attempts, admittedly in a modified and somewhat attenuated way, to do what Christian theology has always attempted to do, take the biblical account of God's acts more or less at their face-value and then ask what they were intended to achieve.

Secondly, however, we have seen what formidable difficulties any such attempt encounters in present circumstances and how it can produce widely different conclusions and very different understandings of the nature of Christianity and Christian discipleship.

Thirdly, in view of all this, a doubt may arise whether the whole attempt is well conceived. In the light of what was said in earlier lectures, this doubt might be formulated as follows: the notion of a special divine intervention in history was one, if I may put it so, which was all of a piece with the New Testament totality, which had its background in the Jewish ideas I discussed in the last two lectures. As a result, though the attempts of the early Christians to describe and explain it might be varied, and even incompatible, they all related it to the cultural context of their day in a way which was readily intelligible and acceptable to at least some group among their contemporaries. Likewise, although subsequent Christian totalities differed in important respects from that of the New Testament, they were, as we have seen, sufficiently similar for many of the explanations intelligible in the New Testament totality to make sense to them, at any rate by dint of some tortuous exegesis and after suitable reformulations, expansions and modifications.

Since our totality is so different from that of the New Testament and of most of our Christian predecessors, it may be questioned whether the idea of a divine intervention of the sort in question is not so alien to it that there is no possible way of relating it to our cultural context which will be intelligible to a large proportion of educated people today. Either, therefore, it has to be accepted in faith as a sheer surd element — an erratic block in the structure of modern man's own understanding; or else Christians can make sense of it only at the expense of being committed to a whole number of beliefs and assumptions about the world in general not shared by their contemporaries and not capable of being intelligibly related to their other beliefs. In that case it would have to be said of us Christians, so far as we seek also to be full-blooded citizens of the modern world: *nobis non licet esse nos*. Being a Christian would inescapably involve a *sacrificium intellectus* in this sense.

Many theologians of course have insisted that some *sacrificium intellectus* is inseparable from being a Christian; and they are no doubt right. On the other hand, a *sacrificium intellectus* is never a thing to be enterprised nor taken in hand unadvisedly, lightly or wantonly, and we have an obligation to ask whether it is a sacrifice of this sort at this point that is required of us. What is the alternative?

A good deal of recent thinking on this matter was focussed for many readers in an important article which Professor M.F. Wiles contributed in 1970 to one of the issues of the periodical *Religious Studies*[5] In it he argued that the biblical writers were doing two distinct things, though they were not conscious of doing so, and could not have recognised the distinction as he puts it because it presupposes ideas derived from the Enlightenment. They were (a) giving an account of the course of this world, and (b) they were telling a story about it; and nothing but confusion can arise from failure to distinguish in any given passage which was being done. In the case of the early narratives in Genesis some such distinction is generally recognised, as we have seen. No one today supposes that the stories in the early chapters of Genesis of the creation of the world and men and women in it, of the naming of the animals, of the fall of Adam and Eve and its dire consequences, of the flood or the subsequent covenant with Noah are accounts of the past. To describe them as a story — indeed in an important sense a true story — expresses a valuable insight, though it would be seriously misleading if it implied that these accounts were intended simply as theological interpretations in narrative form. It may well be that since the Enlightenment we have become so acutely conscious of problems of historicity that we have tended to read back our concerns and distinctions into the minds of earlier generations. If we could ask the writers of Genesis whether they intended history or interpretation, they would not understand our question or be able to answer it. Even if we could ask them whether they really believed that the world was created more or less at one fell swoop in about 4000 B.C. (which date is not simply derived from Archbishop Ussher's calculations in the seventeenth century: such a passage as Lk 3:23—38 for example, shows, if allowance be made for the longevity of the patriarchs, that he had some such time-scale in mind), they would probably find the question baffling. This consideration, however, cuts both ways, and tells as much against the view that Old Testament writers were conscious of speaking only mythologically as it does against the view that they regarded what they wrote as literal truth. The latter is probably nearer the mark than the former; certainly, for example, they will have conceived the world as of comparatively recent origin and have had no conception of the millions of years of pre-history familiar to us. (Biblical man will thus have been spared any of that feeling of near-vertigo induced in many people today by the recognition of the sheer size and age of the universe as revealed by modern science. It would be a mistake, however, to suppose that the world of earlier times seemed 'cosy'. Cp. e.g. Gen.15:5 and many passages in the book of Job.)

We may get more clarification if we take a leaf from the logical analyst's book and ask how the biblical writers would have gone about verifying their account had they understood the need to do so. Why did they give just *that* account?

Obviously it is by now impossible to disentangle their motives in any way that can pretend to be an historical description; but a rough and ready analysis may help. To begin with, they were confronted with a phenomenon, the fact of the world's existence and the conditions of life in it, which seemed to them, as it has seemed to people of most cultures, to need explanation. When it comes to the question: why *that* particular account? even the earliest biblical writers were already dependent on a tradition; and however far back we go, we shall find that people already had traditions on the subject behind them, traditions which, as we have already seen, were partly shaped by the geographical and climatic environment in which they originated and the ways in which they attempted to deal with it (see pp. 4 and 8—9 above). A story of a flood, for example, will clearly have grown up in a part of the world liable to inundation. Then the Jews, like any other people, will have brought to bear their common-sense and powers of observation on the traditions they inherited; but equally, they would not have accepted these particular traditions, with their essentially *religious* explanations, or continued to transmit them, unless they had had what they at any rate believed to be experiences of God or the gods with which the traditions in question seemed to link intelligibly. It is a fact which can easily be documented from the Bible itself that as their conceptions of God changed, corresponding modifications were made in their traditions and narratives about the origin of things.

Mutatis mutandis, what applies to their accounts of the first things can be applied to their expectations about the last things. A people's eschatology, it has been rightly observed, is a function of its doctrine of God.

To return now to Professor Wiles's article, he asks whether the descriptions in the New Testament of Christ's coming and death as a decisive divine intervention should not be regarded as part of the biblical *story* rather than as part of the biblical account of the past, particularly because, as the story of Christ is told in the New Testament, it links integrally with narratives in the Old Testament, particularly in the early part of Genesis. The work of Christ involved a new creation, in more senses than one; Christ was the second Adam who by his obedience reversed the disobedience of the first Adam and became one into whom men could be incorporated, as all men had been in the first. By his death Christ annulled the results of the fall, and so on. As we saw in the last lecture, the New Testament interpreted Jesus by incorporating him into the Jewish story as its final 'fulfilment'.

If this suggestion is at all on the right lines, as I suspect it is, our discussion of the Genesis story may prove illuminating, although it must be recognised that the two cases are by no means entirely on all fours. In particular the Genesis story conveys no factual information in the ordinary sense of the term, whereas in the New Testament account history and story are very closely intertwined — so *inextricably* intertwined in fact that, as we saw last time, it is now impossible to disentangle them and write a history of Jesus independently of the New Testament story about him. Nevertheless, if we allow for these differences between the two cases, we may still get some light from our analysis of the nature and origins of the Genesis story. In the case of the New Testament, as Dr Knox and Dr Pittenger and others have made clear, the phenomenon the early Christians felt called on to explain was the quality of life and relationship to God they enjoyed, and which seemed to them to be completely and marvellously new.

To quote Professor Knox:

The meanings which the images victory and sacrifice were created to express were empirical meanings. They were realities known, at least in principle, or in their first fruits, within the life of the Church and among those who participated in the Spirit. . . . No ordinary terms could express or convey the meaning of this experience. The bitterness, the hopelessness, of the bondage, and the wonder of the release both beggared mere description.[6]

Christians of the New Testament period knew from tradition, and a few from direct personal experience, that this new state of affairs had in some way or other originated with the life and activity of Jesus; and the question they asked, put for the moment in crude and abstractly logical form, was: Who must Jesus have been and what must he have done in order to have made possible the quality of life and relationship with God we now enjoy? The quotation from Professor Knox continues: 'And so there came into being — almost as a part of the event itself — the story of God's sending his own Son into the world to meet our enemies of sin and death, of his struggle with them, of his victory over them.' In order to make the point clear, let us ask ourselves on what grounds a New Testament writer — or anyone else for that matter — could believe or defend the claim that, for example, Jesus was the Word become flesh, or even that he was descended from Abraham through three sets of fourteen ancestors. In principle, the answer must surely be that their present experience — and in the case of the original disciples their past experience of Jesus during his earthly life as well — pointed in that direction. Their experience, or some part of it, would not have been what it was unless Jesus had been the Word Incarnate, or the saviour descended from Abraham towards whose coming God had deliberately, and symmetrically, planned the course of history. (For the Jew the number seven and multiples of it had special significance and their occurrence was often a sign of God's hand at work; e.g. one sabbath every seven days. This fact is a simple but telling illustration of the gap which separates their cultural situation from ours, as is the fact that they had no trustworthy records from which the stages of Jesus' real descent from Abraham, if in fact he was so descended, could be traced or checked. Even the Old Testament evidence has to be 'cooked' by Matthew to get his exact scheme of three sets of fourteen (see the commentaries on Matt. 1:1–17, a passage of great importance for the true understanding of the Gospel; it is in a sense Matthew's equivalent to John's prologue. No doubt Matthew reasoned, or just sensed, that his version was what the Old Testament *must* have said, or meant.)

Or let us look at an example of another sort. On what grounds would it be possible to defend the interpretation of the Christ-event in eschatological terms, as God's *final* saving intervention in history? Only, surely on the grounds that already, in virtue of it, a relationship to God and man was possible for Christians so perfect in principle that nothing further needed to be done save the transformation of the outer man and the outer world.

In other words, when New Testament writers apply to the Christ-event the sort of descriptions I have been discussing, they are led — or should I say driven? — to do so, because if the event had not been of such a character, they do not see how their experience as Christians could have been what it in fact was. It is difficult to find a term for such a procedure which is not open to misinterpretation, but the one I am inclined to use, as being least open to misunderstanding, is one I have found in the work of Professor Amos Wilder —

though I am not sure I shall be using it quite as he does. He speaks of 'imaginatively objectifying' one's experience.

I must explain what the term means as I use it, and first let me forestall a possible objection. In using this term I have no intention whatever of denying, or minimising, the historical events in the New Testament, as I shall show later. My concern is with the way the New Testament writers deal with these events and with what they say about them. Everyone recognises that they do not give a straightforward factual account of them we might expect from a modern historian, and I suggest that if we examine the logic of what they do (*confining* ourselves, for the moment, to the logic) it is, very baldly, something like this.

Our Christian life, they say, derives from a set of historical events which occurred in the recent past. But no ordinary historical events, however remarkable, could be adequate to the production of such results. Therefore, these events must have been more than historical; there must have been more to them than appears on the surface, more to them than meets the eye. The sort of descriptions, or imaginative objectifications, we are discussing are their attempts to express the fact and character of that 'more', but before we discuss that let us notice one implication of what I have been saying.

From our present point of view, when the New Testament writers say that Jesus was the Messiah or the Word made flesh, what they are in effect saying is that the Christ-event must have been whatever it needed to be in order to provide the foundation of their present life and experience. The real heart of the matter lies in their experience, or at least it lies there no less than in the historical events themselves.

But, of course, what I have been giving is a logical analysis, and not a description, of what the New Testament writers did. If we want to give a description of the way they sought to bode forth the supernatural dimension of the events of Christ's life I have long been in the habit of using the word Professor Wiles has also hit on, the word 'story'. They told a story, *prima facie* historical in form, of how God had a Son, a pre-existent supernatural being, distinct from Yahweh, who at a certain point entered the course of history, lived a human life in it for a while under the name of Jesus, died a redemptive death on man's behalf and then was raised again to his proper place at God's right hand to exercise control of the universe, from then onward, on God's behalf. Of course, as we have seen, the story will not be found in precisely that form in any single New Testament writer. Matthew tells a story significantly different from Paul's because his Christian faith and experience were different; what I have given is a generalised summary to illustrate what I mean when I speak of the New Testament writers 'telling a story'.

Also, needless to say, they did not tell this story independently of the historical events; rather, they embedded the historical events in the story, they narrated them in the context of the story. Some examples may help to make clear what I mean. When the Evangelists describe the birth of Jesus they are reporting a historical event; even its virgin character, if it was an empirical fact, belonged to the historical order. But when they speak of the birth as the means by which a pre-existent heavenly being made his entry into history, then they are in effect placing an interpretation on that historical event, they are embedding it in a context of story. As a second example, let us take the story of the stilling of the storm in St Mark's Gospel. In principle this could be a report of a historical incident, inasmuch as it talks of something Jesus did, or might have done, within the historical order. But so far as the Evangelist exhibits Christ here, in the light of Psalm 89, as God's supernatural agent battling successfully against the forces of evil and chaos, typified by the raging sea (see p. 124 above), then history is interpreted by being set in a context of story. Perhaps these examples may suffice, not only to show what I have in mind, but also to suggest how all-pervasive this procedure of the early Christians is. In the epistles, of course, it is to be found everywhere, and the examples I have taken from the Gospels are in no way exceptional. One of the valuable contributions of form-criticism has been to bring home to us that every *pericope* partakes of this dual character; insofar as it is historical at all, it is precisely history *and* story — history embedded in a context of interpretative story.

And because the early Christians belonged to a period before the rise of scientific history, and were mostly unlettered men at that, they not only mingled history and story inextricably together, but it must be confessed they sometimes allowed the demands of the story to modify the details of the history. It may be worth repeating that there was no intent to deceive in this; at that period it seemed perfectly natural, as we have seen, to modify a historical narrative in such a way as to bring out the place of the incident in the total story. As we have also seen, however, this does mean that it is very often impossible for us to get back to the history and see what *our* reaction would have been.

So far, however, our account has remained at a purely formal level. If we wish to understand why the story — or stories — they told were just the ones they were, we must take into account the mental furniture they will have had as first century people of predominantly Jewish background. It was only within very narrow limits that they had any choice with regard to the story they told or the imagery they employed in connexion with the life of Christ. Just consider: if an early Jewish Christian was convinced that through the historical events centring on Jesus, reconciliation with God had been achieved, how *could* he express it except by describing Jesus as Messiah or Son of Man or Son of God or some such term derived from his cultural environment? The term *avatar* for example, and all its implications in Hindu thought lay entirely outside his range of awareness.

One further corollary is important: so far as the early Christians were Jews, they were not so much *telling* a story as *completing* a story. The story in which they embedded the history of Jesus was itself embedded in an older and longer story. They saw their story as the completion, or fulfilment, of that earlier story; they saw it — they could not help seeing it — as the final chapter, or rather, perhaps, the penultimate chapter, of a much longer and more comprehensive story which told of God's dealing with the world from the beginning. Their imaginative objectification of their experience rested back on, and was largely controlled by, the objectifications in which countless earlier generations had sought to give expression to their experience. Still more significant in determining their story was the impact and teaching of Jesus himself. For the reasons I expounded in the last lecture, we cannot now know with any exactitude what exactly that impact was; all attempts to describe it seem to me to have foundered on failure to take seriously enough the differences between totalities. The whole attempt has been to portray a Jesus intelligible and attractive to us, and any Jesus who would be likely to appear immediately attractive to most people in the modern west would have been unlikely to attract first century peasants and fishermen in Galilee, and *vice versa*. That already emerged, as we saw, from Schweitzer's work and it has more recently been documented by Professor H.J. Cadbury, Father Harry Williams and Mr J.C. Fenton among others. It in no way contradicts that to insist that the personality, activity, teaching *and death* of Jesus must have formed a vital factor in shaping the New Testament story. So far as the death is concerned, both Professor John Knox and Professor Willi Marxsen have recently offered plausible, though admittedly speculative, suggestions about some of the ways in which it may have produced its effects, including the story of the resurrection.[7] As for the life and teaching of Jesus, E. Käsemann and his colleagues in the 'new quest' (see above, p. 166 and n. 13) have at least drawn attention to the fact, apt to be underestimated by such as Cadbury, that — to put it prosaically — Jesus and his activity must have been a cause adequate to the effect they produced in the existence of the early church and the quality of its life. In *any* cultural situation, the figure who gave rise to the Christian community must assuredly have been a remarkable one, with a sense of some very special relationship to God. From our present point of view, the importance of this sense of some very special relationship with God on the part of Jesus can hardly be exaggerated. It *can* be exaggerated, however, and has been exaggerated when it has been supposed, for instance by Harnack or the champions of the 'new quest':

(a) that we can now discover with some exactness and certainty what Jesus' beliefs and feelings were, and

(b) that the convictions thus discovered are the essential truths about him.

The objection to this is that the considerations which apply to the pronouncements of the New Testament writers apply equally to the pronouncements of Jesus. Unless we take an impossibly wooden view of his person, and virtually deny the reality of his humanity altogether, his thoughts and words will have been conditioned by the outlook and perspectives of the first-century Palestinian totality as much as those of his followers; and his account of himself and his relations with God will have been a story, an imaginative objectification of experience − in this case *his* experience − just as much as later accounts of him were. What else could it have been? (see above, p. 11. *Mutatis mutandis*, what was there said about a boy brought up in a primitive society must apply also to the historical Jesus.)

Let us grant that the life and influence of Jesus, whatever men may have made of them, were one of the chief means used by God in his concern to contact and help the human race; that the life of Jesus was the instrument of God. Yet being the people they were, the early Christians did not respond in the way we should have done, however that would have been. They responded by producing poetry and telling stories. For example they told stories of how Jesus on the cross had conquered the devil and paid a ransom to release men from his power. They also told a story about his birth and childhood. I do not mean to suggest of course that any of them deliberately sat down and made up these stories as answers to consciously-formulated questions. Their stories are unselfconscious expressions of the *corporate* Christian experience of Christianity as it developed during the period after his lifetime, often independently in different Christian centres. For that reason we should not expect in such stories the sort of consistency appropriate to a unified dogmatic theory, or even a coherent attempt to explain rationally the workings of an objective divine intervention. One story told of Jesus as having been a sacrifice which had dealt once and for all with sin and guilt of every sort. Another told of his life and death as a victory over the evil powers by which men were in principle released from their thrall, even if there were still pockets of resistance to be mopped up. We should not try to harmonize these stories as if they were so many steps in an argument or explanation; we should accept them as stories — imaginative objectifications of the various types of release and freedom their respective authors felt.

These are matters which deserve, and are receiving, detailed discussion such as is impossible here. What I want to do is to draw your attention to this way of looking at the matter and to suggest briefly some of its extremely radical implications for the study of the Bible and the nature of theology.

On this showing, the task of theology will not be to start from an alleged objective divine intervention and then, with such aid as we can get from biblical and post-biblical writers, work out the meaning and mechanics of it. It will be to explore the significance for us of the fact that a certain community at a certain period felt moved to tell a number of stories about God which, at any rate in a loose way, link together into a single story.

On any sober historical assessment we shall no doubt conclude that among the paradigmatic events which helped to spark off these stories were many of the incidents described with greater or less accuracy in the Old Testament, and still more in the New. But the question of historicity — to what extent the paradigmatic events in question were in fact as they are related in the Bible and whether others of equal importance may have been omitted from the biblical records — will not be of so much moment to us. And we shall not be committed *a priori* to the belief that God has ever acted — in the biblical period or any other — in a way different *in principle* from the way he acts in ours. (Of course the belief that God acts at all, in ours or any other age, is one which needs defending; but its defence is the province of philosophical theology and it would not be appropriate even to begin to attempt it here.)

We shall no doubt be impressed by the way the story has survived by approving itself to generation after generation of Christians of very different types. Honesty will compel us to confess, however, that in this context the word 'story' means something different for us from what it meant to them. To them, as we have seen, our distinction between history and story would not have been natural or indeed intelligible; and if it could have been explained to them, they would certainly have wanted to maintain that, however valid the distinction, the *supernatural* past events of the Bible were every bit as real and actual as the *natural* past events. The suggestion I am making is precisely that, notwithstanding Barth and so many others, this is a position which can no longer be maintained. Of course that is not to concede T.W. Manson's point and say that some metaphysical plate-glass partition prevents any active intercourse between God and the world. Rather it is to suggest that supernatural events in the sense of divine-human dealings of a sort different in kind from anything in current experience can be accepted only on the basis of very strong warrants indeed, and that we have no warrant, which satisfies modern standards, for being sure that they have ever occurred.

The church would be bound to need time to assimilate a suggestion with such far-reaching and radical implications. Yet my suspicion is that as members of the church — particularly perhaps non-theologians — began to absorb all that was implied, one of their strongest feelings would be a sense of relief. The cultural differences between our age and those of the Bible are now so great that every Christian, at any rate in the west, is bound to be acutely conscious of the extent to which the Bible belongs to the past — that it is very 'old fashioned' as some of them might put it. (And incidentally, as could have been foreseen, but often was not, modern translations of the Bible have only served to emphasize this truth by making clear to all what the biblical writings were really saying.) What a relief then to be able to acknowledge its pastness frankly. In the next lecture I shall have to discuss some of the admittedly far-reaching consequences of all this for our understanding of Christianity; first I should like to say something about its releasing and enriching effects on our immediate approach to the Bible.

In this connexion there is considerable illumination to be got from some words of Professor Lionel Trilling: 'It is only if we are aware of the reality of the past as past', he writes,

that we can feel it as alive and present. If, for example, we try to make Shakespeare literally contemporaneous, we

make him monstrous. He is contemporaneous only if we
know how much a man of his own age he was; he is
relevant to us only if we see his distance from us. Or to
take a poet closer to us in actual time, Wordsworth's
Immortality Ode is acceptable to us only when it is
understood to have been written at a certain past moment;
if it had appeared much later than it did, if it were offered
to us now as a contemporary work, we would not admire
it; and the same is true of *The Prelude*, which of all works
of the Romantic Movement is closest to our present
interest. In the pastness of these works lies the assurance
of their validity and relevance.[8]

Here surely we have our marching orders. Can we be
relaxed enough to accept the Bible for what, at one level, it
certainly is, a story about the world and its relation to God —
or rather a series of stories — told by writers all of whom
believed that the world had existed for only a finite number
of generations and would continue for even less; some of
whom, indeed, believed that its end was already at hand?

All of them wrote from within what was broadly a single
religious tradition, but on the view expounded here we are
under no obligation to construe their stories as a unity except
insofar as they naturally allow of it and we feel able to do it
without disloyalty to the canons, literary, critical and
historical, which our integrity and inescapable convictions
dictate. We are not, for example, compelled to accept
promise and fulfilment or type and anti-type, as categories
we can recognise as valid, at any rate in all cases where they
figure in the Bible; we are under no obligation to see certain
events as moral consequences of earlier events except in cases
where we should do the same if they occurred in secular
narratives.

On this view we should be free in fact to see the Bible as a
kaleidoscope of writings, traditions and fragments which are
often rather artificially stitched together, the products of
prophets, poets, visionaries, wise men, historians, liturgists,
theologians and many others, and reflecting, at first or
second hand, some vivid experience of life, usually, though
not always, life touched by the hand of God.

Another quotation from Lionel Trilling may take the argument a further stage. He writes: 'De Quincey's categories of *knowledge* and *power* are most pertinent here; the traditional scholarship, in so far as it takes literature to be chiefly an object of knowledge, denies or obscures that active power by which literature is truly defined.'[9] Does not this comment on literature in general apply with full force to the biblical literature? Our approach to the Bible in recent years has been predominantly one which has sought to use the Bible as a source of knowledge — knowledge of historical facts and circumstances, and so knowledge of exceptional divine acts. Has it not, for all its value, prevented the immense *power* the Bible possesses from making its full impact upon us? If we could let go our almost compulsive hold on the historian's — and to some extent the philosopher's — hand, we should be in a position to take the hands of psychologists, literary critics and others skilled in exploring the full meaning of words and images. With their help, and using their methods, we should be able to let the Bible be the Bible, make its full impact on us, including its imaginative and emotional impact, and reveal to us the profound depths and power of many of its stories and images.

Dr Austin Farrer was right in his effort to focus our attention more on the images of the Bible, though when he talked of *the* biblical pattern of images he showed that he too was influenced by the traditional use of the Bible and the desire to find in the Bible an essential basis on which Christianity could be authoritatively defined, and orthodoxy indisputably distinguished from heresy.[10] Images, however, there certainly are abundant and profound — many of them, even in the New Testament, derived from far back in the various religions and cultures on which Judaism and Christianity both drew. It is the age-old history and almost world-wide prevalence of many of these myths and images which accounts in part for the appeal the Gospel has had to peoples of such very varied periods and civilisations.

Our first task, then, should be to explore these images, myths and stories with all the sensitiveness we can muster and help we can get; studying the use and modification of them in the biblical text and tracing their linkages and developments. For I do not wish to be misunderstood; I am not for a moment denying the essential unities and developments which run through the structure of the biblical material and are vital to the proper understanding of it. Even type, anti-type and similar relationships were undoubtedly present, consciously and unconsciously, to the minds of biblical people, and are therefore highly significant for the understanding of what they wrote, impossible though it may be for them to overflow directly into our 'primary life' as Collingwood called it.

That links with another important point. The way of reading the Bible I desiderate would release us from an impoverishing feature of much recent biblical work, the tendency to confine our study to a search for *the* meaning of the passage we are studying and of the Bible as a whole; by *the* meaning, or the literal meaning, seems usually to be meant the meaning the original writer is thought to have intended to convey to his first readers. Obviously the attempt to discover that has its proper place (see the remarks of Prof. Trilling quoted on p. 103 above) but any search for *the* meaning of such symbolic and poetic texts as the Bible mainly consists of, would be dubbed by most literary critics today as the intentionalist fallacy; and they would deny the propriety of talking about '*the* meaning' in this way. Thus Professor Dame Helen Gardner, for example, comments on Miss Lascelles's excellent book on *Measure for Measure*: 'the success of her book is that it does not arrive finally at the meaning of *Measure for Measure*. She has been content to leave the play more meaningful than it was before we read her study.'[11] And Sir Maurice Bowra quotes these words from the poet Valéry: 'Quand l'ouvrage a paru, son interprétation par l'auteur n'a pas plus de valeur que toute autre par qui que ce soi.'[12]

This approach would thus have the result of allowing us to discover in the context of our totality meanings in the text perhaps not intended or recognised by the original writer in his totality; and it would also make us heirs to the many insights (though not of course the vagaries) of the traditional *sensus plenior*. More than one recent biblical commentator has told me how much enlightenment he has obtained from studying the *Gnomon Novi Testamenti* of the eighteenth-century writer Johannes Bengel and other comparable works from the pre-critical period.

If I am asked about the criteria for distinguishing between insight and vagary, either in modern or traditional interpretation, I can only answer in the sort of way Professor Graham Hough once did when I asked him a similar question about the interpretation of the more modern literature on which he is a specialist. There are, he said, no statable or mechanically applicable criteria. Any critic who believes he has discovered new meaning in a text can only submit his interpretation for the opinion of those with the knowledge, experience, sensitivity and other qualifications which entitle them to judge. Very often it may be a long time before it becomes clear whether the alleged discovery of new meaning in a text is a genuine insight or not; but in the long run the consensus of those qualified to judge seldom has much difficulty in deciding where the area of legitimate and illuminating interpretation ends and the lunatic fringe begins.

I shall have a lot more to say about that later, as I shall about the use of the Bible as a whole; but I should be sorry to leave you now with any impression that I regard this preliminary approach to the Bible, studying the biblical writers as you would begin to study any other comparable writers, as the only religious use that can legitimately be made of the Bible. However, although it is not the only use, I believe it is an essential preliminary to any other use.

I should like to see Christians nowadays approach the Bible in an altogether more *relaxed* spirit, not anxiously asking 'What has it to say to me immediately?', but distancing it, allowing fully for its 'pastness', accepting it without anxiety as an ancient story about God and the world, told by people who regarded the world as a phenomenon of at most some five thousand years' duration and believed in God's constant saving interventions in its affairs from creation day to Doomsday. I should like to see us, by a fully willing suspension of disbelief, give it a chance to say to our conscious and unconscious minds all that it said to its original readers, and much more beside.

This can be done at various levels. No doubt achievement of the deepest understanding requires a knowledge of the history, languages, customs and thought-forms not only of biblical times, but also of the periods in which older exegetes worked; but anyone who has witnessed the impact of *Hamlet,* let us say, on an audience of ordinary theatre-goers knows what an enormous leap of the imagination non-specialists can be stimulated to make, and what a comprehensive, if not necessarily highly instructed, sense of the past they possess.

If all this talk of story seems very thin as compared with the traditional view, I have, as I say, more to add later. Meanwhile, do not underestimate the power of story. Read Edward Muir's *Autobiography,* consider what it means to a child to have been brought up on Hans Andersen; consider the impact on the modern world of the story Marx told, with the help of Hegel; think what Sophocles, and with his help, Freud, made of the story of Oedipus. It is a grave mistake to underestimate the story.

9 The 'incapsulation' of biblical thought

In the last lecture I suggested that an approach to the Bible appropriate to our historicizing age might begin by treating it as in the main a mixture of history and story, story woven round historical narrative, or, if you like, historical narrative embedded in story, told in the context of story. From our historicizing perspective we must 'distance' the Bible, allow fully for its 'pastness' and see it as a story, or congeries of stories (I will say more about that later), expressing the faith of a number of different generations within a single religious tradition about the relation of the world to God, and his continual saving and judging interventions in its affairs throughout the whole five thousand years or so during which even the most sanguine of them expected it to last.

I suggested that if we approached it in that way, we should use all the help we can get from psychologists and literary critics, as well as from ancient historians and linguistic experts, in an attempt to discover what it originally meant and what other meaning a sober and sensitive interpretation can find in it.

Supposing we do all this; what more is there to be said? First something negative: it has been a cardinal principle of all previous Christian theology, in whatever form it may have been expressed, that once the literal meaning of each passage – the *sensus literalis* in the sense I discussed earlier – has been established, then if the truths expressed in all the various passages are synthesized in the right way, the essential truth of the Christian faith will emerge, or will be capable of being deduced by a logic so rigorous that no sober judge will be able to doubt its validity. The way this process of deduction could be thought to clarify the revelation without

adding to it is illustrated by this quotation from Professor
Owen Chadwick: 'If definitions were necessary inferences,
they were perhaps adding . . . a clarification . . . of the faith:
yet no one could assert that they were additions to the
meaning of the revelation — from eternity they followed
necessarily from the revealed data.'[1] In the period covered by
Professor Chadwick's book, and earlier, the point was put in
a rigorously logical form; I have tried to show in these
lectures that though more modern theologians have not
sought to deduce the content of Christianity from the Bible
by such rigorous logical methods, it has nevertheless been the
presupposition of them all that there was somehow to be
discovered in the Bible what Shirley Jackson Case called a
constant quantum of truth, or at any rate a firm basis of
some sort on which the content of the Christian faith in each
generation could be authoritatively and decisively formulated. Case writes about modern biblical scholarship in
terms surprisingly reminiscent of Professor Chadwick's
account of earlier periods: 'quite new statements of faith
were sometimes formulated, but this evolutionary process of
dogma was usually supposed to consist in the mere supple-
mentation of earlier pronouncements. Thus one recovered
the correct original; the truth remained a constant quantum.'[2]
I hope by now it may be clear how far, and in what sense,
that is a fair judgement.

One thing is quite clear; the process never worked.
Professor Hodgson wrote:

> There never has been a time when the Bible could be left
> to explain itself in such a way as to produce universal
> agreement about what it has to teach. It was not so before
> the coming of criticism. Fundamentalism cannot restore to
> us a happy past that never was. The critical wave broke in
> upon a Church in which the successors of the tractarians
> were still disputing with the heirs of the evangelical revival
> while Presbyterians, Congregationalists, Baptists, Friends
> and Methodists [and, we may add, Roman Catholics] had
> their differing interpretations of biblical theology . . . the
> followers of Calvin, Zwingli, Melancthon *et al.*, not to
> mention the theologians of the Council of Trent and the

Orthodox Church of the East, all claimed to be the true interpreters of the Bible in their differing understandings of the Christian faith.'[3]

Mr F.G. Downing has documented that matter decisively in his book *Has Christianity a Revelation?*[4]

On the view we have been putting forward none of this is surprising. As Aquinas said, following Augustine, *figura nihil probat*; he was also following Augustine when he wrote that only from the literal sense *potest trahi argumentum, non autem his quae secundum allegoriam dicuntur;*[5] it would seem to follow that from the sort of story we have discovered in the Bible no irrefutable deductions could possibly be drawn. This conclusion must be faced frankly. From the fact, for example, that the Bible story tells of a pre-existent son of God, distinct from Yahweh, who once entered history and subsequently reascended to his father and sent his spirit into the world, no conclusive argument would lie to the objective existence of three distinct divine hypostases such as are presupposed in traditional trinitarian teaching. And, as we have seen, the same sort of thing would have to be said about the traditional doctrine of a divine incarnation, were that something the Bible consistently, or indeed ever, conceived. The point has already been expressed by Professors Pittenger and Knox — and notably by Professor Cyril C. Richardson in his book *The Doctrine of the Trinity.*[6]

At first sight this might seem to spell the end for Christianity; for it might be argued: 'whatever may be said about the matter of terminology, Christianity is either life in the risen Christ, life in (the power of) his spirit or it is nothing at all. If we may not have our *en Christo* there is no point in having anything at all.' In fact, of course, we must distinguish. St. Paul's faith may have been fully justified; the state he characterized as *en Christo* may have been a real and vital one, and yet the religious terminology he used to describe it — his story — may have been culturally conditioned in a way that makes it unacceptable to us. And the same could obviously apply to any other element in the New Testament story. It is in fact, as we have seen, a question which deserves careful pondering how St Paul — or even one of the original disciples — could have known that the terms *en Christo* or *en pneumati* and the stories they imply were the right way of bodying forth the faith and experience which lay behind them. They were, as we have seen, essentially the language of one particular religious and cultural condition; no Indian, for example, privileged to be a witness of Jesus and a subsequent believer, would have bodied forth his faith and experience in those terms. And even within a Jewish-Christian context how, for example, did one distinguish an experience of being *en Christo* from one rightly to be designated *en pneumati*?

Is the point, then, that what we should take really seriously in the Bible is not the actual words of the writers nor yet the special divine acts to which they ostensibly refer and the biblical interpretations of those acts, but the state of mind, the understanding of the relation to God and the neighbour, of which they are the expression? If so, incidentally, we have yet another version of the idea that essential Christianity is fully present in the Bible; only this time it would be a matter of reproducing states of mind rather than beliefs.

Certainly that seems to me *nearer* the truth, and up to a point it is, I think, what certain modern theologians are saying, for example Professor John Knox and Dr Bultmann; though it is important to remember that for Bultmann *Selbstverständnis* does not mean understanding of oneself and one's relationships in any ordinary, psychological, sense; it means a supernaturally given understanding of oneself and one's true nature such as comes only through the word of God mediated by preaching.

So far as this general idea is entertained, however, there seem to me to be several objections to it. First there is the question, raised by Professor Amos Wilder and others, how far it is possible to distinguish in this way between an attitude or self-understanding and the language in which it is expressed. It is always a mistake to try to render the meaning of a poem in prose and perhaps anything as akin to poetry as the biblical story can only make its point in just the way it does.

Then, closely allied, is the point on which Professor Helen

Gardner and Professor Lionel Trilling strongly insist. Raising the question whether there is sufficient continuity in human nature for us to be able to adopt the attitudes of people in previous totalities, especially remote ones, the latter writes in words we have already quoted, and which Dame Helen quotes with approval:

> It ought to be for us a real question whether, and in what way, human nature is always the same. I do not mean that we ought to settle this question before we get to work, but only that we insist to ourselves that the question is a real one. What we certainly know has changed is the *expression* of human nature and we must keep before our minds the problem of the relation which expression bears to feeling . . . the problem with its difficulties should be admitted, and simplicity of solution should always be regarded as a sign of failure.[7]

Yet how very simple is the solution propounded from the average pulpit ('human nature doesn't change'); and for all their sophistication, do not the views of Bultmann and his followers beg the question, at least to some extent? It is an instructive exercise for example to read with this question in mind the latter part of the great book on Gnosticism by Bultmann's colleague and admirer Hans Jonas.[8]

Thirdly there is the question of autonomy; let me remind you again of the motto of the Royal Society: *nullius in verba*. If we are not in bondage to the *words* of any external authority, it seems unlikely that we are meant to be in bondage to anyone's frame of mind either. For all that has been said to the contrary, I cannot help feeling that it is in this area that we should look for the understanding of Bonhoeffer's talk about 'men come of age'. When a son comes of age, it is not just that he *understands* his relationship to his father differently; the relationship itself has changed. What ground have we for thinking that, although the human race and its nature may have changed greatly, God intends its relationship to him to remain absolutely constant?

Let me give some examples of the sort of thing I have in mind. Professor Leslie Dewart has been much criticized for a passage in one of his books of which this quotation is a fair example: 'I think that the Christian theism of the future might so conceive God as to find it possible to look back with amusement on the day when it was thought particularly appropriate that the believer should bend his knee in order to worship God. For when the eyes of the Christian faith remove their hellenic lenses, what continues to appear sacred about hierarchical relations as such?'[9] Does Professor Dewart deserve to be criticized? He got powerful support from an article in *Theology* some years ago by Fr H.A. Williams dealing with the so-called 'prayer of humble access' in the traditional Anglican Communion rite.[10] The Psalmist wrote: 'Even as the eyes of slaves look unto the hand of their masters and as the eyes of a slave girl look unto the hand of her mistress, so our eyes wait upon the Lord our God' (Ps. 123:2). The fourth evangelist could already see that such an attitude was outmoded (John 15:15) but does it not still largely determine the attitude we think God wants from us, though we should ourselves consider it wrong to own slaves or to expect a slavish attitude towards us on the part of anyone? Are we prevented from being as sovereign in our attitude to the text as the fourth evangelist was?

Or consider the traditional attitude towards the judgement of God. From New Testament times onwards almost all Christians have believed, at any rate until very recently, that at some point – either the death of the individual or the general judgement – God will, as it were, rule a final line under each man's moral account and say, in effect, 'according as you are up to this point (or even *at* this point) so shall your eternal destiny be determined'. Some such notion seems to be shared by nearly all the New Testament writers and a great deal has been made of it in Christian theology and liturgy; but may it not in fact be an element from late Jewish eschatology imperfectly assimilated by Paul and his successors, which is not only not essential to Christian belief but inconsistent with it at its best and most profound?[11] Is there not good ground for thinking that in fact 'God hateth nothing that he hath made' and that he will *never* cease to be patient with his children? Here again it would surely be wrong to adopt the New Testament frame of mind.

A third, and closely allied, example is one about which Professor Hodgson wrote in a number of his books, what he called the 'Ark theory' of the Church and salvation. So ingrained is self-interest that men have taken it for granted that their religion exists to promote it. If the root of religion consists in a call by God, the Old Testament makes clear how the Jews interpreted their calling as putting them in a position of advantage with respect to divine favour in this world or the next. Similarly in the New Testament the question was: what must we do to be saved? and the church was conceived as a body which exists for the benefit and salvation of its members. According to the Gospels at least, it would appear that such an attitude was shared by Jesus. If he ordered the rich man in the Gospels to sell all his goods and give the proceeds to the poor, it appears that that was for the good of the man's soul, rather than for the good of the poor. Professor Hodgson writes:

> Inevitably this outlook influenced the thought of the first Christians on the doctrines both of the atonement and the church. It is the source of the notions that the importance of the atonement is summed up in its offer of salvation to penitent sinners, and the importance of the church in its being the society within which this offer is secured to its members. Its roots lie so deep in fallen human nature that nearly two thousand years have not been enough to expose its inconsistency with the revelation of God in Christ and to eradicate its influence from Christian theology. [12]

Hodgson's words seem to me cogent, though I suspect he exempted Jesus from their scope in a way that I have just shown to need questioning if he is accurately represented in the Gospels.

Similarly, there are many New Testament stories which, as they stand, suggest an experience of God as more concerned with his honour, or at least with abstract justice, than with forgiveness radically understood. He seems to be one who cannot remit a debt, but must wait until it is paid by someone — and that is not forgiveness properly so-called. (See below, p. 210 for further discussion of this.)

Examples could be multiplied, but the point seems clear;

in this area also we who inherit the consequences of the Enlightenment cannot with integrity divest ourselves of our autonomy. However much help we may get from the Bible, however reluctantly we part company with it, as we should from the advice of a long trusted friend, in the last resort we must, like Søren Kierkegaard's man of faith, 'constantly launch out upon the deep and with 70,000 fathoms of water under us', *decide for ourselves,* with the help of such light as we can get, what our stance before God, and our attitude to our neighbour, should be.[13]

If I quote Leonard Hodgson again, it must be on the understanding that quoted out of context he may seem to be saying more than he intended to; or should I say that he spoke more wisely than he knew? 'For too long', he writes, 'study of the biblical writers (and, for the matter of that, of patristics, scholastics, reformers and the rest) has been based on the assumption that someone, somewhere, at some time in the past, really knew the truth, that what we have to do is to find out what he thought and get back to it.'[14] It may be significant that the statement occurs in Hodgson's last book; for years he had been moving towards it. My only doubt is whether even in the end he applied it with quite sufficient rigour either to Jesus or to the architects of trinitarian and Christological orthodoxy.

Of that more later; meanwhile there is another very important question. When I emphasized the potency of *story* at the end of the last lecture, some at least of my examples referred only to the impact a story can have on the emotions and the imagination. Can a story also report reality? Can it ever be a window into the way things objectively are? That, as you will probably know, is a thorny and much debated question, but fortunately I do not need to argue it at length because it is admirably discussed precisely with reference to our subject in the excellent appendix to Chapter 2 of Professor Amos Wilder's book *New Testament Faith for To-day.*[15] Briefly, it may be worth noting that two of the examples I quoted last time, the stories produced by Marx and Freud, both purport to tell us something about the way things are, and Professor Wilder argues powerfully in favour of the possiblity that stories can, in their own way, do just

that. 'The chief obstacle', he writes, 'to the proper validation
of religious myth and all cognate mythopoetic portrayals of
life and history is the stultifying axiom that genuine truth or
insight or wisdom must be limited to that which can be
stated in discursive prose, in denotative language stripped as
far as possible of all connotative suggestion, in "clear ideas",
in short, in statement or description of a scientific character.'
But, as he points out, 'the proponents of this thesis are
increasingly uncomfortable since students of semantics and
of science itself have pointed out the symbolic character and
fluidity of even the most objective terms and discourse'.[16]

Probably that would be even more widely conceded now
than when Wilder wrote it in 1954; the denial of the truth
value or representational function of symbols and myths is,
as Wilder says, related to the general divorce of intellect and
imagination, of sense and sensibility since the seventeenth
century,[17] a divorce which is more and more widely
recognised as a disaster, but luckily also recognised as not
necessarily being more than a temporary phenomenon. On all
that there is much sense in Michael Roberts's book *The
Modern Mind*.[18] Here, therefore, it will suffice simply to refer
you to Santayana, Richard Kroner and the other writers
Wilder cites, especially perhaps Arnold Toynbee who quotes
in his support both Plato's myths and Aristotle's statement
that 'fiction is truer and more philosophical than history',[19]
and writes: 'fiction is the only technique that can be
employed or is worth employing [in dealing with certain
kinds of data] . . . In such circumstances the data cannot be
significantly expressed except in some notation which gives
an intuition of the infinite in finite terms; and such a
notation is fiction.' It is interesting that in connexion with
certain Old Testament narratives he adds that mythology is 'a
primitive form of apprehension and expression in which — as
in fairy tales . . . or in dreams dreamt by sophisticated adults
— the line between fact and fiction is left undrawn'.[20]

Yet, granting for the moment that a story can be a window
on to reality, how can we learn about the way things *are*
from a story told by men of an ancient totality about the
way they believed things *were*?

I must be frank and say at once that even so far as I think I

know, I do not find it easy to express clearly or concisely.
First, may I expand what I said at the end of the last lecture
about reading the Bible as a story? Perhaps I can best express
it with reference to R.G. Collingwood's view of doing
history, which, you will remember, included essentially
thinking the thoughts of our predecessors after them. The
example we took, you may remember, was Collingwood's
attempt to think Nelson's thoughts after him as he stood on
the deck of the *Victory* at the battle of Trafalgar; and you
will recall with what seriousness he spoke of plunging
beneath the surface of his mind and there living a life in
which he not merely thought about Nelson but was Nelson.[21]

Perhaps that may provide a clue. What we have to do first
is to get as near as we can to thinking the thoughts of the
biblical writers after them as they wrote their books. As the
example of an audience watching *Hamlet* was meant to
suggest, that is something which can be done perfectly
adequately at a certain level by the ordinary Christian reader
without any wealth of special knowledge; but if it is to be
done with the maximum effect, it will require not only the
help of the text itself, but of every other source the exegete
càn lay under contribution. As Dr Johnson observes, 'all
books which describe manners require notes in sixty or
seventy years or less'.[22]

The reader of the Bible must remember that the meaning of
words is always relative to the situation and experience of the
person who wrote them and of his contemporaries. In trying
to discover these he will need a wide and detailed range of
knowledge. Here, for example — and here alone, *I* should say
— lies the importance of discovering as far as possible who
was the writer of each book and of being scrupulously honest
about pseudepigraphy where it seems to be indicated. If the
Fourth Gospel, for instance, is located in the wrong context,
chronologically, theologically or philosophically, to that
extent the exegete's attempt to think the author's thoughts
after him will be frustrated. But it is not only a question of
the author's *individual* history and experience, it is a question
of the hopes and fears and presuppositions, the limitations,
the outlook on things natural and supernatural which he
shared with his fellows. The exegete cannot delve too deeply

into all these; for let him remember that in order to understand the meaning of what St Mark wrote, he has in effect to become St Mark for a while.

I emphasize this so strongly because I believe this is the place, and the only place, from which the further stages of exegesis can proceed.

But before I develop it further, there are some other things I want to say on our present topic. If the exegete will begin to work in the way I have described, he can be confident of finding many passages revealing undertones and overtones he had never suspected before. For example, if he knows how Jews of the first century thought about history and its relation to God, and if he understands the fascination of numbers for the ancient world and the significance then attached to certain 'perfect' numbers, he will find a wealth of meaning in the genealogy of St Matthew's Gospel. He will see that it is written in a spirit of triumph, with a great sense of its importance and its full fitness to stand as the introduction to the Good News; that it is, in fact, Matthew's equivalent, or part of his equivalent, to John 1:1–14. For it means that God is in total control of history, and that He has exercised that control so as to order history hitherto according to a specific plan and make it all an introduction to the life and work of Jesus, who is thus the crown and fulfilment of the whole creative activity. The Evangelist is saying in fact: if you really want to understand what is happening here you have to see that its real beginning lay way back in history which was, as it were, tailored by God to this end. And if a reader's researches take him on, as they surely will, to question the historical trustworthiness of the genealogy, he will come to see that it was the Evangelist's conviction of God's lordship over history, and Christ's centrality in it, which gave the passage its shape and constituted the message it was meant to convey. (See p. 185 above.)

To take another, more obvious, example, if an interpreter knows something of the terrible way in which many people in the first century were hag-ridden by the fear of demons and felt themselves to be in bondage of all kinds to various evil supernatural powers; if he appreciates that this was a central feature in many of their lives — rather as some people nowadays are obsessed with the fear of some particular disease — then, as he reads the exorcism stories in the Gospels or the descriptions in the Epistles of how the supernatural powers of evil were overcome through Christ's death, he will detect the note of urgency in what he reads and be able to connect it with the writers' deep sense of triumph and gratitude that as a result of Christ's life they and their fellow Christians are now quite free from one of the most terrible oppressions imaginable. It is a matter of a deep feeling of having been a helpless creature under the bondage of Satan and now, as the result of Jesus' life and activity, being completely released; and as the feeling is central to the writers' faith and experience, so it is central to what they wrote. In a sense it is what these passages are about; it is their meaning. And the same is true, as Professor Knox suggests, about the passages which speak of Jesus' death in sacrificial terms. The presupposition was that men could only be released from guilt if sacrificial blood had been shed. 'Without the shedding of blood', says the writer to the Hebrews, 'there is no forgiveness' (9:22); to him and most of his contemporaries it seemed simply axiomatic, rather as the law of gravitation does to us. It was not so much part of the argument as a presupposition of it, and one which many of us will not feel able to accept. We need to recognise, however, that sacrificial blood-shedding is not in the last resort the subject of such passages; sacrificial terminology provides the mode of expression through which the writers express their experience and conviction of release. If the reader recognises this, he will see behind the passages which expound Christ's death as a sacrifice the writers' conviction that whereas they had been responsible sinners, sunk in guilt, now, as a result of what Jesus had been, they were totally forgiven. Once again we have a clue to the meaning of the passages.

These last two examples suggest a further reflection. Those who discuss these two New Testament motifs — of Christ the Conqueror and Christ the Victim — often point out incompatibility between them and then go on to suggest that one or other is given greater prominence in the New Testament and represents the 'real' New Testament view on the atonement. About the incompatibility they are no doubt right, but do they not draw the wrong conclusions from it? I must insist once again that what we are dealing with is a story, and we must not therefore expect the sort of consistency appropriate to a unified dogmatic theory. Perhaps indeed the point should be put more strongly; perhaps I have been over-hasty in speaking of *the* biblical story, and we should rather say that each passage has its own story to tell, and that though sometimes these individual stories can be unified in terms of a longer story, the Bible contains a number of stories and other types of material which we should not too readily attempt to harmonize. Even an individual writer may express himself in terms of more than one story. Perhaps therefore we should not propose to the reader that he try to discover *the* meaning of *the* story, or even *the* meaning of the individual stories, but rather that he recognise stories for what they are and find ways of discovering all the meaning he can in them.

One further consequence of this conception of the exegetical task may be mentioned here. We may sometimes suspect that the terms in which a New Testament writer expresses himself do not do full justice to the faith and experience which appear to underlie them. Such a suspicion will arise if we find other writers, or the same writer elsewhere, using expressions which suggest a different and incompatible faith and experience. This may happen on a large scale and a small scale. On the large scale, there are, as I mentioned briefly before, stories which, as they stand, suggest an experience of God as more concerned with His honour, or at least with abstract justice, than with forgiveness. He seems to be one who cannot simply remit a debt but must wait until it is paid by someone. Such may indeed be the real conviction of the writers, though elsewhere, for example when they speak of God Himself as the one who offers the sacrifice and pays the debt, they sometimes seem to reveal an experience of total and radical forgiveness. One part of the New Testament experience seems to be of forgiveness, and yet it is doubtful if the attitude ascribed to God in the first group of passages could really be called forgiveness at all.[23] On a smaller scale, but still of great significance, is the example Professor Knox believes he can detect in Paul's statement of his beliefs about justification by faith. Paul's deep distrust of law, Professor Knox believes, has led him to express himself with regard to justification in a way that does not do justice to his own deep conviction about the place of law in Christian living.[24] Whatever may be thought about these two examples, the possibility here opened to the exegete of 'correcting' one impression in terms of another and, on occasion, of discovering what a biblical writer means despite what he says, is surely of great importance. One of the most significant and unfortunate moments in the development of Christianity came when Christians began to treat the idea and imagery of the New Testament writers as if they were exempt from the inadequacy-to-its-subject from which all human language inevitably suffers. Most of the New Testament writers themselves would fully have understood the following words of Charles Clayton Morrison:

> God's revelation is in history, that is, in the continuum of events as experienced by a human community, and the ideas with which the community seizes upon these events and receives them as revelation are no less human thoughts than the thoughts of a scientist in explaining a physical phenomenon or an archaeologist in explaining the sig- nificance of a vase unearthed by the spade . . . Every doctrine of Christianity, no matter how venerable, is thus a human construct . . . They are human ideas thrown out — shall I say? — toward the ineffable revelation of God. We can make no exception . . . as ideas, [they] are not revealed. They are the work of men to whom God's revelation came.[25]

The examples I have used in these lectures so far may possibly have suggested to you that the word 'story' applies only to passages dealing with the nature and activities of God. I should like now to make clear that it applies also to statements dealing with the nature and activities of men, that is, to the ethical statements in the Bible — or at any rate that the interpreter's way of dealing with these should be the same as in the case of 'stories'. The truth that the meaning of words is relative to the circumstances and experience of those who use them is as applicable to ethical statements as to any other. Perhaps a rather extreme example may help to show what is involved; let us take St Paul's teaching at the beginning of I Corinthians 11 about the duty of women to have their heads covered in church.

The older exegetes treated this passage in their usual literal way and took its meaning to be a timelessly valid instruction that females of the species should always wear a hat of some kind inside a church building. The modern Church has rightly become suspicious of this, but I think I am right in saying that it has also come to doubt whether the passage has any meaning at all for contemporary Christianity. In this, as we shall see later, it could in principle be right, but the exegete ought not to be put off so easily. He will have to ask what the Apostle had in mind in issuing this particular command, and the answer will obviously demand a wide knowledge of the customs in this connexion in contemporary Corinth, as well as a careful following of Paul's complicated theological reasoning in the surrounding passage. The interpreter may well come to the conclusion that the Apostle's words here are not an altogether satisfactory expression of his true mind, particularly perhaps in verse 16; but it would not be surprising if, as a result of full study, he came to see that the passage reflects a good deal of Paul's convictions about the danger of causing unnecessary offence and scandal to others, as well as, more profoundly, about God's purpose in creation and the relation of the sexes. From these in turn ethical guidance for various situations might emerge. In itself, the example may be a trivial one, but because of its character as a limiting case, it may suggest how other ethical statements in the New Testament should be treated. (The point being made here is not affected by the exegetical difficulties arising from 1 Cor. 11:4 etc.) In the case of divorce, for example, it could well be that if the different, and formally incompatible, statements on the subject attributed to Jesus by the different evangelists were interpreted in this way, it would be found that they were different ways of expressing a common underlying conviction; or even that they expressed different underlying convictions, each with its own validity. What those convictions might be cannot be discussed here, and since my concern is with method rather than detailed application, I hope my extremely brief reference to the question of ethical statements may be adequate.

Perhaps this is the point at which to touch on another aspect in which it seems to me that a good deal of recent biblical scholarship has been somewhat impoverishing. Since the whole Bible has been seen as a history of divine acts culminating in the great act of Christ, there has been a tendency to insist on relating everything, both in the Old Testament and the New, to the Christ-event as interpreted by orthodoxy, before it can be allowed to speak.

Professor Barr, as we have seen, has rightly protested against this facile unification of all the Old Testament material under a single perspective. Although for convenience of exposition, I frequently refer to 'the biblical story', it is I hope clear that on the view I am suggesting it is not in the least surprising if on occasion individual stories, or material which does not naturally come under that description at all, make a direct impact upon us and seem bursting with meaning for us, whether they occur in the New Testament or the Old. That this happens is the experience of most readers of the Bible, and perhaps accounts for the remark which I have heard recently from more than one source: 'In certain respects I find the Old Testament more congenial than the New.'

10 The Bible and doctrine

The exegete, then, must think the thoughts of the biblical writers after them. But does that exhaust his task? Perhaps as *exegete* it does, but not as either theologian or Christian believer.

At this point exegesis is still close to history, at any rate as Collingwood conceived it. 'In the kind of history', he writes, 'I have been practising all my life, historical problems arise out of practical problems. We study history in order to see more clearly into the situation in which we are called upon to act.'[1] But how is the desired insight arrived at?

Will you permit me one further quotation from Collingwood?

> If what the historian knows is past thoughts, and if he knows them by re-thinking them himself, it follows that the knowledge he achieves by historical inquiry is not knowledge of his situation as opposed to knowledge of himself, it is a knowledge of his situation which is at the same time knowledge of himself. In re-thinking what somebody else thought, he thinks it himself. In knowing that somebody else thought it, he knows that he himself is able to think it. And finding out what he is able to do is finding out what kind of man he is.[2]

In other words, an historian or exegete who has 'plunged beneath the surface of his mind' and really knows what it is to be St Mark or St Paul will come back into the present a changed man, alive to new demands, opportunities, problems and possibilities in every sphere. May I give a few, perhaps rather feeble examples? The exegete or other Christians of his acquaintance, may have been oppressed with fear — fear, perhaps of some particular disaster. But as one who knows what it is to be St Mark, with his conviction of Christ's having overcome the evil powers, he will have known what it is like to be freed from fear, even fear of what the most hostile fate or evil powers could accomplish. He will be bound to recognise, therefore, that St Mark, under the immediate impact of the saving event, would never have been in bondage to the exegete's fear; he would have regarded it as incompatible with his confidence in God through Christ. 'Perfect love casteth out fear.'

Or again the exegete may be a man who is afraid of God, so conscious of his own imperfections that he cannot believe he will be accepted by God until he has made himself a very different person. But as one who knows what it is to be St Paul, with his conviction of the sacrificial efficacy of Christ's death, he will have known what it is to go to God in full recognition of his sin, and yet in full assurance of being accepted. This cannot help throwing in question his present fearful, merit-ridden, attitude to God and opening up new possibilities of relationship to God before him, though it need not involve him in accepting Paul's conviction that reconciliation with God depends on the shedding of sacrificial blood.

Or it may work in the opposite direction. The exegete may have been one who interpreted the findings of modern psychology to mean that we have virtually no responsibility for our actions. In that case, having known what it is to be almost any one of the New Testament writers, with their deep sense of man's responsibility before God, he cannot help raising the question in his mind whether he has not misinterpreted the truth in modern views and failed to see 'of how great weight sin is'.

Those three examples will have to suffice; I hope they will be enough to clarify the point I am attempting to make; that thinking the New Testament writers' thoughts after them, if it is done with full seriousness, opens up to the exegete all sorts of possibilities — possibilities of self-knowledge and of relationship to God, man and the world. The New Testament becomes an invitation to pilgrimage, as John Baillie might have put it, an invitation to explore new possibilities and open up new relationships; a recommendation to take up a new stance in relation to God and so to the neighbour. It challenges us with a demand for faith, opening up what it claims is a new possibility for men in relation to God and life, and demanding that we enter into it.

In the language of Bultmann — Bultmann, this time, as distinct from Barth — some things in the Bible are *geschichtlich,* as opposed to *historisch,* that is, historic as opposed to merely historical, or past; like other things which we call historic, they still have influence and significance for our time. The writer being dead, yet speaketh.

Yet it must be insisted once again: because we live in so different a totality we cannot accept the writer's words or his attitude as they stand, nor allow our stance to be dictated by him. As Collingwood would put it, even when we have understood his meaning, it remains 'incapsulated'; even in cases where we have been deeply influenced by it, it cannot overflow directly into our present, what Collingwood calls our 'primary' existence, because of the primary, or surface knowledge which keeps it in its place and prevents it from thus overflowing.[3]

Can we be any more precise about how the thoughts of these men of the past, as we rethink them, affect and illuminate our own thought and belief? One of the main contexts in which this question has been talked about in recent times is the long tradition of German debate about hermeneutics stretching back to Schleiermacher and behind him to earlier Lutheran discussions. The best known modern contributors to this debate are Professors Heidegger and Bultmann. Bultmann explicitly acknowledges the kinship of his views and Collingwood's.[4] Just as Collingwood said 'we study history in order to see more clearly into the situation in which we are called upon to act'[5] Bultmann claims that everything depends, in the interpretation of a thing, on your *Vorverständnis,* your 'pre-understanding', that is, the set of preoccupations, questions and expectations with which you approach it. Just as you cannot understand a book written in Greek unless you have some familiarity with the Greek language, so you cannot understand any writing unless you have some sort of understanding of the subject-matter and problems with which it is concerned.

So far so good. Everyone in the modern west who reads the Bible in a religious interest (and it is only with such readers, you will remember, that these lectures are concerned) will approach it with at least two sorts of thing in mind.

First there will be some of what I may loosely call the characteristic mental furniture of a modern western mind. It is a pity Bultmann affects to be able to give a summary inventory of it; in fact, as we have seen, that is impossible, though it is obvious that it will include knowledge, beliefs and assumptions of all kinds about medicine, psychology, ethics, natural science, archaeology and a hundred and one other things, which are none the less influential for being in many cases unconscious, and will certainly prevent our accepting a great many biblical statements at their face value.

Secondly, no one today would engage in religious study of the Bible unless he already had some faith in God, or at least some experience which led him to think that Bible study might be a fruitful activity. Such faith or experience will seldom have been derived mainly from the Bible direct, and never entirely so. It will have come, in one way or another, directly or indirectly from the Christian community through parents, friends, preachers, written sources or Christian art. Professor Hodgson, for example, has some interesting things to say about how the majority of Anglicans in the nineteenth century derived their Christianity *directly* from the Prayer Book catechism, and when they read the Bible, read it through the spectacles of that catechism.[6] 'The Church to teach, the Bible to prove' as it often used to be put.

What all that means is that any person or group of people in the modern world who can be conceived as undertaking serious religious study of the Bible will have at least two characteristics. First they must already have some experience of God, however inchoate, or at least some idea of what experience of God would be. Secondly, they will share some of the assumptions, questions and problems characteristic of modern culture, especially if they live in the west. It will make comparatively little difference whether they are self-conscious or unself-conscious people or whether with the

tops of their minds they claim to have remained untouched
by what they may regard as the arrogant pretensions of
modern culture. The sort of questions and presuppositions
with which we are concerned here are active at too deep a
level to be escaped in that sort of way.

It follows that if the Bible is to have any meaning for such
readers, or be of any help to them, it will be as the result of a
certain interaction between the three factors involved. The
experience of God, personal or vicarious, from which they
start will provide the *Vorverständnis* which enables them to
recognise the truth in what the biblical writers say about
relationship with God; it will make it possible to 'think the
God-related thoughts of the biblical writers after them' in
such a way that when we re-emerge into our primary
existence, it is with our own relationship with God clarified,
deepened and expanded. On the other hand, the problems
which we have seen to be associated with the process of
re-emergence cannot be ignored. The situation into which we
emerge, with our new relationship to God, is one in which
we, as well as others, believe certain things to be true and
others false, make certain assumptions, hold certain presuppositions. We may not simply flout these beliefs,
assumptions and presuppositions. Of course there are some
assumptions and presuppositions — even quite deep ones —
which can be changed, or need to be challenged, and some
hitherto neglected needs and concerns which can be recognised, without our being brought into conflict with the
fundamental stance of our culture. At times, however, men
will feel driven by the Bible to changes beyond those; on
such occasions they must obviously follow the *logos* where it
leads and adopt the attitudes and patterns of behaviour it
directs, rather as we have seen Galileo persevering in his
researches even when they seemed in basic contradiction of
much in the cultural outlook of his day.

Here, however, two things must be added. If men speak of
being driven by the Bible in this way, they must be sure that
what is moving them is a compulsion which engages them at a
deep level and not just a desire for continuity with the past in
the sense of holding on to the terms in which earlier Christian
ages expressed their orthodoxy. Secondly, in a culture as

self-conscious as ours, if we are moved to think and act in ways incompatible with normal cultural assumptions we must make every effort to pinpoint which of the assumptions and presuppositions defining our culture need to be changed and to show where exactly the influences which produced them have been wrongly estimated or understood. As we have seen, the presuppositions of any culture in Collingwood's sense of the term — 'the doctrines felt as facts' — lie so deep that it is very difficult to become conscious of them, let alone to change them. Yet this is what we must try to do; and we must try to carry our fellows with us in the changes we propose. It is neither consonant with our integrity nor helpful to others simply to claim that the Bible demands belief or behaviour unfamiliar or unintelligible in our cultural totality without a determined effort to show precisely where and on what grounds we regard the canons of that totality as being at fault, or at least as less than compelling.

But I am getting into a philosophical area I have neither the time nor the competence to explore. So suffice it if I offer a simple model of the sort of way I understand the matter. Suppose I am brought into contact with a man whom I find in some ways attractive and intriguing and yet whom I find it hard to understand and like, and with whom I manage to establish only a superficial relationship. And then suppose I meet his old nanny — assuming him to be old enough and rich enough to have had one. She may tell me, in her simple way, stories about his past — about his mother's death when he was young, for example, and about his and his father's reaction to it and to one another.

Age may have blurred and distorted her memory, and if I know anything about psychology, I may realise that her interpretation of what happened is far from adequate. Yet what she tells me may help me to understand the man and launch me into a new and deepening relationship with him; from time to time I may still find him puzzling, but a combination of greater maturity on my part, of the deeper understanding the old lady's story has made possible, and further recollection and understanding of what she told me may eventually lead to the ripening of the relationship into one of the closest intimacy. In the light of what I then learn, the nanny's stories may seem in retrospect to need still more allowances made for them, yet they will have had an indispensable part to play in bringing about the ultimate situation.

As that model will suggest, I myself believe in God and the possibility and reality of relationship with him, the creative and redeeming one, a relationship in which the initiative comes always from him — 'all is of God'; and I believe in the indispensability of the biblical story, and of Jesus and the others who gave rise to it, in making possible the sort of relationship which a twentieth-century Christian can have with God. However much else the resurrection story means, it means that without Jesus, whoever or whatever he may have been, there would not have been a community of men and women reconciled and related to God, to perpetuate and pass on a story in which it communicated its understanding of itself. The origination of that continuing community out of the Christ-event is in itself enough to distinguish the ancient Jewish-Christian story from any other ancient religious stories, for example those of the Greeks or the Egyptians. A believing relationship to those latter stories is not now a live option.

From what I have been saying it will be obvious that I am sympathetic to Bultmann so far as he insists that no understanding of our relation to God will do permanently so long as it remains what he calls mythological, that is, in basic conflict and discontinuity with contemporary beliefs and assumptions. He seems to me to err, however, in two respects. First by assuming that the assumptions and pre-suppositions of any age are an absolutely unalterable 'given' for those who live in it; and secondly by working with too narrow and rigidly defined an understanding of the contem-porary cultural situation. He contends not just that there is great insight in the existential type of phenomenological analysis of the human situation associated with Heidegger, but that no other will help to illuminate the Bible. Please do not misunderstand that criticism; that Heidegger's type of analysis can provide the biblical student with a most valuable heuristic principle, a key to unlock many doors, a way of discovering meaning in many otherwise opaque passages, seems to me to have been proved beyond a peradventure by the enlightening work Bultmann and his school have done in the interpretation of the Bible and of gnostic and other texts. Bultmann's mistake, as I see it, is in his tendency (whatever he may say to the contrary) to regard this as the only key and to dismiss as irrelevant, or meaningless to us, anything in the Bible which will not make sense in these terms. And is not the cause of his inclination the influence of the past, which makes him feel that if only we use the right techniques for discovering it, there is something which can be called '*the* meaning of the New Testament', the sole sufficient criterion for defining the Christian faith? In the last resort Bultmann too is a biblicist.

In fact the position, as I see it, is both more open and more complicated. The proper use of the Bible today could perhaps be analysed for purposes of description as a two-way process. On the one hand, if a man is soaked in the biblical story in the sense I have described in an earlier lecture, and he takes seriously the business of living today with its problems, moral, metaphysical, social and personal, he will constantly find his thinking about the situation (though he does it in an entirely modern way fully compatible with intellectual integrity) enlarged, questioned, judged, given new perspectives by the biblical story and by particular stories and sayings within it. Sometimes the impact will make itself felt more or less spontaneously, as he reads or listens; sometimes it will be a matter of deliberately confronting the contemporary situation with the biblical story, or some part of it which he thinks likely to prove illuminating. There will be times, in such cases, when the oracle remains silent; no light will emerge from the confrontation; and often we shall come across biblical passages which, study them as we may, seem to have nothing to say to us. Anyone of my persuasion will not be unduly worried by that. Many ancient texts have no meaning today in any normal sense of the word 'meaning' even though they will usually afford interesting reflexions of some sort if we ponder them long enough; why should the biblical text always be an exception? That is something the neophyte preacher may often remember to his comfort, if he finds himself expected to extract relevant ideas from some passage, just because it happens to have been appointed to be read in the course of the liturgy on the day of his sermon.

On the other hand, if the modern world should be brought into confrontation with the Bible, the Bible will have to be confronted with the modern world. If we are sensible, we shall not lightly assume that we are wiser than our fathers; we shall *start* from all they, with their many deep insights, have made of the Bible. Bultmann surely impoverishes himself by *appearing* at least to dismiss all this too summarily. Yet, though we are not necessarily wiser than our fathers, we are different. As Dean Inge was fond of quoting from Joshua 3[4], we 'have not passed this way heretofore' and we must take on our shoulders the full burden of the novelty of our situation. It is not for our fathers – even our biblical fathers – to determine what the truth is now. We must fully accept that responsibility for ourselves, while giving full weight to their testimony and wisdom. Professor Hodgson has been criticised by Canon J.A. Baker on the score of his often repeated question: 'What must the truth be now if people who thought as the biblical writers did put it like that?'[7] The justice of Canon Baker's criticism depends on how Hodgson meant us to understand his question. If it meant that there is a fixed quantum of truth which has only to be reformulated today, the criticism is just. It is possible that that is what he meant, though I am not entirely convinced that it was, at any rate in the later period of his life. Certainly when I have quoted his words in the past, I have taken them to mean: what light can we get on our present situation from the stories told about God and man by people of the biblical era?[8]

It is important to recognise that in all ages of the continuing community, Christians have treated the biblical story *as story* in the sort of way I have suggested. One need point only to Augustine, for example, and especially to the last few books of his *Confessions*, to establish that. But as we have seen, until recent times they have also attached to it a literal sense – treated it as in some sense literally true; and there we must recognise that we are not bound by precedent. We need not, and should not, treat the story on any other terms than those which come naturally to us as people of our period.

On this view, what the Bible, and especially the New Testament, mediates to us is that possibility of, and demand for, self-awareness and relationship with God and man which God intended should issue from the life of Christ. And here I am most anxious not to be misunderstood; nothing I have said is intended to minimise the central importance of Christ's life in this connexion. The possibilities of which I speak have resulted from the life of Christ, and only become possibilities because of it. That is why the Church will always want to discover all it can about that life from those who lived under the immediate and full impact of it.

But to say that is to raise a question which I have already glanced at several times but must now attack frontally. The burden of what I have been saying in these lectures is that the vital 'story' element in the New Testament is, in the last resort, an interpretation of the new experience and way of life which the career of Jesus made possible for the early church. From that it follows, first of all, that we can never dispense with, or replace, the New Testament story; if we did that, we should have no means of discovering many of the Christian possibilities or demands. Professor Knox puts the point very well in his book *The Death of Christ.*[9] The New Testament story, he says, 'is true and irreplaceable, not because it explains in a causal or instrumental sense the deliverance which God through Christ makes available to us, but because it conveys something of the concrete meaning of the deliverance, its quality and its transforming power, and because that quality and that power can be conveyed in no other way.'

But that, you will notice, leaves wide open the question *how* exactly Jesus' life produced the results it did. What was it in, or about, Jesus which made his life the originating point of a new community with so new and distinctive a spirit and way of life? In one important sense, I think, we have to say we do not know. When the New Testament speaks about the matter it does so in first century terms, most of which we can no longer accept; and we have very little basis on which to build any alternative account. On the basis of such evidence as we do possess, Professor Knox has some very illuminating things to say in the book from which I have just quoted, and so, among others, has Professor Bornkamm in his book *Jesus of Nazareth*. But for the most part, the answer is hidden in the mists of history and the wisdom of God. As I tried to explain earlier, it does not seem to me to matter greatly; through Christ God achieved what he set out to achieve, and if, so far as method goes, He has kept His secret to Himself, I cannot see that we are the losers. Most of what I should want to say on this topic is said far better and more briefly in these two further quotations from Professor Knox: 'It is *God* who made the event significant . . . and . . . it is impossible for us to explain just how He did so or to identify the precise locus of His action' and, more fully,

> That this event had the particular result it had — a new community in which are found a new forgiveness, victory, and hope — is a matter of empirical knowledge in the Church; *but why this particular event had this particular result is a matter altogether beyond our knowing. God's thoughts are not our thoughts, and his ways are not our ways. The event was a whole event and its effect was a whole effect. We cannot break the event into parts and attribute the whole effect to one part, nor can we ascribe any particular part of the effect to any particular part of the event. Both event and effect are one and indivisible; and moreover, they belong indissolubly together. Of this whole the remembered death of Jesus is the poignant centre. And the death of the Son of God is the all but inevitable symbol of its ineffable meaning.[10]

The last quotation may help to explain why I am laying so much emphasis on this aspect of our question and dealing so fully with it. As I see it, this is the vital distinction between the old tradition in the use of the Bible and the new tradition

---

* By the last nine words I take Professor Knox to mean, not that the Church as seen from outside — or even inside — is an obvious proof of the divine status of the events from which it originates, but that within its life and tradition its members can achieve a deep certainty of a new forgiveness, victory, hope and so on.

for which I am pleading. According to the older tradition what had to be done *was precisely* to discover 'why this particular event had this particular result', to 'break the event into parts and attribute the whole effect to one part', and to ascribe particular parts of the effect to particular parts of the event. Earlier scholars believed, at any rate with the top of their minds, that their task was to discover as far as possible the nature and structure of the Godhead and then to show how, in relation to that, the various elements in the Christ event produced the results they did. That for them was what the Bible is about. On our view its real concern is with the new life and love and relationship with Himself which God through Christ made possible to the early Church; that is the significance of the new chapters which the early Christians added to the Old Testament story in order to expound and explain their new relationship.

If I were asked to cite a theologian who uses the Bible in the way I desiderate, and incidentally, by the contrast between his approach and Bultmann's, demonstrates the excessive narrowness of the latter's interpretative categories, my choice, I think, would be Fr Harry Williams, especially in his remarkable book of sermons *The True Wilderness*[11]. Fr Williams is well seen in philosophy, though his philosophical formation no doubt owes more to Professor Wisdom than Professor Heidegger; he has a deep knowledge of modern psychological theory and practice, partly as a result of personal experience, and a profound and sensitive understanding of modern literature and drama. He is a modern man and not ashamed of it. As such, he makes no secret of the fact that he finds certain quite central elements in the biblical story unacceptable, and indeed, if allowed to overflow directly into our self-understanding, potentially highly misleading. Examples taken from his writings are the pre-Freudian understanding of responsibility and blameworthiness[12] or the way the New Testament teaches, or implies, the complete saintliness and total sinlessness of Jesus.

He explains himself in these words:

What has Christ to give us? . . . We cannot think of it in terms of some spiritual essence or celestial power, for as

thus considered it is meaningless. Must we not rather
search the Scriptures, believing that the word of God
therein set forth will be made flesh in our own day and
generation? This is not the search for historical objectivity
— for what really happened or for what was really said.
That search has been tried and failed. It is rather faith that
the Bible can speak God's word to us now and that the
word will incarnate itself in terms of our own contemporary views, taking as always the form of a servant.[13]

That is just what Fr Williams in his sermons and lectures
helps the Bible to do, never, as he says,[14] transmitting
second-hand opinions, whatever their source, the Bible,
Aquinas, Paul Tillich or Charles Gore, but consistently
throwing light, at least for me, on words which, as he puts it,
'he has proved true in his own experience'. He says in effect:
'As I try to practise the Christian faith in a way and form
fully compatible with modernity, I find my understanding of
this, that and the other matter, enlarged, deepened and
stretched by familiarity with the biblical story in such and
such ways. As a result, this is how I see it; can you not see it
like that as well?' That seems to me the proper approach.
Indeed in the present situation I cannot see how anyone can,
in the last resort, adopt any other, however differently the
matter may be phrased.

It needs to be added at once that Christianity remains as it
has always been, essentially something corporate. What
Fr Williams, Professor Bultmann, Professor Knox,
Dr Robinson and others should be seen as doing is offering
what seem to them to be their various insights for the
guidance or judgement of their fellow Christians. In each
generation it will be for the *consensus fidelium* to determine
as best it may, with God's help, what truth emerges from
what are claimed to be the insights and interpretations
offered to it. Provided it is not pressed too far, Dr Charles
Davis's model of the natural-scientific community examining
and testing the various papers and reports offered to it, and
so gradually moving forward along the path of knowledge,
seems to me a good one. Like him, I cannot see why the

Christian community should feel any more need for an external, normative, and allegedly objective criterion than the scientific community appears to do.

Obviously, on such a basis, any creeds, any definitions of what being a Christian means and commits us to in any generation, will henceforth have to be less sharply defined than in the past, though on sociological grounds alone they will surely be an essential continuing element in any foreseeable church life; and we shall have to accept that creeds and liturgies will change at a rate and to an extent hitherto unparalleled. For it will continue to be true of our successors that they 'have not been this way heretofore'. The creeds of the past could claim to be timelessly valid because they could be seen as brief expositions or summaries of *the* meaning of the Bible. If we can no longer believe in anything called '*the* meaning of the Bible' in that sense, the nature of creeds will change accordingly, though that of course is not to say that there will be no stability or continuity. As we saw earlier, a literary critic knows the lunatic fringe when he sees it; and Christians of any generation would know, for example, what to make of a so-called Christianity which invoked the name of Christ over, let us say, a doctrine of universal hatred or organized selfishness.

Some weeks ago, when I was discussing such matters with a distinguished English biblical scholar, he remarked: 'Not to put too fine a point on it, what you are saying is that Christianity is at any period what Christians say it is.' Well, yes and no; may I leave that question for discussion later? Meanwhile there is at least one question I could rightly be accused of having begged so far. I have talked a good deal, in one way and another, about genuine modernity, and what is, and is not, compatible with it. Who is to decide what is '*genuine* modernity'? I have already quoted with at least qualified approval Dean Inge's aphorism 'He who marries the spirit of the age will soon find himself a widower'; it is notoriously difficult to distinguish what is inescapably demanded or excluded by valid modern insights from what is simply passing intellectual fashion.

About all that I have time to say only two things. The first is this. Let us hear no more of the suggestion that a modern approach to the Bible is arrogant and that it is the business of the true theologian to submit to the Bible and not sit in judgement on it. Such talk rests simply on a confusion. The aim of every genuine theologian — or other scholar — is to grasp the objective truth about his object of study, to submit his whole self, with all his presuppositions and prejudices, to whatever demand may be made on his understanding by the facts. When well-based evidence is such as to drive a theologian to question or revise some traditional under-standing of the Bible, he is not arrogantly sitting in judgement on his creator, but submitting himself to the Lord who bids us prove all things in order to discover where we are to hold fast.

Secondly, it is *not* easy to distinguish lasting truth from fashion, but we have to do the best we can, and it is idle to pretend that the Bible can settle the matter for us in any but the most indirect way. For example, there are those who study the Bible with full religious seriousness without being theists at all (the 'death of God' theologians, for example), or without being theists except in what they themselves would agree is a very Pickwickian sense (for example, Professor R.B. Braithwaite). For my part I believe they are mistaken; the truth lies with a much more robust theism and doctrine of creation; I am not sure that I should even go by any means all the way with the so-called 'process theologians'. The important point is, however, that these are not matters which can be settled by direct appeal to the Bible. I cannot say to Professor Hartshorne, for example: you are wrong because there is no direct statement of your position in the Bible, or even because there is no passage directly compatible with it. What I *must* do — and all I *can* do — is to understand his viewpoint, or any other, as fully and sympathetically as I can; and if I find it unacceptable, explain why, and offer my alternative, on the basis of a full acceptance of what I take to be genuine modern insights as illuminated and transfigured for me by the biblical story and the relationship with God into which it has launched me.

Such a position as I have outlined would, if accepted, obviously have very wide implications for all readers of the Bible, for preachers, liturgiologists and many others; though who can doubt that in any case our liturgiologists need to take an altogether more radical view of the task of liturgical revision than any of them shows signs of doing at present?

The great majority of Christians today are more than half aware of the character of the Bible as story, much of it true story. There are many circumstances in which it would be entirely proper to assure Christians, both simple and sophisticated, of the truth of the Bible story, or some part of it. The chief need, however, is first to help people to articulate their implicit feelings about the Bible without loss of faith and to cease feeling guilty because they no longer regard it as a 'sacred' book in the sense that phrase bears in the comparative study of religions. Fr Williams writes:

> The discarding of the old bottle and the provision of the new has been interpreted by some Christians as a denial that there is any more wine at all. That is because they have imagined that God can be contained within the limits of a definition as though wireless waves were identical with a certain type of receiving set. Yet the fact that God cannot be thus contained or identified was for St Paul part of the scandal of the cross. The Greeks, he said, seek after wisdom; yet the world by its wisdom failed to find God, who is not known in intellectually satisfying systems of thought . . . [15]

Here preachers could help, not only — not perhaps so much — by explicit discussion of the matter as by exemplifying in their sermons the way in which the biblical story is related to Christian faith for today, and how the Bible should be used now that it is no longer a 'sacred book'; by showing, for example, that we are not tied to any literal acceptance of biblical statements or logical deductions from them, and that it is no way of settling ethical problems for people in the twentieth century simply to try to behave in ways which may have seemed natural — and may indeed have been right — in the first.

An interesting example of this was brought to my attention the other day by my former colleague Professor G.C. Stead, who had just been to a Christian conference at which a mature and sympathetic lecture and discussion

session about the problems of homosexuality today happened to be followed by a service containing a passage from
Paul roundly condemning all homosexual practices as contrary to the will of God. It was significant of contemporary
attitudes to the Bible that a number of lay members of the
conference found themselves perplexed and troubled by the
juxtaposition. That was because they had not been shown
how to 'distance' the Bible and allow for its pastness. They
still sought detailed ethical guidance directly from its text.

The preacher's part is the more important because just as
people of many sorts, but not all, will watch and appreciate
Shakespeare's plays, so it is not the vocation of all Christians
to read and appreciate the biblical story for themselves. To
them, *pace* the new Anglican catechism, the faith is properly
mediated through other books and other means, including
the sermon.

Also including the liturgy — very much including the
liturgy; and that gives the liturgy a vital role. It could perhaps
fulfil it if it would abandon its implicit fundamentalism in
appearing to assume that the way to body forth the Christian
faith corporately today is by doing as near as makes no
difference what the ancient Jews did in their synagogues and
doing exactly what Jesus is said to have done at the Last
Supper. By all means let new meaning be shown in old texts
— that is presumably the case for the continued use of the
paternoster (on that see further p. 259 below); but let the
liturgists select their biblical passages with an eye to the
impact they are likely to have on those unsophisticated in
matters of interpretation; and let them contextualise such
biblical readings as they appoint with modern music and
action and with non-biblical readings (there is plenty of
precedent in the breviary, if precedent is needed!). That will
help a congregation to understand what they hear and to
realise that they are not bound to the literal acceptance of
any of it, still less of the sub-Christian sentiments of many of
the Psalms for example. Liturgists, quite as much as dogmatic
theologians, need to free themselves for what has rightly been
called 'the curse of the canon'.

The question of the canon is obviously too long a one to
be entered on fully at this stage. It may, however, be pointed

out that the notion of the canon and the notion of a constant quantum of truth which is the essential content of Christianity, go very closely together. If the latter is questioned, the former is bound to come into question as well. The canonical books cannot cease to have a peculiar status, at any rate for the foreseeable future, because they have been evaluated and studied for centuries as having an 'authority' not attaching to other writings, however ancient or 'sound'. That fact undoubtedly influences profoundly the position from which any modern Christian *starts*. It is, however, a quite different question whether in our efforts to reconstruct and understand the ancient Jewish-Christian story, we, from our standpoint, should distinguish between available source material on any ground other than its usefulness for the purpose in hand. If the Wisdom of Solomon, or even the Qumran Scrolls, prove more useful, in certain contexts, than, let us say, the book of Nahum, we should use them in those contexts without feeling under any necessity to provide a doctrinal justification as a basis for our procedure.

If the notion of inspiration is here brought into the argument, it can only be replied that if the notion is used here in the same way that it is in connexion with other writings we might describe as 'inspired', our criterion is a subjective one and my position is not affected. We could apply to this particular aspect of the matter the words of Troeltsch: 'At the present time people rightly turn with ever-increasing agreement to the Christian experience of salvation and to the totality of a religio-ethical philosophy of life for the grounding of Christian belief.'[16] This is really a special application of the modern position we have already discussed that 'faith is only to be guaranteed by the inner necessity of the human spirit'. If an objective doctrine of exclusive inspiration is advanced, it is hard, from a modern standpoint, to see it as anything but a dogmatic re-assertion of positions about timeless truths, the status of certain writings as *auctours* and the like, which we have already found to be untenable.

I have said that most Christians are at least half aware of the story character of the Bible. Their awareness needs to be completed and made articulate at whatever is the appropriate level in each case; then they need, rather desperately, to be helped to know what to do with story in an age which, as we have seen, has come so to divide sense and sensibility that even poets scarcely know what their function is. I know of no higher priority than the production of a liturgy which would help forward such an understanding and the preaching of it, instead of making them seem, by contrast, a betrayal of the faith.

The fact is that the Jewish-Christian community is like a river; the branch to which Christians belong took a decisive turn at the Christ-event, which has determined the direction of the flow ever since. Newman long ago saw through the claim that a stream is clearest near the spring. There is still a great deal that is worth pondering in his statement: 'Whatever use may fairly be made of this image, it does not apply to the history of a philosophy or belief, which on the contrary is more equable, and purer, and stronger, when its bed has become deep, and broad and full. It necessarily arises out of an existing state of things, and for a time savours of the soil'.[17] Perhaps the last words may suggest a more modern analogy suggested also by Troeltsch's observation that in the course of passing through, and allying with, various cultural situations, Christianity has become a number of totalities. There has been 'an interweaving of Christian and extra-Christian material, a dependence upon the total situation.'[18]

As the water of the Christian faith has flowed through the various stretches of the river, it has indeed in some respects got clearer and stronger and it is still the water of life. But from the upper reaches it has also received elements which make it, as it reaches us, *eau non potable* until we have added to it, and killed things in it, as only our generation knows how to do. Our fathers had different palates and other stomachs. Only after appropriate treatment can the water of any river be health-giving and thirst-quenching to our generation.

11 The Bible and the future of the faith

The discussion after the original delivery of these lectures which revealed the omissions I have now tried to repair in the Introduction also revealed that many members of the audience would have liked a clearer picture of the way I envisaged the Church functioning in the future, if my position with regard to the Bible, or anything like it, came to be accepted. To meet that demand the present chapter is being added as a kind of postscript. In this case, however, the reason the audience was left in doubt was not simply lack of time; I did not — and to a considerable extent still do not — see my own way at all clearly in the matter.

If there is any substance in the sort of problem raised in this book, the situation is not one capable of being cleared up quickly by any single mind; it is one that will have to be dealt with by the Church as a whole, and even the Church will need time to live with it and ponder it. If the problem is to be solved, it will be very much a case of *solvitur ambulando*. What follows is therefore offered for consideration and frank criticism by my fellow Christians simply in the hope of indicating a possible way forward.

I

At the beginning of the lectures, when the question whether the Church's attitude to the Bible contributes significantly to the contemporary Christian problematic was first raised, the analogy was suggested of an individual whose proper psychological development has been arrested and distorted because he has remained fixed in his attitude to some person or institution. The implication was that the attitude in question was one of unquestioning acceptance or obedience, which although it had been healthy and helpful at an earlier stage was no longer appropriate. In a sense the analogy was, quite deliberately, tendentious; yet few modern theologians would refuse all validity to it. For the sort of reasons discussed in the lectures, it is now generally recognised that the situation since the onset of the modern cultural revolution demands of Christians a different relationship to the Bible from any appropriate or possible before; and most theologians would also agree that no fully appropriate relationship has yet been discovered or defined.

In the lectures we have discussed various suggestions for change in this connexion which have been made in the last century or so, and, brief though our discussion has been, it has sufficed to make clear what very varied attitudes to the Bible have been advocated. One thing, however, all these suggestions have in common: they all recommend some *modification* in the traditional attitude to the Bible rather than the substitution of a radically new attitude for it. They all agree that being a Christian involves bowing before the authority of the Bible and allowing one's fundamental beliefs and attitudes to reality to be dictated by it in a more or less direct way, as if the Bible somehow contained *in nuce* the whole Christian faith. Those who make these suggestions are all like psychological advisers who recommend conservative treatment; they are what we described earlier as minimisers, and we saw some reason to think that in this context the role of the minimiser might be that of the tempter. (see pp. 43–4 above.)

When it comes to the question *how* exactly we should be controlled by the authority of the Bible, we have seen that the various suggestions differ widely. Pope Pius XII, for example, appeared to suggest that a Christian is still committed to believing everything the Bible says provided only that it is understood in its true sense as determined by expert philological and historical investigation and the traditional teaching of the Church. Protestant versions of a similar view could also be quoted.[1] Others suggest that what the Christian is committed to is belief in the occurrence of certain of the historical events reported in the Bible and acceptance of the meaning ascribed to them by the biblical writers and elaborated by later Christian thinkers.[2] By contrast, others doubt if it is possible for a modern Christian to understand the biblical events quite in the ways the biblical writers did; according to them, what a Christian is committed to do is to accept that these events contain the decisive clue to the nature and meaning of reality, and to make an appropriate modern response to them, as reconstructed on the basis of modern historical study.[3] Others again see it as the mark of a Christian that he should model his life on the teaching of the historical Jesus about the fatherhood of God and the brotherhood of man, while still others place their emphasis on the biblical *attitudes*, especially the attitudes towards the future and towards man's responsibility for his past. The Christian, they say, must discover the essential character of these attitudes, which he can do by a proper interpretation, or demythologization, of the biblical text and then reproduce them, or some of them, in his own life. The authors of all these suggestions, it should perhaps be added, insist that the grace of God is a pre-requisite for discovering the meaning of the Bible and responding to it in the way they suggest.

The very variety of these suggestions is bound to give us pause, especially when we remember that each theologian who has put forward a suggestion has only done so because he found reasons for being dissatisfied with the others. There must obviously therefore be considerable grounds for dissatisfaction with every one of these suggestions, and in the course of the lectures we have seen what the chief grounds of the dissatisfaction are. In the broad sense they are all historical.

If, for example, we are asked to pattern our life and beliefs on the teaching and attitude of Jesus, it is not at all clear that we have sufficient evidence to be sure what his attitude or teaching was. As we have seen, it is possible to summarise his teaching under such rubrics as 'the fatherhood of God' and 'the brotherhood of man', or to sum up his attitude by describing him as 'the man for others', 'the one who was completely open to God and the future' (Bultmann), 'a man who dares to act in God's stead' (Fuchs) or 'the one in whom existence was completely transparent to essence' (Tillich);

but if we could get back and observe Jesus in the days of his flesh or — what is equally impossible — reconstruct his life and teaching in their full historical particularity, it is not at all clear whether such formulas would not prove misleading abstractions from the total impressions he made and sought to make — whether indeed he would have recognised himself in them at all. They are all suspiciously modern and there is at least a danger here of deciding what the true attitudes are and then calling them after Jesus.

Likewise with the resurrection of Jesus and the other historical events interpreted in the Bible as special revelations of God; it is not at all clear, as we have seen, whether we can now reconstruct them, even in cases where they actually occurred, with enough accuracy and detail to be clear what an appropriate modern response to them would be.

The nub of the problem in fact lies in what we have said about cultural change. Our unreflective reaction, given our cultural circumstances, is to expect from the biblical documents a degree of historical accuracy it was not natural or possible for documents of that culture to possess; and what is more, we have to ask how far attitudes and teaching deriving from the biblical and early post-biblical totalities, however appropriate or profound they may have been in their settings, are capable of determining in any direct way what our beliefs and attitudes should be in our very different cultural totality. No one pretends that that is an easy question to answer, and our aim has simply been to put the reader into a better position to answer it for himself.

It is, for example, possible to produce formulas of a very abstract sort such as C.H. Dodd's 'God at work in judgment and redemption, challenging man to respond and thus to shape the course of events to ends beyond his surmising',[4] and to argue that such a phrase aptly characterizes the belief of the biblical writers and can also determine and express our attitude. The trouble with formulas of such a high level of generality, however, is that they tell us virtually nothing either about what the biblical writers *did* believe or about what we *should* believe. And as soon as we try to unpack them and extract detailed guidance from them, we come up against formidable difficulties. In the case of the formula just mentioned, for example, biblical writers already understood it in different senses, and for our part we cannot understand the word 'God' in any of the ways in which Old Testament Jews understood the name Yahweh or even in the way, or ways, New Testament writers understood the word *theos*; and similar difficulties will arise in connexion with 'at work', 'challenging', 'judgment' and 'mercy'. The lectures have emphasized the internal coherence of cultural totalities and shown the impossibility of isolating our religion from the rest of our culture in such a way as to be able to adopt religious terms and responses precisely in the senses in which they expressed the mind of people of earlier cultures. The possibility has therefore to be faced that in religion as in other spheres, our twentieth-century beliefs and responses will have to be our own. The Bible will no doubt prove to have a very important part to play in determining what they should be, but that is a very different matter from their being directly dictated by it in the way that all pre-critical, and most critical, theologians have demanded.

In the interests of sharpening it up, the point may be put as follows. Modern sociologists and religious anthropologists, if faced with New Testament Christianity in any of its forms — or for that matter with the Christianity of the patristic, or of the medieval or of the Reformation period — will examine it in exactly the same way as they would any other of the religions from alien cultures they are accustomed to examining. In the light of such examination most of them will pronounce it an outmoded religion in the sense that its belief-system, rituals and legitimations seem irreconcilable with a great deal of what we know, or are compelled to believe, as modern western human beings. In the light of their general presuppositions and their knowledge of the development of other religions, these sociologists will feel that the account the biblical religion gives of itself is unacceptable at too many points to form the substance of their own attitude to reality, or even the fundamental basis of it.

What are we to do in the face of such a situation? Many Christians nowadays would go a long way with such sociologists, especially where the more primitive elements of Old Testament religion are concerned, but they would almost

all want to call a halt at some point and claim that beyond
that the sociologists have overpressed the evidence. They
would insist that some of the things said in the Bible are as
true now as when they were written. An example many of
them would be likely to take, at any rate in England, would
be the Incarnation. 'If God became man', they would say,
'He became man, and no amount of change in culture or
outlook can change that.' We have already seen the difficulty
about any such position. Quite apart from the fact that the
incarnation of God is not something the New Testament
reports (see above, p. 155) the statement that God became man
is not a statement about the past in the ordinary sense and
does not possess the sort of irreformability such a statement
would have. It is an interpretation of certain events believed
to have happened in the past, and an interpretation which is
arguably as impossible in our cultural setting as it was in that
of the New Testament writers. (see pp. 95 ff., esp. p. 97.) As we
saw there, it is not a question of *logical* impossibility; yet, as
we have seen in connexion with Barth, it is an impossibility
which can be denied only on the basis of some 'positivism of
revelation'.) For us to make this statement in the sense
intended by those who first formulated it would involve
mythological discourse or a philosophy of substance such as
many of us find we cannot relate intelligibly to the rest of
what we know to be true. Nor will it avail to invoke the
category of mystery at this point. Belief in the Incarnation in
the traditional sense would involve us in mystery in a quite
different sense from any it involved for those who propounded it. We may take our cue from William Chillingworth
who wrote in 1638, 'following the Scripture, I shall believe
many Mysteries but no Impossibilities; many Things above
Reason, but nothing against it.'[5]

To some, therefore, it will seem that we have no
alternative but to go all the way with the sociologists. The
question is whether it is possible to do so, to 'distance' New
Testament Christianity and allow fully for its pastness and
remain a Christian. Can we say of the biblical books what
Lionel Trilling says of some of the poems and plays he studies:
'In the *pastness* of these works lies the assurance of their
validity and relevance'? (see p. 193 above; italics mine.)

The aim of this chapter is to suggest that we can, and indeed to claim that it is possible on such terms to be a profoundly biblical Christian who ascribes to the Bible a very central place in the providence of God. In order to understand this claim it is necessary first to be clear about one thing. To describe a religion as 'outmoded' or as 'a religion of the past' is (at any rate in our understanding of the words) simply to say that it cannot now be accepted or practised as it stands. It does not for a moment involve denying that the adherents of the religion in question may have had a genuine relationship with the true God or that their meaning-system and rituals may have formed a perfectly appropriate expression of it for their times.

If that is recognised, nothing that has been said in these lectures prevents us from seeing in the New Testament writings, and the practices they describe, expressions — some no doubt more adequate than others — of genuine and deep relationships with God. At this distance of time we may not be able to say at all exactly at the historical level how these relationships came into being; obviously the faith of Judaism will have had a great deal to do with it, and, as we have seen, it is hard to believe that the life and personality of Jesus did not play a larger part than some modern scholars have allowed (see above pp. 189 and 223).

However, questions of that type will not unduly worry us if we define the Christ-event in the sort of way we have seen Professor Knox does, as embracing not only the words and deeds of Jesus himself, but the effect they had on his contemporaries and the response of his followers to him, including their thoughts, activities and influence during the century or so after his lifetime (see above, p. 169). So defined the Christ-event is, as we saw, an indubitable fact, and equally indubitably it resulted, or even in a sense consisted, in the emergence of a group of new communities, the Christian church, within which the relationships with God were experienced, expressed, pondered, discussed and shared, to their mutual enrichment. *Is it not possible to see the nub of the whole matter in the origination of this relationship and the fact that the Church has survived by introducing men of every succeeding generation and culture to it, or rather, to a version of it appropriate to their varying circumstances?*

So impressed were the first Christians by the richness and reality of their newly experienced relationship with God that they felt a passionate urge to make it available to as many others as possible, and in this they were remarkably successful — partly no doubt through force of example, but also by their use of the spoken and written word. Indeed their primary aim in putting pen to paper was to clarify their faith and make it intelligible and attractive to others. So far as the New Testament writings are concerned, we have argued that they were produced, not so much to 'document' the rise of the Christian faith in the sense in which we should understand the word, as to 'legitimate' it, which means, as we have seen (see pp. 8 ff. and 164), to account for its existence in ways which would ensure its being taken seriously as of divine origin and also make clear what its acceptance and practice promised and demanded.

However such legitimating accounts may strike us, they served in that totality to introduce converts to a relationship with God which proved itself so fully in their experience that many of them in their turn were moved to spread it both by the spoken and written word, with the result that the faith was passed on from generation to generation in ever widening circles. Already at this point it is important to note a vital feature of the process. The new generations of Christians undoubtedly sought most earnestly to understand and practise their relationship with God in precisely the ways defined in the New Testament; and because their cultural situation was in many cases so similar to that of the New Testament writers, they succeeded to a considerable extent. Nevertheless, as we have seen, the canonization of the New Testament and the harmonization of the various New Testament outlooks in a single 'faith', and a faith moreover which no longer envisaged the speedy end of the world, was already an act of interpretation which to some extent altered the character of what it interpreted. Nor is this anything like an isolated example. It is impossible to read carefully the Christian writings of the second, third and fourth centuries without realising that, quite unconsciously and in the belief that they were simply drawing out the full implications of the original revelation, their authors gradually introduced changes which had the effect of making the Christian relationship to God, as they understood and practised it, intelligible and acceptable in the somewhat different cultural conditions of their day. It was for this reason, humanly speaking, that they could successfully evangelize others who shared their cultural outlook.

The same process is evident in every subsequent period of Christian history, and it is safe to generalise and say that one of the essential reasons why the relationship to God proclaimed by the Church has been able to commend itself to people of so many different periods and cultures is because in the form in which it has been offered to each community it has been intelligible and acceptable to the members of that community without loss of integrity. (It goes without saying that acceptance of Christianity involves radical changes in any convert's previous assumptions and values, and always has. The point is that the changes in question must never be such as to involve flat contradiction with the rest of what the circumstances of his time compel him to regard as factually true. See Chillingworth as quoted above and *passim*.) Since the communities have varied, the relationship, or at any rate the understanding of it (see pp. 242 and 250), has in practice differed from time to time. Until comparatively recently, however, as we have seen, the communities in which Christianity has been accepted have been culturally speaking relatively homogeneous, and therefore the differences we are discussing were not great enough to attract much attention. (In one sense, allegorical and other non-literal methods of interpreting scripture were ways of attending to them, but they were not recognised as such.) In the forms in which it was preached and practised up till, let us say, the middle of the eighteenth century, the Christian relationship to God was still everywhere capable of being comprehended under the original biblical categories and images without any impossibly strained interpretation being called for.

Nevertheless, as the lectures have shown, it *was* often necessary to interpret the terminology and imagery of the Bible in what we can only regard as forced and artificial senses in order to make it appear applicable; and the fact is inescapable that if we ask what in practice Christian belief and discipleship have meant in the life-contexts of believers of different periods — what it has felt like on the pulse, so to speak, to be a Christian of the New Testament, or the patristic, or medieval, or Reformation periods — significant differences reveal themselves.* If, for example, it were possible to imagine bringing together in one room representative Christians of different cultures in the period up to 1750, for instance Matthew the Evangelist, Cyril of Alexandria, Scotus Erigena, Bernard of Clairvaux, Melanchthon and John Locke, we should soon find that even if they could learn to speak one another's languages in the literal sense, they by no means spoke the same language in the metaphorical sense. 'The faith once delivered to the saints' which most of them held in common — in a sense of course Matthew would ante-date it — would prove a unifying factor only to a relative degree and at a somewhat abstract level. Their conceptions of the God and the Christ they all worshipped would differ significantly.

If that was true of Christians before, or at the beginning of, the modern cultural revolution, how much more will it apply to those who have lived since? One of the differences which distinguishes those living before the flood from those living after is that the latter have become fully conscious both of the necessity for understanding and expressing their relationship to God in new ways and of the degree of novelty involved. The process has sometimes been resisted and held up for longer or shorter periods by time-lags and rearguard

---

* What modern Christian, for example, can conceivably imagine Christ on the cross uttering to the penitent thief sentiments of the kind which the Crusaders felt it entirely natural to attribute to him?

> My friend, he said, the race is yet unborn
> That shall avenge me with their sharpened spears.
> The French will then deliver all the land,
> And they who share in that great pilgrimage
> Will enter with their souls to heaven itself . . .

Professor Colin Morris, who quoted the words in a university sermon at Oxford, commented, 'A work of God, planned on the Cross to avenge the Cross — that was the Crusade.'

actions of various sorts; but it is because it has on the whole been persistently maintained that Christianity has survived and reached our generation in a form which made its acceptance a live option for us.[6] As we learned of it, whether from parents, friends, clergy, books or broadcasts, it was a form of belief not so obviously or inherently at odds with truth derived from other sources that we were compelled to reject it.

In one instance this is generally recognised and welcomed. If the faith had been presented to almost anyone now alive in the traditional form insisted on by Bishop Wilberforce and other English churchmen only just over a century ago, in which it demanded rejection of the theory of evolution and the acceptance of the Bible as an inerrant authority even on matters of natural science, it would not have been a live option. All too often the re-thinking on this point in the last hundred years is treated rather grudgingly as an isolated instance. Instead we should see, and welcome, it as one example among many of the way in which the faith has had to be, and has been, reformulated even in the last few decades, in such a fashion that we have been able to take Christianity seriously and have been introduced by the Church to a relationship with God which we value more than anything else in life.

What we have to recognise is that although this relationship is not by any means identical with the one described in the New Testament or those expressed in most post-biblical Christian writings, it could not have existed or been what it is but for the whole process we have just described, including — very much including — the events behind the Bible, and the biblical interpretation of them.* To speak thus surely implies no low view of the Bible; for we are expressing our recognition that in the providence of God the biblical events and the biblical transmission of them have played a decisive part in bringing about the relationship with God which forms the very centre of our lives. Whatever our cultural differences

---

* It implies no lack of respect for humanists or adherents of non-Christian religions to claim that dependence on the biblical writings and the Christian tradition produces a quite distinctive type of character.

from our predecessors, it is still the same God with whom we are in communion and it is still recognition of him in the Christ-event which reveals his love for us and has made our present communion with him possible.

If we do not, in the traditional way, claim a unique status for that event or for any of those who took part in it or the transmission of it, that will be for several reasons and will imply no underestimation of it. In the first place, although no one, even of Bultmann's persuasion, is likely to doubt that the activity and personality of Jesus had an essential part to play, a part without which the events would not have been what they were or had the results they did, the same is true of the positive response to him and the creative understanding of him on the part of Paul and John and many other primitive Christians — or for that matter of the interpretation put on him by Athanasius in his day. What warrants have we for pegging out certain stretches of the series of events as uniquely significant in the providence of God, and how should we know where exactly to put in our pegs?

Secondly, some of the most important movements of thought which have contributed towards the development of our present cultural situation have made us acutely, and salutarily, aware of the limits of meaningful discourse where the extra-natural is concerned. (Wittgenstein's well-known aphorism 'Whereof one cannot speak thereof one must be silent', *Tractatus Logico-Philosophicus*, § 7, is symptomatic.) We are in general much less inclined than our fathers to suppose that we can chart the workings or explain the mechanics of the unseen world. 'God's secret to himself.' We may well feel therefore that we have neither the historical nor the philosophical grounds for essaying a Christology or a theory of the atonement in the traditional sense, and be content simply to say with John Knox that the 'divinity' of Jesus 'was the purpose and activity of God which made the event which happened around him, but also in and through him, the saving event it was'.[7] That it was a 'saving' event (however exactly we unpack that word) we shall know for ourselves, for our present relationship with God is an issue of it.

II

However, if we left the matter there, we should seem to be ascribing to each Christian's relationship with God the status of an absolute criterion for determining religious truth, and to do that would run counter to our whole thesis. It is not just that we know as a matter of principle that our successors' understanding and practice of their religion is bound to differ from ours, as their diagnosis and treatment of what we call diabetes will. The seeds of future change are already present and germinating in our consciousness.

Our first instinct with regard to our relationship with God is, quite naturally, to treasure and enjoy it. We seek to foster, deepen, extend and perfect it by every means at our disposal — or more accurately, allow it to be deepened, extended and perfected by God — and we are apt to get defensive when questions are raised about it. All that is natural and proper enough; but nevertheless if this relationship is genuine, we cannot but we aware of an obligation to make it available to others, and that is certain, sooner or later, to involve defending its authenticity against those who question it. We shall not get very far with that, if our opponents know their business, without being made to recognise that our present understanding and expression of it are inadequate. (Inadequate, that is, in a sense in which the inadequacy could in principle be overcome. There is of course a sense in which all human accounts of relationship with God must always be inadequate.)[8] Even apart from recognitions forced upon us by apologetic and missionary activity, every thoughtful Christian is bound to recognise that there are certain elements in the faith, even in the contemporary form in which it was presented to him, of which he has to say 'that I can't believe'.[9] It is always true that the shoe pinches somewhere; the fit is never perfect, and in a period of rapid change such as ours it is apt to be especially poor. Just how poor it seems and where the pinch is felt, will vary from person to person, partly as a matter of temperament and partly in accordance with the aspects of contemporary culture familiar to each. As we have seen, the modern cultural situation is far too complex for anyone to be aware of all its aspects, and the problems or enlightenment they contain for Christianity. It is partly because so many of these aspects are bound to be closed books to the clergy and other theologians that it is so vital for lay Christians, who do know about them, to play a much larger part in theological debate than they have done hitherto and do even now. The time is past when sermons and other contributions from lay members of the Church could be regarded as an optional extra; they are now vital for a faith with potentiality for survival.

'That — at any rate as expressed — I can't believe.' No one will accept such a verdict as final till he has consulted others older and wiser in the faith, who may — or may not — be able to convince him that his supposed difficulty is groundless. The fact remains, and must be fully faced, that there are today elements in the faith with regard to which some of the most thoughtful and instructed Christians have come to feel that radical reconsideration is necessary. It must equally be recognised that some of these elements are among the most central. To take the most striking example, many have come to feel that, as a recent writer puts it, 'God is the problem'.[10] Their experience will not for a moment allow these Christians to deny the reality of the transcendent, and yet their familiarity with modern science and philosophy, and in some cases their deepest moral certainties as well[11] prevent them from conceiving it any longer under the forms of traditional supranaturalism, as a separate reality, some sort of immaterial person alongside and over against, the rest of reality. They find they have no more need of any 'realm of the divine over and above or behind the processes of nature and history which perforates this world and breaks it by supranatural intervention' — of what Leslie Dewart calls 'absolute theism' — than the Marquis de Laplace had in the early nineteenth century.[12] Indeed they cannot accept at all what John Robinson calls 'the supranaturalist projection'.[13] The question of God, they say, is not the question 'whether some entity or other exists but . . . whether Being has such a character as would fulfil man's quest for grace'. The 'Beyond', as Bonhoeffer put it, is found 'in the midst of our life'; or as Teilhard de Chardin has it, the transcendent is the 'within' of all things 'coextensive with their without'.[14]

Now it is true that there is a Christian tradition

exemplified in such writers as Ruysbroeck, Eckhart and Boehme with which such language harmonizes very well, but it is not on that account that the language is being recommended today; still less would those who use it claim that it is 'really' what the Bible was saying, or seek to vindicate a non-supranaturalist perspective for the biblical writers. The language is used because it is the only adequate, or at any rate the most adequate, language in our situation. The question at issue arises out of the whole character of the modern sensibility and there is therefore no hope of dealing with it simply by conforming ourselves to New Testament writers or any others who lived, experienced and wrote in terms of a quite different sensibility. Here, as in natural science, we must insist on a proper autonomy. There is no choice but to wrestle with the matter in the way that such theologians as Kaufman, Hartshorne, Macquarrie, Ogden, Robinson and many others are doing until we have an understanding of the nature of the transcendent which is not 'impossible' in relation to our sensibility.[15]

Perhaps a further example is only an extension of the last. Many modern Christians wrestle in the sort of way just described with what has traditionally been called the doctrine of creation, and ask how we today are to image the causal relation of the transcendent to the world of phenomena. Here authors such as Raven, Coulson, von Weizsäcker, Teilhard and Arthur Peacocke among many others have made their contribution, and they have had to take into account not only that the natural world is of a size, age and developing character (on the last see pp. 253–4 below) quite inconceivable by Jesus or any of the biblical writers, but also the near-certainty that it contains innumerable self-conscious beings besides ourselves. There must therefore be 'other Christs for other worlds'. As Alice Meynell saw in her poem *Christ in the Universe*[16] any satisfactory picture of the relationship between God and the universe today has to contain room for 'His pilgrimage to thread the Milky Way' and 'his bestowals there', and for the guise in which 'He trod the Pleiades, the Lyre, the Bear' and 'the million forms of God those stars unroll'. Simply to rehearse the matter is enough to make clear that there can be no question of conforming ourselves to the thought of writers for whom these eras and areas of reality did not exist. In one very real sense, we have to say to the biblical writers 'Your God is too small'. Our understanding of the matter must be our own. It is not enough simply to draw from the narratives in the early part of Genesis the truth that the world is totally God-dependent; the question is to discover how in our totality that dependence can and should be imaged. Must our picture, for example, depict change and movement on the part of the transcendent? Some of the most eminent modern theologians believe so, and their debate with their opponents cannot be settled by appeal to writings for whose authors neither the data nor the questions had so much as appeared over the horizon. It would for example be completely irrelevant to quote against 'process theologians' the words attributed to Yahweh in Malachi (3:6) 'I the Lord change not' — just as it is illegitimate to quote the anthropomorphic-dynamic imagery of the Bible against supporters of a doctrine of impassibility. It will be clear why the quotation of biblical passages does not, and cannot, play any very large part in such discussions. It should also be clear that the two examples discussed were chosen almost at random out of a practically limitless selection. In a similar way, for instance, we must reserve the right to understand the person of Jesus and the results of his activities in ways which make sense, or at least do not make nonsense, in relation to our total cultural context.

All this leads on to an important but, so far as I know, little discussed question. Most modern theologians, even if they are prepared to concede the sort of point just made, combine their agreement with a significant distinction. For purposes of apologetic, of formal exposition and intellectual discussion of the faith, they agree that new formulations such as we have been describing are necessary and proper. But at the level of the imagination, which is the level of prayer and practical piety, they seem to feel that our needs are best met by continuing use of the biblical story.

Professor Knox, for example, after a discussion very much along the sort of lines we have been setting out, of what the ministry of Jesus can mean today, concludes with the statement that 'the death of the Son of God is the all but inevitable symbol of its . . . meaning'. Elsewhere he describes the New Testament story as 'true, . . . indispensable and irreplaceable' on the grounds that 'it conveys something of the concrete meaning of the deliverance' and that 'the quality and transforming power [of that deliverance] *can be conveyed in no other way.*'[17] It is easy to appreciate what he has in mind. As we have seen (pp. 182–3, 188 and 194), one of the reasons why the gospel has appealed effectively to people of so many different cultures is because the imagery of the biblical story is primordial; and by now that imagery has penetrated so deeply into the consciousness of western man that it can articulate his relationship with God in a way that no newly devised imagery could possibly do, while on the other hand its very archaism obviates any danger of its being mistaken for literal statement of fact. All talk of God, indeed all statements of an ultimate attitude to things, must take the form of story. The basic Marxist account of things, for example, is a story and so is the humanist account; so it is inevitable, and in no way objectionable, that the primary Christian account should be in story form. A.N. Whitehead, we have seen (p. 120; cp also p.68), made a distinction between the concrete image cast up by a paradigmatic event and the concepts that are abstracted by the reason. Is it not therefore best for the Church to retain the images originally cast up by the biblical events and to leave it to the individual theologians or apologists of each period to abstract the appropriate rational concepts? In this way the essential continuity and continuing identity of Christianity are ensured, while an appropriate understanding and exposition of it can be provided for each generation and cultural situation. A case can be made along similar lines for keeping unchanged the traditional verbal imagery and symbolic actions of the Christian liturgy.

There is obviously a great deal of truth in all this and no one doubts that the biblical story should, and will, be kept in the widest possible circulation. Yet is there not another, and complementary, side to this matter? So far as continuity is concerned, a great deal depends on the type of continuity envisaged. If the word implies persistence in remaining completely unchanged despite changing circumstances, it is not clear that it is a thing to be aimed at. It was persistence of that sort which brought about the extinction of dinosaurs. Is it not rather the sort of continuity which links an acorn, a sapling and a full-grown oak that we are after?

Then again the question must be raised whether the view we are considering does not ask of the biblical story something it cannot possibly be expected to do. A story, like a poem or a play, is produced, or grows up, to express a certain meaning. We might even go so far as to say that a story *is* its meaning. At any rate, if it is a well told story, no other way of expressing things will convey what it is intended to convey anything like so fully or exactly. (We may be reminded how T.S. Eliot, when asked by an undergraduate what he meant by writing the line 'Lady, three white leopards sat under a juniper tree' replied 'Lady, three white leopards sat under a juniper tree', and how Lionel Trilling urges us to 'keep before our minds the problem of the relation which expression bears to feeling' (p. 39 above). We may remember too Dame Helen Gardner's praise of Miss Lascelles for eschewing any attempt to reproduce *the* meaning of *Measure for Measure* in an alternative, twentieth-century mode of expression.) But by the same token — and this cannot be too strongly emphasized — a story intended to express one meaning will not normally be a suitable vehicle for the expression of a different meaning. In view of that, and of what has been said earlier in the chapter, what exactly are we asking modern Christians to do when we invite them to make the biblical story their own? Austin Farrer had no doubt. Teach people how to interpret stories, or indeed poetry, he said, and they will be able to get from the biblical story all they need.[18] As we shall see, there is some good sense there, but in the present context there are at least two serious difficulties about it. In the first place it is quite Utopian; only very very few people, ordained or lay, are capable of extracting the meaning of verbal symbols and imagery with anything approaching Austin Farrer's acuteness and sensitivity, or even of being trained to do so. (It is tempting to say of him what he says of Bultmann, ' "modern man" means for the purposes of this question a being sufficiently sophisticated to appreciate the approach which is his offered remedy; say one man in five thousand'!) Second, and more significant, is the point that if we discover what the biblical story was designed to convey, what we shall have discovered is how people between 2,000 and 3,000 years ago responded to reality. The whole argument of these lectures has carried the implication that we cannot respond to reality in precisely that way, and this is something of which preachers constantly show themselves aware when they warn their congregations against taking the biblical story 'literally', that is, in the way the biblical writers and their first readers took it. (As we have seen, people in the biblical period were quite innocent of the distinction made in these lectures between history and story; they firmly believed the truth of what they wrote about the past — and the future — and for them the story *was* the meaning of reality.)[19] Modern congregations are thus advised not to suppose that God created the world in six days flat, for example, or that he intervenes in history to keep the sun stationary in the sky for periods of several hours. What they are *not* told is how they *should* envision God's creative or providential relations with the world, or indeed any of his other dealings with it as we now know it to be.

It can be argued, it seems to me, that the place where contemporary Christianity is weakest is at the level of the imagination. Men find it hard to believe or pray because they have no imaginative framework genuinely compatible with their modern sensibility in which to envisage what the existence of God and relationship with him can mean. They have no story which does for them what the biblical story did for men of biblical times, provide food for the imagination which is also digestible by the mind, unite sense and sensibility, imagination and understanding. Is the unprecedented popularity among non-theologians of the — far from easy — writings of Teilhard de Chardin and Dr John Robinson partly due to the fact that they gave some promise at any rate of plugging that gap? (The case of Teilhard is perhaps instructive. Would it be fair to say that in his concern to provide food for the imagination which would also be digestible by the mind he sometimes forgot that it was food for the *imagination* he was after, and dressed it up as a strictly scientific account? Hence, maybe, some of the charges of pseudo-science made against him.) Critics of Dr Robinson have leaped in to insist — correctly or incorrectly — that the modern Christian does not really imagine God as a distinct, individual person 'up there' or 'out there'. What they significantly fail to tell us is how he does, or should, imagine him.

Yet it is certain that 'where there is no vision (in this sense) the people perish'. There can surely be little doubt what the biblical writers would have done in such a situation. We have seen (e.g. pp. 23 and 183) that when their understanding of God and his activity was modified or extended in any significant way, they modified or extended the traditional story about God in such a way as to do justice to the new dimension. It is also worth noting how they allowed new insights to produce modifications, often radical modifications, in their liturgical worship. What advice would they give us? Would they perhaps see our difficulties as one more aspect of the 'curse of the canon'?

III

If, however, we were to follow their example and take their advice, what new story should we tell? This book is not the place, nor has its author the competence, even to begin to answer that question; suffice it for us if we have made clear that it is a cogent question which demands to be taken up. Even the more restricted question of the sort of relationship the new story should bear to the biblical story cannot be fully discussed in the final section of a book such as this; but it is so important a question, and one subject to so much misunderstanding that something must be said about it.

The first and most important thing to say is that the relationship will be an unprecedented one. 'We have not passed this way heretofore.' There is so far as I know no precedent for producing one story about reality, partly on the basis of an earlier story which professed to reveal the ultimate nature of things and partly on the basis of other data. (Perhaps a partial parallel might be found in the activity of a modern philosopher who calls himself a Platonist. What will be the relationship between his system and that

expressed in Plato's original dialogues? The philosopher may
be fully justified in claiming to be a Platonist in the sense
that his view of things has been moulded to a large extent by
repeated and appreciative meditation on Plato's dialogues.
Yet since, as we have seen (pp. 101–2), his claim cannot mean
that he views reality today exactly as Plato viewed it in
fourth-century Athens, it is legitimate to ask him just how,
given all he owes to Plato, *he* sees things *now*.) All the more
credit, surely, to Bultmann that he has essayed so daunting a
task. It is no doubt true, as his critics allege, that his
demythologized version of Christianity will not serve for
what we are after. Quite apart from its covert biblicism, it is
not sufficiently a story, it does not encompass enough of
God's dealing with the world, its imagery (if that is the
word![20]) is too restricted, and it lacks the universality and
simplicity which characterized a lot of Luther's writing, for
example, and will have to characterize any new story which
is to feed our imaginations as well as our understanding. (In
fairness to Bultmann it should be added that his motive
has been a good one. It was wise of him to confine his account
of our relationship with God to those elements which seemed
to him of existential significance. We may not necessarily
agree with him what these elements are, but we shall do well
to limit our story to 'what we feel, what we smartingly do
feel'. See further pp. 254–5 and meanwhile cp. R. Gregor
Smith, 'We cannot speak of God in himself . . . We can only
speak in terms of the ways in which we actually encounter
otherness'.[21]) The translation metaphor is wholly misleading
in this context. Apart from anything else, it would commit us
to the assumption Leonard Hodgson rightly deprecated that
'someone somewhere at some time in the past, really knew
the truth [and] that what we have to do is to find out what
he thought and get back to it.' (See p. 205 above.) It is
inextricably involved in the 'fixed quantum of truth' view of
Christianity.

So far from the one story's being a translation of the
other, it is not even true that the subject-matter of the two
stories will completely overlap. As we have seen, our story
will have to take account of God's dealings with whole eras
and areas of reality completely unknown to the biblical
story. To add a further example to those already given, the
story we are after will have to do full justice to the reality of

development. According to the biblical story, all creatures, both animate and inanimate, had simply persisted or reproduced themselves, in exactly the form in which they had been created. The only essential change which had occurred had been a moral declension or 'fall' which affected the entire creation; and that in turn went a long way towards defining the form God's *redemptive* activity would take. For according to the biblical and comparable mythologies, the *Endzeit,* the end time or condition of salvation, would in some sense be a restoration of the *Urzeit,* the beginning time or period of original perfection. For us, however, development appears to be a basic activity of a God who has worked patiently for inconceivable millions of years to produce even the present stage in the development of the universe. We shall not, therefore, be surprised if we find it operative in our relationship with him in a way the biblical writers did not, and could not, do. As we have seen, an adolescent son does not merely *understand* his relationship with his father differently from the way he did when he was three years old; the relationship itself is different. For all that its outlook is in many ways basically static, the biblical story contains at least the germs of a developmental view, and we shall not hesitate to go much further; our story may well suggest that the relationship to which God calls us is in some respects very different from that to which he called people of earlier times. In many contexts at any rate, we may even agree with Bonhoeffer that he calls us to live and act *etsi deus non daretur.*[22]

If the story we are after may thus contain many things of which the Bible knows nothing, it may for various reasons have little or nothing to say about matters which do figure, and figure prominently, in the Bible. Parts of the biblical story may prove, for example, to be concerned with questions and problems no longer of any interest to us — for instance the question whether it is necessary to become a Jew before becoming a Christian, over which Paul agonized and in connexion with which he so elaborated the story of Abraham.

Again, as we have seen, ours is an age acutely and healthily aware of the limits of its capacity to speak intelligibly about the extra-natural, and we shall perhaps distrust our ability to say more than a very little, by biblical standards, about such topics as the end of history and its supernatural aftermath. Our experience of God may compel us to repeat after Mother Julian and T.S. Eliot our conviction that 'all shall be well and all manner of thing shall be well', but we may feel incompetent to specify much further and produce any equivalent for the vivid and often detailed biblical portrayals of the coming and character of the kingdom.

What we are after is thus emphatically not a 'translation' of the biblical story. Even where the subject-matter coincides, our story should not be expected to 'do justice' to the biblical story in the way that a translation can properly be expected to 'do justice' to the original. It is by now a commonplace among historians that we can often understand the past better than it understood itself. A modern scholar may offer an interpretation different from — and often, it must be added, superior to — any offered by those who took part in it or first wrote about it. There is a good deal in that for us to reflect on. It has been customary for Christians to suppose that the interpretation of the biblical events in the biblical story was *the* true interpretation, on the grounds that the meaning it saw in the events was either a meaning somehow inherent in them or else divinely revealed as the true meaning. We have seen grounds for doubting whether any such trans-cultural claim is in principle possible; but even if it were, the question would still have to be faced how *the* meaning disclosed in persons or events by the biblical writings should best be expressed in writings belonging to our cultural totality. For example, the claim that 'Jesus is the Christ' clearly plays a vital part in the New Testament, but it gets the meaning it carries there from its context in the biblical story, and indeed the biblical culture, as a whole; and if it is taken over direct as part of the modern Christian story, so far from helping to prove the substantial identity of the new story with the old, it will inevitably take on a new meaning from its new surroundings and the question will arise what that meaning is and whether this particular formula is the best way of expressing it.

It follows that the inclusion or omission of particular

biblical (or for that matter patristic) imagery or phraseology will not by itself give any guidance as to whether our story is genuinely Christian or not. It will thus be no good attempting to discredit a suggested version of the modern story on the grounds that it does not contain some phrase or idea which may be central to the biblical story. One cannot argue as follows, for example: the New Testament makes clear that Jesus was the Son of Man and therefore no story is authentically Christian which does not say so. The new story will quite possibly, and if so, without any impropriety, have been framed on the assumption that Son of Man is a mythological term in Bultmann's sense and so not suitable for inclusion in the Christian story as we tell it.

This point is well brought out by Dr Knox in a book from which we have already quoted. He recalls an occasion when an academic colleague, engaged in a discussion about the difficulty of supposing that Jesus regarded himself as Son of Man, was asked, 'But suppose he *was* the Son of Man?' Knox comments,

> Now I find such a question very hard to deal with, not because of what it asks for, but because of what it seems to presuppose. It seems to ascribe to the 'Son of Man' objective and personal reality. It seems to assume that there was, and is, a Son of man. But what does the phrase 'Son of man', in the context of apocalypticism (and no one can deny that context in many of the Gospel statements), really designate? Must we not say that it stands for an idea, or an image, in the minds of certain ancient Jews? One can trace to some extent the beginnings and development of this idea or image in Jewish culture. But do we for a moment suppose that it is the name of any actual person — that the Son of man in fact exists or ever existed?[23]

(Our point remains substantially unaffected if, with Dr Vermes and others, we take a different view from Dr Knox of the precise meaning attaching to the phrase *Son of Man* in New Testament times.)

IV

The last few pages have been almost entirely taken up with ways in which the Bible cannot, or should not, be used. In conclusion we must face the question of the ways in which it *can* be expected to help toward the deepening of our relationship with God and the making of that relationship all-pervasive of our lives, both individual and corporate.

It is important first to be quite clear that the Bible can exert great influence despite the fact that we cannot specify with the precision our ancestors attempted either the methods by which the influence is best brought to bear or the ways in which we expect it to have its effect. Essentially, what the modern student of the Bible is doing is the same as what Christians of all earlier periods have done when they have searched the scriptures. He is engaging in what the Germans describe by the expressive word *Einfühlung,* that is, literally, 'feeling one's way into' another's meaning with the aid of all the imaginative sympathy and all the knowledge one can command. Obviously this is something which can be done, at their different levels, by specialist scholar and ordinary Christian alike. Indeed, since no amount of factual information is a substitute for imaginative sensitivity, a non-professional well-endowed with the latter, may often get a good deal further than the scholar.

What principally distinguishes the modern Bible reader from his predecessors is that, at any rate if he is a historically-minded westerner, he will start with the realisation that the biblical beliefs and attitudes into which he 'feels his way' will almost certainly prove alien to him in important respects. He will recognise that the further he feels his way into the minds of the biblical writers and those they describe, the more likely he is to be conscious of sailing in strange waters. He will certainly be able in many cases to achieve a measure of what, to use another Germanism, is known as *Nacherleben,* experiencing the experience of a biblical writer or character after him. As we have seen, it is a mistake to exaggerate the extent to which such identification with another's experience is possible; and in any case, what is more important, the modern reader will not expect the experience to be one which he can bring back into the present, as it were, and incorporate just as it is into the rest of his contemporary experience.

That will not surprise or discourage anyone who has grasped what writers such as Collingwood have to say about the inevitably 'incapsulated' character of any thoughts we 'think after' people of the past. On the contrary, to anyone who has really made this insight his own, it may be a source of great relief. It will mean that he is freed from any obligation to attempt — or if he is a preacher, persuade his congregation to attempt — to reproduce or conform to biblical beliefs or precepts today, however sensitively or accurately he may have intuited them.

On the other hand, to say that they cannot be brought directly into the present is not for a moment to deny their influence, or the importance of feeling one's way into them. Readers may care to look back to the words of Collingwood quoted on p. 214, some of which are worth reproducing here. 'In rethinking what somebody else thought', he wrote, the historian 'thinks it himself. In knowing that somebody else thought it he knows that he himself is able to think it. And finding out what he is able to do is finding out what kind of a man he is.' Perhaps an analogy may help.

Suppose an Englishman goes to live for several years in Italy and finds the experience enjoyable and stimulating. He may come to speak Italian and to live, dress and feed after the Italian fashion. Supposing him to be a man of any sensitivity, we may be sure that if he eventually returns to live in England he will be a very different person from the man he was before he went. That does not mean that he will attempt to reproduce his Italian way of life on the English scene. If he is wise, he will not speak Italian all the time, eat exclusively Italian food, dress after the Italian manner or even adopt Italian attitudes to politics in the English political situation. When in England he will do as England does, and the influence of the Italian experience will manifest itself in various differences *in his way of being English,* differences of which in some cases he will be aware, though in some cases they may be more apparent to others than they are to him.

It is in some such way as this that the influence of the

Nacherleben of biblical beliefs and attitudes should be understood. We saw in an earlier chapter how an imaginative-ly sensitive study of a Gospel passage might lead to the exorcising of a characteristically modern fear, or how a thoughtful reading of St Paul might lead to a conviction of sin fully compatible with the insights of modern psychology and sociology. We may perhaps add a further example now. A modern Christian who reads the Book of Ruth cannot hope fully to fathom, let alone adopt towards anyone today, the attitude of a young Moabite widow in the eleventh century B.C. towards her widowed mother-in-law; yet reading about Ruth's loyalty to Naomi may well give the reader a salutary jolt in connexion with his insensitive attitude toward some elderly relative or even toward old people in general. The example is trivial but the point it exemplifies is of universal application. [Not in the sense that every biblical passage can be relied on to speak to our immediate condition or give us a salutary jolt, but in the negative sense that no passage will ever provide direct unmediated guidance, or items that can be incorporated as they stand into our belief-system. How much misery might have been saved if only Augustine had realised that the words 'compel them to come in' in Lk. 14:23 did not apply directly to his situation or provide any guidance about the way the Church should treat heretical or schismatic Christians!) A more striking example which may serve to drive the general point home is provided by the Lord's Prayer. Whether or not it goes back to Jesus – and that is very much in doubt – the incorporation of modern translations of it into liturgies has made many Christians aware that some of its clauses cannot be taken over today in their original sense, e.g. 'do not bring us to the test' – no one today expects an imminent universal ordeal of the kind in all probability originally envisaged. (The alternative rendering in the Anglican Series 3 service is to some extent an evasion of a genuine difficulty.) In fact the problem is of wider scope than most people realise. Anyone familiar with the most probable translation and interpretation of the prayer will be aware that comparatively little of it can be used today in its original sense.[24]] In one of the most important theological books of recent times the American

Roman Catholic scholar, Father John S. Dunne, has explored with great thoroughness and insight the various vital but subtle ways in which men can be changed as a result of what he calls 'passing over' into alien religions and cultures, that is, entering with the fullest imaginative identification into their manner of life and thought.[25]

Our analogy may have further light to shed. The kind of influence which the experience of foreign travel has on people depends principally on two things: the places to which they go and the sort of questions, interests and concerns which are uppermost in their minds before they set out. A period in Florence, for instance, is not likely to have much effect on anyone who knows and cares nothing about painting and architecture; or at any rate it will have a very different effect from what it would have had on a passionate art-lover. I want to suggest that both these things have their analogues in connexion with the Bible; and in the case of the first I am not thinking simply of the obvious truth that the influence the Bible has on a reader will depend on which part of it he reads.

There is a much more interesting sense in which different readers may be said to read different parts of the Bible, or even to read different Bibles. What that sense is may best be made clear if we begin by looking at another important passage from Professor Trilling. It comes from the work already quoted[26] and for ease of reference I have ventured to label each of the possibilities it enumerates with a bracketed letter. In the course of a discussion about the true nature of a poem he points out that the question is constantly being raised 'What is the real poem?'. He goes on:

Is it (a) the poem we now perceive? Is it (b) the poem the author consciously intended? Is it (c) the poem the author intended and his first readers read? Well, it is all these things, depending on the state of our knowledge. But in addition the poem is (d) the poem as it has existed in history, as it has lived its life from Then to Now, as it is (e) a thing which submits itself to one kind of perception in one age and (f) another kind of perception in another age, as it (g) exerts in each age a different kind of power. This

makes it a thing we can never wholly understand — other
things too, of course, help to make it that — and the
mystery, the unreachable part of the poem, is one of
its . . . elements.

It is not only the last part of this statement that is relevant to
the Bible — though would that people had heeded the truth
in that and never supposed that they could completely
comprehend the Bible or get it 'taped'. *Mutatis mutandis*,
practically everything Professor Trilling says here is relevant
and important for our enquiry.

The Church as a whole must take pains to ensure that it
lays itself open to the whole Bible in the sense of the word
'whole' Professor Trilling implies; but it is inevitable, and
quite natural, that individual members of the Church should
concentrate primarily on one or other element in the whole,
on one or other Bible in Professor Trilling's sense. The
modern biblical critic, for example, is concerned almost
exclusively with (b) and (c) and only with the others so far as
they throw light on these. The fruit of this concentration has
been an astonishing increase in our knowledge of what
biblical books and passages meant to their writers and first
readers — often something very different from what had
traditionally been taken to be their meaning. Most ordinary
church people on the other hand, and most dogmatic
theologians to date, take it more or less for granted that (d),
(e) and (f) are what really matter. (So far as dogmatic
theologians are concerned, many of them have made sincere
attempts to take the work of the biblical critic into account,
but it has generally been within the context of the
assumption that he would prove to do no more than dot the
'i's and cross the 't's of the classical interpretations, and
would not bring the latter radically into question. Exceptions
must of course be made for theologians such as Paul Tillich).
This is because the great majority of clergy and their
congregations have been brought up to believe, and are still
encouraged by their forms of worship to believe, — something else which is 'nought for the comfort' of liturgiolists
and liturgical revisers, all too often, alas, the same people —
that the 'real' Bible is the Bible which 'submitted itself to

being perceived' at whatever post-biblical period or periods are regarded as doctrinally authoritative in their denomination. For most Anglicans, for example, the real Bible is the Bible as seen through the eyes of those who framed the creeds and definitions of the 'undivided Church'[27] with the viewpoint of some later group, such as the Reformers or the 'Caroline divines', added as partially corrective spectacles.

It is an open secret that this situation leads to tension and mutual suspicion, the ordinary churchman* suspecting the biblical critic of unnecessarily and arbitrarily undermining the biblical foundations of such doctrines as those of the Trinity and the Incarnation[†] while the biblical critic suspects traditional believers of reading into the text what he can only regard as illegitimate and arbitrary meanings because they could not by any stretch of the imagination be supposed to have been part of what the original writers intended or their readers understood, nor are they derived from the Bible by the use of reputable modern scholarly methods.

If there is any substance in the argument of these lectures, it will be seen that all these fears and suspicions are groundless. Once it is recognised that there is nothing properly described as '*the* meaning' of the Bible, no fixed quantum of truth which it contains and which we have only to take over as it stands, then both groups will be able to continue with their approaches without any suspicion on the part of the other. The traditional believer can only be grateful to the biblical scholar for having uncovered hitherto unsuspected layers of beliefs, attitudes and relationships to God to be explored and intuited under his guidance in the way described just now. The biblical critic on the other hand, must first grasp that it is perfectly legitimate to find in a document meanings which go beyond what the original author consciously intended, and that in any case estimates of

---

* And all too often, it must be admitted, his leaders as well; cp. e.g. the letter to *The Times* of 15 May 1974 by the Bishop of Chester, which reveals as complete a failure to understand the situation in modern biblical study, and indeed historical study generally, as could well be imagined.

† A blatant example of the unsupported assertion that biblical critics are irresponsibly motivated and work on arbitrary assumptions, without any concern for the effect their studies have on their fellow Christians, is to be found in the *Church Times* leader for 25 April, 1975.

what a writer originally intended are themselves to some extent functions of the cultural situation in which they are made. (It is, for example, widely recognised that the meaning Barth found in the Bible had close connexions with the tragic and chaotic character of the times in which he lived; similarly we can be sure that whatever meaning interpreters of the twenty-second century find in the Bible will be different from those we find. We may fairly claim that genuine progress is being made in getting nearer the original meaning of the biblical text, but the process can never be more than asymptotic.) He will then be in a position to give up all claims to be the sole possessor of 'the meaning' of the Bible and therewith all objections to what the ordinary Bible reader, and at a deeper level the dogmatic theologian, wishes to do.* It will by now be clear that what these latter are doing, or should be doing, is to feel their way into the meaning of writers who interpreted the Bible in patristic and later times, and into the relationship with God those writers sought to express. The fact that their interpretations were not on lines which would have been possible in any of the biblical totalities and are impossible in ours, does not mean that they do not betoken genuine relationships with God, the *Nacherleben* of which, if we may put it so, can help to deepen and extend our own relationship with him in the manner described just now. The point is important enough to warrant brief elaboration.

In the preface to her study of *Measure for Measure* Miss

---

* Unfortunate though its results may have been, the attitude biblical critics have tended to take up is intelligible enough against its historical background. When modern biblical criticism first arose, the idea was still more or less universally accepted that the Bible was directly normative of Christian belief and conduct. Seeing the unscientific and often fanciful interpretations of the text to which Christians were being expected to conform, biblical critics said in effect: If we are to be controlled by the biblical teaching and history, let it be by the original teaching, and the history *wie es eigentlich gewesen.* In effect they thus set up something which corresponded in intention to the old 'literal' meaning. By now however, the mistake of trying to define *the* meaning of the text should be apparent.

Lascelles defends the frequency with which Dr. Johnson's views are quoted in the body of the book. 'Veneration for his critical sagacity', she writes, 'compels me to attend to what he says, even when I believe him to be in error.'[28] Something comparable often needs to be said about the biblical interpretations of such men as Augustine or Luther, for example. If we study their interpretations, we shall frequently have to say that they do not, and cannot, embody the meaning of the Bible for us; we may even on occasion doubt if they were primarily derived from the Bible at all. At the same time, we shall ask why Christians of their stature attributed to the Bible the ideas they did, and we shall often find that what they say may still contain, couched in its own terms, truths which are deeply significant for us. If, as Leonard Hodgson used to insist, the Bible should always be approached with the question: 'What must the truth be now if people who thought as they did put it like that?' there seems no reason to suppose that the posing of the same question with regard to these later interpretations of the Bible would be any less fruitful, or at any rate that it would be entirely fruitless. In this connexion it must be remembered how essential it was in earlier ages to be able to cite biblical authority for any views one wished to get accepted, and so how easily men could, quite unconsciously and with no intent to deceive, attribute to biblical writers opinions and doctrines which they felt *must* be true and of which they were passionately anxious to convince others.

It is a weakness of much contemporary theology, especially in Germany, that it affects at least to take little account of earlier interpretations of the Bible and makes it its sole aim to bring about a direct confrontation between the original meaning of the biblical text, so far as it can be discovered, and the modern western world, as if for the first time. (So far as German theology is predominantly protestant, the origins of all this in the *sola scriptura* are too obvious to need emphasizing; nor does it need to be emphasized that implicitly, modern German theology is as much influenced by earlier biblical interpretation as any other. In fact, apart from the influence of Luther much of it would be hardly intelligible.) As the work of Bultmann, for example, shows, such a confrontation often proves highly creative and can lead to something of an understanding explosion. Similarly, as Dr Kathleen Bliss has pointed out on the basis of her experience in India, when people of a non-western culture, hitherto uninfluenced by the Bible, are confronted with it, insights are often generated which prove illuminating to westerners and non-westerners alike. Yet to confine the legitimate interpretation of the Bible to such situations would be like limiting 'the real poem' to 'the poem we now perceive'.

To ignore earlier interpretations of the Bible is to betray a basic failure to understand how things work either sociologically or psychologically; it is a symptom of the excessive individualism and the failure to apprehend the community dimension of the Christian religion which characterizes much existentialist theology. Whatever else it is, the communion of saints is an important sociological reality, and many of the truths derived, at least purportedly, from the Bible by earlier exegetes have become so much part of the Christian consciousness that any position which simply writes them off will prove unacceptable, and rightly so. Contemporary Christians must be prepared to have these truths confronted with some such question as Hodgson's;[29] what they are rightly not prepared to do is to see them simply ignored.

All these approaches then are legitimate and complementary, but it would be a great mistake to regard them, even taken together, as excluding any other. It is worth noticing that in the passage from which the present phase of our discussion began, Lionel Trilling gave pride of place to 'the poem we now perceive'. Likewise we must make no attempt to hide or depreciate 'the Bible we now perceive'. Just as earlier generations were right to look at the Bible in their way in their day, so we must look at it, and at subsequent interpretations of it, in our way in our day. Which means looking at it steadily and looking at it whole through the spectacles provided by modern historical, psychological, sociological, religious-historical and other studies. What we shall see will be very different from what our predecessors saw — a mass of religious traditions and beliefs of varying types and stages of development, many of them closely paralleled in other religions, brought into unities we shall sometimes regard as artificial, and 'legitimated' in ways we shall often be unable to accept. Yet not only must we be allowed to look at the Bible like this, there must be no suggestion that it is impious to do so. On the contrary, we may expect important new insights to emerge from the process. We may for example come to see that God, having created an *historical* universe (that is, one subject to the conditions of historical change and development) relates and reveals himself to people of each historical situation in a — or rather the — appropriate way. (Taking account, of course, not only of men's stage of cultural development but of the situation produced by their *sin* at any time. It hardly needs to be added that it is fully compatible with all this to believe that one of God's principal media for revealing himself to any generation may be the story of how he has dealt with earlier generations). Whatever may be thought of this particular suggestion, we must accept in principle that 'the Bible we now perceive' is just as fruitful a source of insight as the Bible 'as it has existed in history' and submitted itself to various kinds of perception by previous ages. As Lionel Trilling goes on to say, 'each new age makes the pattern over again, forgetting what was once dominant, finding new affinities; we read any work within a kaleidoscope of historical elements.'

If the influence of the Bible on the reader thus depends on which Bible he reads, it also depends, as we have seen, on the mental 'set', the assumptions, concerns, questions and expectations he brings to his reading of it. About this matter of *Vorverständnis* a good deal has already been said, and only a few comments, or rather perhaps examples, need to be added here. Even among professional students there will be variety; some, with a primarily linguistic background, will be mainly interested in the exact meanings and overtones of the words and phrases in a passage; others, with more historical interests, will be more concerned with reconstruction of the incident or incidents that lay behind it, and the meaning of those incidents. Still others, perhaps with a background in literary criticism, will concentrate more on the biblical books as wholes, asking what their authors or final redactors meant to convey by selecting just that material, and arranging and expressing it in just the way they did. Others again will concern themselves with the whole sweep of the Bible, perhaps being fascinated, as Austin Farrer was, by the complex interplay of the imagery it contains, or being moved by its basically narrative structure to the conviction that only narrative discourse of some sort can ever do justice to the reality of God's dealings with the world.[30] They may even be moved, as Erich Voegelin, for example, was, to try to *produce* some such narrative, though it will be a narrative retailed from a genuinely modern perspective and not an attempt such as the biblical theologians made, to re-vindicate the narrative of the Bible itself.[31]

Yet however great the variety — and we have not begun to do justice to it — one thing these approaches have in common. None of them confers on those who adopt it the right to say to their fellow Christians 'the meaning which emerges in the light of my *Vorverständnis* is *the* meaning, and you entertain any other at your peril'. The most — and also the least — that any of them can rightly do is to offer the insight he believes himself to have attained for the judgement and, if so be, the enlightenment, of his fellow Christians. The matter can hardly be better expressed than it was by Father Laurence Bright O.P. in a letter to the *Times*:

> Isn't the real situation much more like that of literary criticism? The critic looks more closely at a text than others have done, brings new ideas to bear from a wider experience, and points out what the rest of us have overlooked. But in the end our agreement is necessary. As Dr Leavis once pointed out, the characteristic critical judgement takes the form, 'This is so — isn't it?' Where something authentic has been said, the rest of us eventually answer 'Yes, of course'.[32]

We cannot help being reminded of Hodgson's repeated insistence that the characteristic theological judgement is of the form: 'This is how I see it; can you not see it that way as well?'

But how do we know whether what has been said is 'authentic'? 'If this is your final conclusion', I may be told, 'your whole discussion has been one long begging of the question. The members of the Church, whoever they may be, are to be asked to adjudicate among the various allegedly 'biblical' insights offered to them, while at the same time they have been robbed of any objective, universally agreed, criterion by which they could confidently make any such judgement. Who in practice are the Church in this context and on what basis would they make their judgements?'

By way of such reply as space allows four things may be said:

(*i*) The question of the means and channels by which Christians come to a mind about where they stand today is on any showing an open and much-discussed one in all the churches. We have given reasons for thinking that church members who are not ordained and not theologians should play a much larger part than they have done hitherto; but that is something which would be widely agreed in any case, on a number of grounds.

Even when many of its members have thought it was doing so, the Church has never in practice used the Bible or anything else as a body of objective data from which the truth could be extracted on a basis of logical entailment; it has always taken many factors into consideration. Had it been otherwise, the rise of biblical criticism would not, as Leonard Hodgson pointed out, have found the Church so deeply divided as to have split into a variety of denominations and confessions. Even the most biblicist Christian has in fact appealed to what he and his group *took* the Bible to mean.

(*ii*) The desire to settle things by an appeal to authority is itself a culturally conditioned phenomenon. In the period before the emergence of the modern world when it was customary to settle matters of all kinds by appeal to authority,[33] it was natural to follow the same procedure in religion* but modern culture, as we have seen, is essentially

---

* In order to make clear just how strong belief in (especially written) authority was, it may be worth pointing out that in the Middle Ages people believed on the authority of Aristotle many things about animal life which a few hundred yards' walk into the woods would have shown them to be untrue. Even as late as the Renaissance, when dissection showed that the *rete mirabile*, a structure described by Galen as part of the human body, did not in reality exist at all in

autonomous in all its forms. Natural scientists and literary critics (to single out only two groups who happen to have been discussed earlier) manage to reach at least as much agreement about truth as Christians have ever succeeded in doing without appeal to any sort of knock-down external authority. If in an autonomous age the Church were to take upon itself, under God, the burden of discovering and deciding the truth without claiming to have any infallible external arbiter, it would be doing no more than the primitive Church did when it forged its belief-system without benefit of authoritative creeds or conciliar definitions. To be sure, the early Christians took such Old Testament and other Jewish traditions as they had very seriously, just as we have argued the modern Church should take its traditions with great seriousness; but it felt free to reinterpret them creatively, sometimes to the point of virtual negation. Why should we not do the same? 'Hath God forgotten to be gracious?' To the extent that we are called to live *etsi deus non daretur* we can hardly expect him to provide us with ready-made and incontrovertible criteria of judgement!

(*iii*) However it decides to come to a mind, the Church will have many factors to take into account, not least its members' present experience of God. Some years ago, after describing how the theologian should draw upon the insights of others disciplines in advising the Church, I wrote:

> In particular he should concentrate upon . . . the Church's prayer life. For if there is one defect more than another of which I am conscious in what I have been saying, it is that I have concentrated too exclusively on one focus of what is in fact a sort of ellipse. The meaning of the biblical revelation for to-day is given not only through the Bible itself and reflection upon it, however acute that reflection may be. It is also given through contemporary prayer — prayer which is based upon the revelation and in turn illuminates it. And so it has been in every generation. The

---

man, respect for the written authority was so great that a change in the human anatomy since Galen's time was assumed. See e.g. A.G.R. Smith, *Science and Society in the Sixteenth and Seventeenth Centuries* (Thames and Hudson, 1972) p. 21.

truth we are after is, if I may put it so, out of the Bible by the mystics. Consequently the student of divinity must give full weight to what, for want of a better term, I must call the 'religious experience' of the present and the past.

I also wrote, 'the problem of biblical authority cannot be cleared up in isolation. The authority of the Bible is inextricably connected with other authorities — the authority of the Church, of the saints, of the liturgy, the conscience and the reason.'[34] The list could easily be extended, but the point will be clear. There is a perfectly proper place at the appropriate level for authority — both the word and the thing — but the process of weighing authorities and giving each its due weight, can never be one which affords much opportunity for the use of unanswerable, knock-down arguments.

(*iv*) Finally, since I have started on the slippery slope of quoting myself, perhaps I may be allowed to conclude with this extended quotation from a lecture delivered in 1969:

> It is, I think, worth noting that Karl Barth, of all people, at least twice in his *Dogmatics* discusses the theoretical possibility that God might have adopted modes of revelation different from the one to which, on Barth's own view, he has in fact exclusively confined himself.
>
> In one place he envisages the possibility that revelation might have been laid up for us, as it were, within human nature itself, and so taken the form of a 'timeless essential state of man himself, namely his relationship to the external and absolute', in which case proclamation would have been a process of *anamnesis* — a 'heart searching', by which a neglected or hidden part of human nature would be re-discovered and unfolded.[35]
>
> More apposite for us is the following statement:[36]
>
> > ... it might also have pleased God to give His Church the canon in the form of an unwritten prophetic and apostolic tradition, propagating itself from spirit to spirit and from mouth to mouth. It will not be disputed that there is something of this kind in the Church apart from the real canon. But it would have to be said that, so far as it had pleased God to make this unwritten

spiritual-oral tradition the cannon of His Church, the
canon would be as faintly distinguishable from the life
of the Church, as we can distinguish the blood of our
fathers which flows in our veins from our own blood; in
other words, the Church is . . . left to her solitary self
and concentrated upon herself, upon her own aliveness.

Precisely. But in the former quotation Barth simply concludes with the bald statement: 'in fact the matter has
been contrived differently' (he does not say how he
knows), and after the second passage he writes: 'Whatever
of such spiritual-oral tradition there may be in the
Church, obviously it cannot possess the character of an
authority irremovably confronting the Church. In the un-
written tradition the Church is not addressed, but is engaged in a dialogue with herself.' With all due respect, do
not these quotations beg the question? Barth nowhere, so
far as I know, considers the possibility that God may have
chosen to work through a combination of all three of these
modes; and that is because he does not consider the
possibility — which is precisely the question at issue — that
God does not *wish* His self-revelation to 'possess the
character of an authority irremovably confronting the
Church'. What if God, taking history really seriously, actually wants the Church in the twentieth century to be
'engaged in a dialogue with herself'?[37]

Notes

Chapter 1

1 P.L. Berger and T. Luckmann, *The Social Construction of Reality*, English ed. (Penguin Books, 1972) p. 210.

2 T.E. Hulme, *Speculations* (Routledge and Kegan Paul, 1949) pp. 50–1.

3 See especially Collingwood's *Metaphysics*.

4 B. Willey, *The Seventeenth Century Background* (Pelican Books, 1972), particularly the first chapter.

5 P.L. Berger, *Invitation to Sociology* (Pelican Books, 1968) p. 104.

6 The way the matter is discussed in this Introduction may suggest a 'functionalist' approach of the kind associated with the names of Lévi-Strauss, Evans-Pritchard or Mary Douglas. However, the essential points being made here are unaffected by the disagreements on such matters among sociologists and could equally well be stated in terms acceptable to such writers as Roger Grainger — see, for example, his book *The Language of the Rite* (Darton, Longman and Todd, 1974).

7 See J.H. Plumb, *The Death of the Past* (Macmillan, 1969) and below p. 42, and p. 107 and n. 14.

8 On this see H. Richard Niebuhr, *Christ and Culture* (Harper, 1951).

9 M. Halbwachs, *Les cadres sociaux de la Mémoire* (Presses Universitaires de France, 1952) p. 296: 'La pensée sociale est essentiellement une mémoire' .

10 P.H. Bagby, *Culture and History* (Longmans, 1958) p. 191 — see also pp. 53 and 82. These considerations explain why a full understanding of the Bible demands familiarity with the languages in which it was originally written.

11 Berger, *Invitation to Sociology*, p. 25.

12 H.S. Hughes, *Consciousness and Society* (Vintage Books, 1961) p. 8.

13 For a brief account see E.H. Gombrich, *In Search of Cultural History* (OUP, 1969), and note the instructive diagram on the front cover.

14 Cp. Hughes, *Consciousness and Society*, p. 187.

15 Cp. Gombrich, *In Search of Cultural History*, p. 36: 'Oswald

Spengler . . . assigned different psyches to his different cultural cycles. It was an illusion due to sentimentalizing humanitarians to believe that these different species of man could ever understand each other.'

16 Hughes, *Consciousness and Society*, p. 8.

17 Cp. the works of such scholars as T.S. Kuhn and D.A. Schon. The criticisms of the use of the concept by writers such as Roger Trigg are not such as to affect the use made of it below.

18 L. MacNeice, *Autumn Journal* (1939) ix.

19 A.D. Galloway, *Faith in a Changing Culture* (Allen and Unwin, 1967) p. 70.

20 H. Gardner, *Religion and Literature* (Faber, 1971) pp. 43–4.

21 Goethe, *Faust*, Part I, 1220ff.

22 S.T. Coleridge, *Biographia Literaria*, ed. J. Shawcross (OUP, 1949) ii, p. 6ff.

23 R.G. Collingwood, *Autobiography* (Penguin Books, 1944) p. 77.

24 Quoted without reference by C.M. Bowra in *The Heritage of Symbolism* (Macmillan, 1954) p. 73.

25 Gardner, *Religion and Literature* pp. 116–17.

26 See *A Rumour of Angels* (Penguin Books, 1971) especially pp. 43ff.

27 Recognition of that will at least save us from the false position exemplified in the statements of R.P.C. Hanson and R.H. Fuller in their book *The Church of Rome*, circa p. 95, and discussed by me in *The Use of the Bible in Modern Theology* (John Rylands Lecture) John Rylands Library, Manchester, 1969, pp. 184–5.

28 Sir Isaiah Berlin, *Art and Ideas in Eighteenth-Century Italy* (Edizioni di Storia e Letteratura, 1960) iv, p. 182.

29 L. Trilling, *The Liberal Imagination* (Mercury Books, 1964) pp. 187 and 189.

Chapter 2

1 Cp. *Confessions of an Inquiring Spirit*, ed. H. St J. Hart (Black, 1956) Letters 1 and 2, pp. 42–3.

2 J.K.S. Reid, *The Authority of Scripture* (Methuen, 1957) p. 139; John Charles, S.S.F., *The Franciscan* xii, p. 104.

3 For a fully documented historical treatment along the lines envisaged, see the volumes of *The Cambridge History of the Bible*.

4 C.S. Lewis, *The Discarded Image* (CUP, 1964) p. 5; and see p. 61 below.

5 Ibid., p. 11.

6 C. Smyth, *Church and Parish* (SPCK, 1950) p. 159.

7 Ibid.

8 R.B. Tollinton, quoted in G.L. Prestige, *Fathers and Heretics* (SPCK, 1948) p. 59.

9 Cp. L.A. Schökel, *The Inspired Word* (Burns and Oates, 1967) p. 315.

10 *De actis cum Felice manichaeo*, ix, Migne, PL xlii, col. 525.

11 L. Hodgson, *The Bible and the Training of the Clergy* (Darton, Longman and Todd, 1963) p.4. Italics mine.

12 *Sermons*, ed. Potter and Simpson, vol. vi (1953) p. 62, quoted from Dame Helen Gardner, *The Business of Criticism* (OUP, 1959) p. 137.

13 A.N. Whitehead, *Religion in the Making* (CUP, 1927) p. 39.

14 Tertullian, *Apol.* 46 and *de prescrip. her.* 7.

15 Lewis, *The Discarded Image*, p. 10.

16 See his essay in *Christianity in its Social Context*, ed. G. Irvine (SPCK, 1967).

17 C.G. Darwin, *The Next Million Years* (Hart-Davis, 1952) p. 49.

18 O. Chadwick, *From Bossuet to Newman* (CUP, 1957).

19 G. Tyrrell, *Through Scylla and Charybdis* (Longmans, Green, 1907) pp. 7 and 8.

20 Cp. the following passage from Foakes Jackson and Kirsopp Lake, *The Beginnings of Christianity*, vol. ii (Macmillan, 1922) pp. 193–4: 'Ancient and mediaeval theology erected a doctrinal edifice by means of the application of logic and metaphysics to the [biblical] data . . . but the productive work of the future will consist chiefly in the attempt to go behind these descriptions to discover the actual facts'. So far as the latter part of this quotation is concerned, see later in the lectures, especially pp. 184ff.

Chapter 3

1 C.S. Lewis, *They Asked for a Paper* (Geoffrey Bles, 1962).

2 G.K. Chesterton, *Orthodoxy* (Bodley Head, 1949) pp. 18–20.

3 See Lord (J.E.E.D.) Acton, *Essays on Freedom and Power* (Thames and Hudson, 1956) p. 43.

4 von Ranke, 'Geschichten der romanischen und germanischen Völker', *Werke*, vol. xxxiii–xxxiv (Leipzig, 1874) p. vii.

5 Cp. W.G. Kümmel, *The New Testament* (SCM, 1963) pp. 58–60.

6 Whitehead, *Religion in the Making*, p. 45.

7 See e.g. Bradley's first published work, *The Presuppositions of Critical History* (1874), now to be found as the first item in his *Collected Essays* (OUP, 1935).

8 See George Tyrrell, *Christianity at the Cross Roads* (Longmans, Green, 1910) p. 44, who pictures the Protestant scholar looking down a deep well constituted by 'nineteen centuries of Catholic darkness' and thinking he sees Christ's face reflected at the bottom.

Chapter 4

1 *The Interpretation of the Bible*, ed. C.W. Dugmore (SPCK, 1944) pp. 96–7 and 93–4. The quotations in it are from Harnack, *What is Christianity?* pp. 83 and 52.

2 By A.G. Hebert (OUP, 1950).

3 See J. Knox, *The Death of Christ* (Collins, 1959) ch. 2, especially pp. 38ff.

4 *Boswell's Life of Johnson* (OUP, 1933, 2 vols. in 1) i, 484.

5 Although Kähler's position was not Barth's, the very title of his

famous and extremely influential little book is significant: *The So-called Historical (=historische) Jesus and the Historic (=geschichtliche) Biblical Christ* (E.T., Fortress Press, 1964).

6 Cp. *Church Dogmatics*, iii/1, 81 and 88.

7 Cp. ibid., 82.

8 *Downside Review* lxxii (1954) p. 94.

9 That applies at least as much to the more flamboyant modern revivals of such theories as to the relatively sober versions of them current around the turn of the century! If exception is made to some extent for G.A. Wells, *The Jesus of the Early Christians* (Pemberton, 1971) it must still be said that he has convinced scarcely a handful of other scholars, whether Christian or non-Christian. See the still relevant discussions in A. Schweitzer, *Geschichte der Leben-Jesu-Forschung*, 2nd and subsequent eds, ch. 23 (e.g. Siebenstern Taschbach Verlag, 1966, pp. 500–60); and H.G. Wood, *Did Christ Really Live?* (SCM, 1938).

10 See Nineham, 'The Use of the Bible in Modern Theology', *Bulletin of the John Rylands Library*, vol. 52, no. 1 (Autumn 1969) 186–7.

11 See his discussion in his edition of *Lessing's Theological Writings* (A. & C. Black, 1956) circa p. 31.

Chapter 5

1 F.R. Tennant, *Philosophy of the Sciences* (CUP, 1932) pp. 99f. The point Tennant is making in the immediate context is rather different from ours, but quoting him in this context does not misrepresent his overall thought.

2 F. Nietzsche, 'Jenseits von Gut und Böse', §224, *Werke in Drei Bänden*, ii (Hanser, 1966) pp. 686–7.

3 Terence, *Heauton Timorumenos*, I, i, 25.

4 Cp. the quotations from C.S. Lewis on p. 45 and the discussion on p. 84.

5 Troeltsch, *Gesammelte Schriften*, III (Tübingen, 1922) p. 33, cited in A.O. Dyson, *Who is Jesus Christ?* (SCM, 1969) p. 32.

6 R.W. Southern, *The Making of the Middle Ages* (Hutchinson, 1953).

7 *kontinuierlicher Werdezusammenhang*, e.g. *GS* III, 54.

8 See p. 273 n. 22.

9 L. Trilling, *The Liberal Imagination* (Mercury Books, 1964) p. 184. Italics mine. The essay from which this quotation and a good deal else in the paragraph are taken, is of great suggestiveness for our subject.

10 R.G. Collingwood, *Autobiography* (Penguin Books, 1944) p. 77. Cp. also *The Idea of History* (OUP, 1946) especially pp. 282ff.

11 *Autobiography*, p. 77.

12 Ibid.

13 Ibid., pp. 77–8.

14 J.H. Plumb, *The Death of the Past*. Having succeeded in

establishing first that 'every literate society which has so far existed has needed to use the past for the same fundamental purpose . . . to justify authority, to create confidence and to secure stability' (pp. 39—40), he points out by way of contrast on p. 42, that 'for the new scientists and technologists, the men who man or run nuclear power stations and computer services, this so-called past of their society can at best be no more than nostalgic. It can have no social validity, it cannot give them a sense of purpose. It cannot provide a framework to their authority or a justification for it . . . '

15 Schweitzer, *The Quest of the Historical Jesus* (E.T. 1910) p. 397.

16 K.E. Kirk, *Marriage and Divorce* (Hodder and Stoughton, 1948) pp. 74ff.

17 Ibid., p. 74.

18 Ibid.; see also the rest of his remarks on p. 75.

19 Troeltsch, *Christian Thought* (University of London Press, 1923) pp. 23—4. Italics mine.

20 R. Trigg, *Reason and Commitment* (CUP, 1973).

21 For the universality of this recognition according to the Bultmann school, see e.g. Hans Jonas, *The Gnostic Religion*, enlarged ed. (Beacon Press, 1963), and cp. the same author's explicit postulation 'of an unchangeable fundamental structure of the human spirit as such' (*einer unausweichlichen Fundamentalstruktur des Geistes als solchen*) in *Augustin und das paulinische Freiheitsproblem*, 2. Auflage (1965) p. 82. *Selbstverständnis* as used by the Bultmann school carries overtones not conveyed by the English 'self-understanding'. Just as for Barth the faith which describes the occurrence of supernatural interventions in history is a divine gift and not a historical, psychologically explicable phenomenon (see above, p. 87) so for Bultmann *Selbstverständnis* of the sort described above is a supernatural phenomenon made possible only through God's intervention in Christ and not to be produced through any amount of psychoanalysis or purely human meditation.

22 For the evidence, which involves some qualification of that very bald statement, see Bultmann's essays in *Essays in Old Testament Interpretation*, ed. C. Westermann (SCM, 1963), and in *The Old Testament and the Christian Faith*, ed. B.W. Anderson (Herder and Herder, 1969).

Chapter 6

1 Whitehead, *Religion in the Making*, p. 21.

2 Van A. Harvey, *The Historian and the Believer* (SCM, 1967).

3 Ibid., pp. 253—4.

4 Some aspects of that example have been interestingly discussed by Lord Percy of Newcastle in his book *The Heresy of Democracy* (Eyre and Spottiswoode, 1954). I was unaware when I gave the lecture that Bultmann has also discussed the same example.

5 Niebuhr wrote his *Meaning of Revelation* in 1941. For a partial correction to what he said about this American story see now Plumb,

The Death of the Past, p. 43.

6 *The Interpreter's Bible Dictionary* (Abingdon Press, 1962) vol. 2, pp. 195–6.

7 Troeltsch, *GS*, III, p. 156.

8 R.W. Southern, *Western Society and the Church in the Middle Ages* (Penguin Books, 1970) pp. 92–3. Italics mine.

9 Is. 51:9–11 and Ps. 89:8–18, NEB. Cp. also e.g. Pss. 29, 77, 89 and 93 and Hab. 3. Such ideas are echoed in many other parts of the Bible, including the New Testament, cp. e.g. the discussion of Mk 4:35–41 in D.E. Nineham, *The Gospel of St Mark* (Penguin Books, 1973) pp. 146ff. .

10 See *The Interpreter's Bible Dictionary*, vol. 2, pp. 194–5.

11 See ibid., vol. 3, p. 664.

12 The Right Reverend Cecil Allan Warren, now bishop of Canberra and Goulburn.

13 Cp. further pp. 184ff. Meanwhile see now the remarkably similar – and quite independent – statement of the matter by Eric Franklin in his book *Christ the Lord* (SPCK, 1975) p. 177: 'In the Old Testament, we have, in Gärtner's words, "a religious view of history which, practically speaking, is unique". The past is recounted in order to elicit a particular response in the present, and it is the nature of the response which it is hoped to establish which determines how the history is described. The past is seen as the basis for the present, and it is the present which determines the interest in the past. *History is seen through the eyes of what must have been, as the expression of a faith that is*. All Israel must have come out at the Exodus, for all Israel is represented as the possessor of God's covenantal activity. The Settlement becomes a conquest because Yahweh was giving her the land. Jerusalem had to be saved because it was Yahweh's city, but, when she fell, it was because of Yahweh's action to punish her transgression. Even contradictory statements about such things as the Temple treasures represent what "must" have been, as historical events are seen to be moulded by the theological convictions of the writers. The significance – and indeed the understanding – of what must have happened in the past, remains open to the ever new reinterpretation of the present which is the dominant factor in the historical descriptions it calls forth.' (Italics mine) Other modern scholars have put the same sort of point in different ways, e.g. Professor K. Stendahl talks of 'The tendency to *describe* what was originally *believed* (*Beiheft zur ZNTW*, XXVI (1960) 94) and Dr M. Johnson talks of 'The tendency towards the historification of "non-historical" materials' (*The Purpose of the Biblical Genealogies* (CUP, 1969) p. 254). Cp. also this comment of Professor W.D. Davies, although it refers to the Mishnah: 'By itself the evidence from the Mishnah on historical matters is always uncertain, because of the possiblity that it is imaginatively coloured and creates a past which never existed.' (*The Setting of the Sermon on the Mount* (CUP, 1964) p. 283 n.1.)

Chapter 7

1 For the detailed facts see e.g. Howard C. Kee, *Jesus in History* (Harcourt Brace, 1970) or C.K. Barrett, *The New Testament Background* (SPCK, 1956).

2 *Cambridge Ancient History* (CUP, 1936) vol. XI, ch. vii, see especially pp. 272—86.

3 Ibid., p. 275.

4 In their original context, those words refer primarily to the sub-apostolic age, but the whole trend of the article makes clear that similar considerations applied to the New Testament period. Indeed for Streeter 'what demands explanation' in the New Testament period 'is the large measure of *agreement* that persisted' (p. 273, italics mine). For the same sort of point see also R.A. Knox, *The Belief of Catholics* (Unicorn Books, 1939) p. 167.

5 See the careful discussion by G.F. Moore in *Beginnings of Christianity*, ed. Jackson and Lake, I (Macmillan, 1920) 346ff., and compare F.C. Burkitt, *Christian Beginnings* (University of London Press, 1924) e.g. p. 27 'Christians have been too apt in the past to assume that there already existed among the Jews a fairly definite and uniform conception. . . That is presupposed in many Christian documents, particularly in the fourth gospel, but it is not borne out by a study of Jewish literature.'

6 According to many scholars, when the eschatological agent was thought of in this sort of way as a pre-existing heavenly figure, he was often described as the Son of Man; this, however, is disputed. For the two sides of the argument see e.g. S. Mowinckel, *He That Cometh* (Blackwell, 1956) and G. Vermes, *Jesus the Jew* (Collins, 1973).

7 E.g. Rom. 1:4 on which see A.M. Hunter, *Paul and his Predecessors* (Nicholson and Watson, 1940).

8 *Monarchia*, I, xvi, 2. (*Le Opere di Dante*, 2nd ed., Florence, 1960, i, p. 344.)

9 Streeter, *CAH*, XI, p. 284.

10 Cp. once again Streeter's chapter, this time at p. 285, for a vivid expression of the latter view. 'The point of the fourth gospel will be missed by a reader who approaches it primarily as a historical authority. It should be read as a book of devotion, as one would the *Imitatio Christi*; and the writer's attitude of mystic adoration may at times be better apprehended by a change of pronouns in the great discourses ascribed to Christ: "*Thou* art the vine, *we* are the branches"; or "*Thou* art the Resurrection and the Life".'

11 For an exemplary instance of how his should be done see C.H. Dodd, *History and the Gospel* (Nisbet, 1938).

12 S.G.F. Brandon, *Jesus and the Zealots* (Manchester University Press.)

13 Cp. e.g. E. Fuchs, *Studies of the Historical Jesus* (SCM, 1964) p. 22; G. Bornkamm, *Jesus of Nazareth* (Hodder and Stoughton, 1960), and the works of such scholars as E. Käsemann, Hans Schlier and other exponents of the so-called 'new quest of the historical Jesus'.

14 Vermes, *Jesus the Jew*, p. 79.

15 Cp. e.g. H.J. Cadbury, *Jesus What Manner of Man* and *The Peril of Modernizing Jesus* (SPCK, 1962) and E. Trocmé, *Jesus and his Contemporaries* (SCM, 1973).

16 And further was there a tomb at all? What we know of Roman law and custom in connexion with crucifixion makes that at least a debatable point. See e.g. M. Dibelius, *The Message of Jesus* (Nicholson and Watson, 1939) p. 182; J. McLeman, *The Birth of the Christian Faith* (Oliver and Boyd, 1962) ch. 2; and W.E. Bundy, *Jesus and the First Three Gospels* (Harvard University Press, 1955) pp. 549ff. and the literature there referred to.

Chapter 8

1 L. Hodgson, *Sex and Freedom* (SCM, 1967) p. 42.

2 *The Bible and the Training of the Clergy* (Darton, Longman and Todd, 1963) p. 10.

3 Kierkegaard, *Philosophical Fragments*, 2 (Princeton University Press, 1962) p. 130.

4 Not that Professor Hodgson should be seen as the doctrinal fundamentalist for which he is sometimes mistaken; cp. for example his remarks on Nicene orthodoxy, in *For Faith and Freedom*, ii (Blackwell, 1957) p. 181.

5 *Religious Studies*, vi (1970) 69–76, now reprinted in *Christ, Faith and History*, ed. S.W. Sykes and J.P. Clayton (CUP, 1972) pp. 3–12.

6 Knox, *The Death of Christ*, p. 156.

7 Knox, op. cit.; W. Marxsen, *The Resurrection of Jesus of Nazareth* (SCM, 1968).

8 L. Trilling, *The Liberal Imagination*, p. 186.   9 Ibid., pp. 181–2.

10 Cp. e.g. Farrer's Bampton Lectures, *The Glass of Vision* (Dacre Press, 1948).

11 Gardner, *The Business of Criticism*, p. 154. The whole surrounding passage is instructive.

12 Quoted without reference in *The Heritage of Symbolism* (Macmillan, 1954) p. 73.

Chapter 9

1 Chadwick, *From Bossuet to Newman*, p. 25.

2 S.J. Case, *Jesus through the Centuries* (University of Chicago Press, 1932) p. 347; the whole book is extremely instructive in relation to the subject under discussion.

3 Hodgson, *The Bible and the Training of the Clergy*, pp. 12–13.

4 F.G. Downing, *Has Christianity a Revelation?* (SCM, 1964).

5 *S.T.*, pars 1, quaestio 1, art. 10.

6 C.C. Richardson, *The Doctrine of the Trinity* (Abingdon Press, 1958); cp. also M.F. Wiles, op. cit. and J.L. Houlden in *The Church Quarterly*, clxix (1968) 4–18.

7 Trilling, *The Liberal Imagination*, p. 189; and see Helen Gardner, *The Business of Criticism*, p. 25.

8 H. Jonas, *The Gnostic Religion*, 2nd ed. (Beacon Press, 1963), and see further above, p. 114 and n. 21.

9 L. Dewart, *The Future of Belief* (Burns and Oates, 1967) pp. 203—4.

10 *Theology*, (Oct 1958) 401—4.

11. Cp. B.H. Streeter's words, 'it may be suggested that Augustine largely reared his system of theology on just that element in Paul which represents a survival in the Apostle's mind of a pre-Christian conception of God'. op. cit., p. 281.

12 Hodgson, *The Doctrine of the Atonement* (Nisbet, 1955) p. 16.

13 Kierkegaard, *Stages on Life's Way* (OUP, 1940) p. 402.

14 Hodgson, *Sex and Christian Freedom*, pp. 42—3.

15 A. Wilder, *New Testament Faith for To-day* (SCM, 1956) pp. 59—71.

16 Ibid., p. 60.

17 Ibid., p. 61.

18 M. Roberts, *The Modern Mind* (Faber and Faber, 1937).

19 Admittedly a slightly tendentious translation of *Ars Poetica*, 5—6 1451b.

20 Both from *A Study of History*. Abridgement of vols. i—vi by D.E. Somervell (OUP, 1947) pp. 40—6.

21 Collingwood, *Autobiography*, p. 78.

22 Boswell's *Life of Johnson*, i, p. 483.

23 On this, cp. John Knox, *The Death of Christ*, p. 152.

24 John Knox, *Life in Christ Jesus* (SPCK, 1962).

25 C.C. Morrison, *What is Christianity?* (Willett, Clark & Co., 1940) p. 191. The whole of this section of this strangely neglected book will repay study in the present connexion.

Chapter 10

1 Collingwood, *Autobiography*, p. 78.

2 Ibid.

3 Ibid.

4 Bultmann, *History and Eschatology* (Edinburgh University Press, 1957) e.g. p. 130.

5 *Autobiography*, p. 78.

6 Hodgson, *The Bible and the Training of the Clergy*, pp. 15f.

7 Cp. e.g. *For Faith and Freedom*, ii, p. 68.

8 See J.A. Baker, *The Foolishness of God* (Darton, Longman and Todd, 1970) pp. 364—5. With the positive opinion expressed by Canon Baker at this point in his book I have complete sympathy, though I am far from clear that he has drawn the right conclusions from it.

9 Knox, *The Death of Christ*, pp. 156f.

10 Ibid., pp. 171 and 159.

11 H.A. Williams, *The True Wilderness* (Constable, 1965); and see now *True Resurrection* (Mitchell Beazley, 1972).

12 *The True Wilderness*, pp. 152ff.

13 Ibid., p. 158.

14 Ibid., p. 9.

15 Ibid., p. 11.

16 Troeltsch, *G.S.*, II, pp. 227f.

17 Newman, *An Essay on the Development of Christian Doctrine* (Penguin Books, 1973) p. 100. The 1845 edition there reprinted has 'sect' instead of 'belief' which Newman substituted in later editions.

18 *Zeitschrift für Theologie und Kirche*, viii (1898) p. 6.

Chapter 11

1 E.g. Professor J.K.S. Reid writes, 'Biblical authority ... gives meaning to passages commonly neglected as unedifying. What, for example, are we to make of the passages which present the specification of the ark and of the temple, of the detailed legislative regulations in the Book of Exodus, and the long lists of names that occur elsewhere? The answer is that they too bear testimony to the same living and redeeming God ... they have all the authority which God concedes to their testimony'. *The Authority of Scripture*, p. 268.

2 Usually on the ground that the meaning in question somehow 'inhered' in the events. There is a decisive rebuttal of this entire notion, with special reference to the works of C.H. Dodd, in the D. Phil. thesis of Dr Ruth Page, *History and Symbol in the Writings of C.H. Dodd and Paul Tillich* (available in the Bodleian Library, Oxford).

3 For an example of this see Leonard Hodgson's *Doctrine of the Trinity* (Nisbet, 1943) especially pp. 21–2 and 24.

4 See *According to the Scriptures* (Fontana Books, 1965) pp. 128–9.

5 *The Religion of Protestants*, vi § 62, 10th ed. (1742) p. 355.

6 Cp. T.S. Eliot's comment that 'Christianity is always adapting itself into something which can be believed'. Quoted in R. Sencourt, *T.S. Eliot* (Garnstone Press, 1971) p. 116.

7 Knox, *The Death of Christ*, p. 125. It is true that on the same page Knox speaks of 'the absolute uniqueness of what God did through' Jesus, but in the total context of his thought it is not altogether clear how great a difference that implies between his position and ours.

8 Cp. what I wrote in *The Study of Divinity* (SPCK, 1960) p. 27: '... the ultimate object of the theologian's study is an ultimate being who *must* therefore exceed the measure of finite minds ... any human account of this being, and his relations with the world, which formed a completely coherent rational system with no *lacunae* or ragged edges would *ipso facto* betray itself as an inadequate account of him who is — and must always remain — "far above out of our sight".'

9 Cp. the book with that title by Dr John Robinson (Fontana Books, 1967) for some elements which have affected one modern Christian in that way.

10 Cp. Gordon D. Kaufman, *God the Problem* (Harvard University Press, 1972).

11 On the last point see Charles Hartshorne, especially in *Man's Vision of God and the Logic of Theism* (Willett, Clark, 1941) and Schubert Ogden, *The Reality of God* (Harper and Row, 1966).

12 Cp. p. 97 above; the quotations are from J.A.T. Robinson, *Exploration into God* (SCM, 1967) p. 78; and L. Dewart, *The Future of Belief* (Burns and Oates, 1967) pp. 64–9.

13 Robinson, op. cit. pp. 33ff.

14 The first quotation is from Professor John Macquarrie, *Studies in Christian Existentialism* (SCM, 1966) p. 12. See also D. Bonhoeffer, *Letters and Papers from Prison* (SCM, 1953) p. 124 and Teilhard, *Hymn of the Universe* (Collins, 1965) p. 83.

15 Cp. Chillingworth, cited p. 238 above.

16 *The New Oxford Book of English Verse*, ed. Helen Gardner (OUP, 1972) p. 791.

17 Knox, *The Death of Christ*, p. 159 and pp. 156–7. Italics mine.

18 Cp. e.g. his epilogue to *Kerygma and Myth*, ed. H.W. Bartsch (E.T., SPCK, 1953) especially pp. 214–15.

19 For a full discussion see Erich Auerbach, *Scenes from the Drama of European Literature* (Meridian Books, 1959); and *Mimesis* (Princeton University Press, 1953).

20 R. Gregor Smith, *Secular Christianity* (Collins, 1966) p. 123.

21 In an unpublished paper Dr Walter Hollenweger has remarked: 'Bultmann chose a Heideggerian philosophical approach, but his, or indeed any modern philosophical approach, is the language of an insignificantly tiny minority, even within the Christian community. This does not of course rule it out as false, but it rules it out as a major attempt at doing Christian theology. If we believe that Christian theology is done with and for the whole people of God, such a philosophical approach would defeat its purpose from the start. It would in fact be a return to the Roman Catholic tradition of doing theology in Latin — or worse. This is not to say that we have to opt for a superficial "pop-theology" but what? This is what we have to examine.'

22 Bonhoeffer, op. cit; p. 163.

23 Knox, *The Death of Christ*, pp. 71–2.

24 See e.g. E.C. Hoskyns, *Cambridge Sermons* (SPCK, 1938) pp. 18ff. In fairness it should be added that many scholars take a different view: cf., e.g. W.D. Davies, *The Setting of the Sermon on the Mount* (CUP, 1964) pp. 309ff.

25 See J.S. Dunne, *The Way of All the Earth*, (English ed. Sheldon Press, 1973).

26 Trilling, *The Liberal Imagination*, pp. 186–7.

27 Considered in the light of modern scholarship, itself a loaded and tendentious term. On the diversity of the church from the beginning, see e.g. J. Knox, *The Early Church and the Coming Great Church* (Epworth Press, 1957); and Walter Bauer, *Orthodoxy and Heresy in Earliest Christianity* (SCM, 1972).

28 *Shakespeare's Measure for Measure* (Athlone Press, 1953) p. vii.

29 For an example of such questioning in practice see e.g. Professor C.C. Richardson's book *The Doctrine of the Trinity* (Abingdon Press, 1958).

30 This I take to be part of Professor Hans Frei's thesis in his recent book *The Eclipse of Biblical Narrative* (Yale University Press, 1974); cp. what was said on p. 254 about development. One of the impoverishing features of much existentialist writing on this subject is its *a priori* refusal to allow the propriety of any modern account of God's creative and providential dealings with the world; only talk directly relating to I—Thou encounter is to be allowed.

31 Cp. e.g. E. Voegelin, *Order and History*, vol. i: *Israel and Revelation* (Louisiana State University Press, 1956).

32 *The Times*, 18 June 1974.

33 See R.R. Orr, *Reason and Authority* (OUP, 1967) p. 115, who describes as 'a statement describing most seventeenth century minds' the assertion that 'unless men have a sure test of the validity of their beliefs, they will despair of salvation'.

34 *The Study of Divinity* (SPCK, 1960) p. 25; and L. Hodgson *et al.*, *On the Authority of the Bible* (SPCK, 1960) pp. 95—6.

35 K. Barth, *Dogmatics* 1/1, 111f.

36 Ibid., 1/1, 117.

37 *Bulletin of the John Rylands Library*, vol. 52, no. 1 (Autumn 1969) pp. 196—7 (also published separately under the title *The Use of the Bible in Modern Theology*.) All this of course raises acute questions about the role of the Church in doctrinal definition in days to come. On any showing, however, some radical thinking about such questions is long overdue and it could do worse than begin from the profound work by Chillingworth already quoted. See the discussion of his thought by R.R. Orr, *Reason and Authority*, especially around pp. 66ff. and pp. 124ff.

Reference Index

Subject Index

Index of Names